VICTORIAN NEWS AND
NEWSPAPERS

Victorian News and Newspapers

LUCY BROWN

CLARENDON PRESS · OXFORD

1985

Oxford University Press, Walton Street, Oxford OX2 6DP
Oxford New York Toronto
Delhi Bombay Calcutta Madras Karachi
Kuala Lumpur Singapore Hong Kong Tokyo
Nairobi Dar es Salaam Cape Town
Melbourne Auckland

and associated companies in
Beirut Berlin Ibadan Nicosia

Oxford is a trade mark of Oxford University Press

Published in the United States
by Oxford University Press, New York

British Library Cataloguing in Publication Data
Brown, Lucy
Victorian news and newspapers.
1. British newspapers—History—19th century
I. Title
072 PN5117
ISBN 0-19-822624-1

Set by Latimer Trend & Company Ltd, Plymouth
Printed in Great Britain
at the University Press, Oxford
by David Stanford
Printer to the University

Preface

This book would hardly have been possible without generous help from many quarters. I should like first to express my thanks to Times Newspapers Limited and to W. H. Smith and Son Limited, who allowed me to consult their important archives and gave me permission to quote from them. I should also like to thank Mr T. W. Baker-Jones, archivist to the W. H. Smith and Hambleden collections, and Mr Gordon Phillips, archivist to Times Newspapers at the time I was working there, for all the help and encouragement they gave me.

I owe a great debt to those people who gave me some introduction to the technicalities of the subject. Mr Henry Arrowsmith-Brown took me on a tour of Arrowsmith's printing works, and arranged a demonstration of typesetting by hand, and also enabled me to see all the stages of production of the Bristol *Evening Post*. I have benefited from the great fund of knowledge of the provincial press possessed by Mr Kenneth Hirst, formerly editor of the *Oldham Evening Chronicle*. To read the nineteenth-century history of a paper while that day's issue was being prepared was a great pleasure. I am equally indebted for much discussion and advice to two other professionals, former students who had previously worked as journalists, Mr R. Gillings and Miss Elaine Williams.

Much of the work for this book was done in the British Library's Newspaper Library, and I would like to express general thanks to the staff there who make a day in Colindale as pleasant and productive as it nearly always is. At Bloomsbury I am particularly grateful to Dr R. A. H. Smith of the Department of Manuscripts, who three or four times has told me of manuscript sources which it would never have occurred to me to consult, but which invariably yielded something of interest and value. At Bristol I received similar help from Mr John Farrell. Lastly I must thank warmly Mrs Irene Parkin, who typed most of the first draft of the book, and Dr Daniel Waley, who nobly read the whole of the final version.

27 April 1985   LUCY BROWN

Contents

	Introduction	I
I	Production	7
II	Distribution and Circulation	26
III	Party Politics	54
IV	Journalists	75
V	The News	95
VI	News Agencies	112
VII	Social Contacts	127
VIII	Access to Information	144
IX	Political News	170
X	Foreign News	210
XI	Handling the News	244
XII	Conclusion	273
	Bibliography	278
	Index of Newspapers and Periodicals	286
	Index	294

Introduction

THE subject of this book is the news in Victorian Britain—where it came from, how it was handled, distributed, and presented. 'The news' as we understand it is a nineteenth-century creation. It is a package of information on diverse subjects, some appearing for the first time, some the most recent developments of long-running stories: the package is delivered at the same time to the great body of people, and forms the subject-matter of public debate. By the later nineteenth century, thanks to telegraphy, there was, from day to day, a common basis of information among politicians at Westminster (other, obviously, than those with access to confidential information) and average readers in provincial cities: the news would be fuller among the former than the latter, but the same lie of the land would be generally known.

The influences moulding the news—which are many and various—therefore deserve study and analysis. The first question must be the general technical conditions of newspaper production. If materials and printing processes were expensive, the resources which could be spent on reporting and editing would be correspondingly restricted: the shape and tenor of what was printed would be determined elsewhere than in the newspaper office. The introduction of telegraphy also had its effects on the character of news reporting: in giving the provinces instant access to the most recent information it opened up the range of events which could be reported. In another, less publicized, way it restricted it: messages sent over publicly-controlled telegraph networks were at greater risk from interference by governments. Telegrams were charged—very highly if they were overseas cables—at so much a word. This also had its effects on news reporting: the occasional descriptive letter was first supplemented, and then supplanted, by the brief, but much more frequent, telegram. The kinds of readers, and kinds of advertisers, may also influence the

character of news. For all these reasons, therefore, a study of the news involves a survey of newspaper production as a preliminary.

Political traditions are also of great importance in determining the range of news. In any community some kinds of news will be broadcast and others kept secret, but the dividing line between them will be placed very differently in different societies. In the English-speaking radicalism of the late eighteenth century freedom of information was considered as important as freedom of speech: the protection of freedom of speech and freedom of the press was enshrined in the First Amendment of the Constitution of the United States in 1789; in Britain the reporting of trials, and the printing and publishing of Parliamentary Debates, and of Parliamentary Papers, all become established practices in the period of the French Revolution and the Napoleonic Wars. Cobbett put his best efforts into producing a working system which would put this information into the hands of a mass readership. In the course of the middle and later nineteenth century the objective of freedom of information came up against greater, and in the end probably insurmountable, obstacles: William Howard Russell made good use of his opportunities in the Crimea, but freedom to move about in wartime and then to publish freely was hardly likely to become established practice. The freedom to report Parliament was not extended to knowledge of the workings of the Civil Service or of the Cabinet. Mid-Victorian Britain was a place where the freedom of the press was respected, but where important areas could only be penetrated by informal means.

A further important element in the production of news was connected with this political tradition, but to a certain extent independent of it—that is, the degree of social acceptance of the press and of the people who ran it. Editors and political writers mixing easily with the people they wrote about, and anxious to retain their position, might feel things very differently from journalists who were excluded, humiliated, or resentful. Details of political journalists' normal social life, in the narrowest sense of the term, are therefore relevant to the study of the news.

Anyone who attempts to write about newspapers in the nineteenth century quickly comes face to face with the difficulty of
the sources. The files of the papers themselves should provide a
bottomless reservoir of information, in some respects admirable
material on which to work, each issue being numbered and
dated, and much of the contents being simple statements of
fact which can be checked against other sources. Yet the sort of
statistical questions to which these sources seem so well suited—
the space and emphasis given to various kinds of news, the
character of advertisements—are ones that can be answered by
simple methods over very short periods: newspapers were put
together from day to day according to the same recipe. Over a
period of time managements may decide to expand in certain
directions, or do so without a conscious decision, but this is not
difficult to establish.

The difficulties lie in trying to establish the processes behind
the finished result. Journalism was nearly always anonymous,
though authorship can sometimes be found out from memoirs.
But journalists could move from job to job with bewildering
speed, and memoirs are inaccurate. Another source of difficulty lies with politics: it has been clearly established that party
political considerations were very important in the establishment and running of many papers. Nevertheless, just how
much a party standpoint influenced what was actually published is another matter. The business history of the press is
equally obscure: circulation figures were given sporadically for
some papers, but for others not at all. Business records have
not, generally, survived (though it is always possible that more
may appear), and where they do exist tend to be scrappy.

Where the history of the press differs from that of many
other business enterprises is in the absence of consistent and
interpretable information about it. Down to the abolition of
the stamp duty on newspapers in 1855, there were figures of the
numbers of stamps sold, from which calculations of circulations could be made, though these were subject to increasing
uncertainties. In 1947–8 the Royal Commission on the Press
produced a mass of information, in some cases stretching back
to the years before 1914. Between these two poles however
there is no reliable external evidence—no statistics collected in

prescribed form year by year, and no parliamentary inquiries, other than very minor ones, where witnesses would be cross-examined and reported verbatim. Nor are there more than passing references to the newspapers in *Hansard*. The press guarded its freedom, and had no reason to agitate for public inquiries; nor had politicians.

The workings of the press, therefore, must be reconstructed out of the massive deposits of printed newspaper files, and the scattered and often flimsy other records. For this reason, in the present study, certain people and publications may appear in unduly central positions, as may certain episodes, for example the Penjdeh episode in 1885, which happens to be exceptionally well-documented. While particular examples may not be intrinsically the most important, they illustrate the processes behind the formation of the news.

In the history of the newspapers there are, nevertheless, a few landmarks and turning-points round which a chronological history can be shaped. The repeal of the stamp duty immediately made the penny daily paper an economic possibility, and newspaper production as a whole took a great leap forward in the next decade. In 1860 there were nine morning and six evening dailies in London, though only three of them cost a penny. In the provinces there were sixteen dailies, one which came out three times a week (the *Leeds Mercury*), and sixteen which came out twice a week. By the 1880s and 1890s there were, all told, about a hundred and fifty dailies in existence. The slightly later repeal of the paper duties, at $1\frac{1}{2}d$. a pound, at a time when newsprint was costing about $8d$. a pound, would not have as dramatic an effect, but the steady fall in newsprint prices gave a continual stimulus to the cheap press.

The second major landmark must be the formation of the Press Association in 1868. This co-operative agency was formed when the Atlantic cable had been opened, and the telegraphic link with India was imminent. In association with Reuters it brought a cheap service of news, which could be independent of the London papers, to the provinces. Provincial papers were enabled to offer municipal news and regional advertisements, together with a coverage of world events appropriate to the citizen-electors of a great empire. Falling

costs of production, and an easily available supply of tele-graphed information from all over the world, formed the basic conditions in which the news in late Victorian Britain was presented. These were conditions which were quite different from what had gone before.

I

Production

THE period from the 1860s to the end of the century was one of rapid development, and much of this was not peculiar to Great Britain. In France and the United States we have a similar record: theories which explain the expansion of the press in relation to British considerations such as the taxation of newspapers and the Education Act of 1870 fail to take account of this general development. If there is a common cause of the expansion, the most likely explanation lies in the urbanization of these countries and in the speeding up of transport arrangements. Railways, which made the provisioning and the employment of large concentrated populations possible, also made possible the larger markets for newspapers. Circulation areas in which big metropolitan papers could also be those which were the first to arrive on the doorstep with the news, something which was vital in the days before broadcasting, were widening in all industrializing countries.

The newspaper, viewed as an economic enterprise, operates under severe constraints. It has to present an account of events, sufficiently clearly presented to be digestible by a mass audience, and sufficiently correct and considered to withstand the criticism and possible libel action of those people whose doings are being reported. The paper has to be printed and distributed before the news is superseded by other news, or rather by other papers offering later news. In these respects newspaper production is unlike the printing of periodicals or books, where cheapness, or the reputation of writers, or of the publication itself, will be more important factors in the volume of sales. There is therefore in all industrial countries an emphasis on technical efficiency at the expense of the price of the paper if necessary. A big competent newspaper is above all a feat of organization: it involves a large number of people with a common understanding of what it should contain, or normally does contain, pooling a large number of individual items. It involves a quick and uninterrupted production process,

and at the end of the process a distributive network which
puts the paper before a maximum number of people, at a time
when they are able to buy it and are anxious to know what it
contains. This cycle has to be performed regularly, and the
distributive system requires it to be done to a timetable in order
to maintain the relationship with its clientele of regular customers. Such organizational skill seems to have fascinated
nineteenth-century readers. There is no dearth of descriptions
of the productive and distributive system at work; very possibly
because it was a subject that lay ready to hand to descriptive
writers working for the newspapers.

The technical development of newspaper printing has been
described by other writers, and is not the main subject of this
book.[1] The web rotaries were being introduced in England
from the late 1860s. They were made practically possible in
Britain by the repeal of the paper duties. (The technical reason
for this was that the paper duties had been charged at so much
per sheet of newsprint, and the system could not be adapted to
continuous rolls. It was also a question of the strength of the
paper:[2] printing from a continuous roll could not be effective
until frequent breakdowns could be prevented.)

The first web machines were developed in the 1860s, their
invention stimulated by the burgeoning circulations, not merely in Britain but in Western Europe and the United States. A
daily paper needed a fuller printing equipment than a weekly
or twice-weekly one, as the whole circulation had to be
produced in one night's work. Even more, an evening paper
needed to run off its main edition in a very short time, though
the problems of an evening paper became evident rather later.

The first machines were of foreign manufacture—the Mari-
noni, the Bullock, and the Hoe; the Walter press, first used by
The Times in 1868, being an adaptation of the Hoe press. In the
late 1850s and early 1860s the machinery in general use had
involved rotary printing together with the feeding in of
newsprint by hand. The speed of production depended on the
skill of the operative.[3] Small provincial papers would have
'two-feeders', papers of larger circulation 'six-' or 'eight-

---

[1] See especially Ellic Howe, *Newspaper Printing in the Nineteenth Century*, 1943.
[2] *Printer's Register*, Jan. 1875.
[3] Ibid.

feeders', or even 'ten-feeders'; the operatives standing on tiers of cast-iron platforms on either side of the very large machines. The web rotary represented an unequivocal improvement. It saved labour; the *Glasgow Herald* for example reduced its machine operatives from 23 to 4 unskilled men. Output was regulated by the speed of the machine. In February 1870 it was claimed that, at *The Times*, 7 men working two Walter presses could produce the same output as 48 working on hand-fed Hoe machines.[4] The new machines occupied much less space and they were faster, though conflicting figures are given. They were expensive, but not much more so than the largest hand-fed models. They were chiefly of interest to the London papers with the largest circulations, until the appearance in 1878 of a small Victory web machine costing £1,200.[5]

They represented a rapid technical development: to change from the massive eight- and ten-feeders to the first web rotaries involved large investment decisions and uncertainty whether the new machines would effectively supersede the old. Sometimes a paper re-equipped itself with ten-feeders in the 1860s and found them superseded while they were relatively new. This happened to the *Daily News* and the *Manchester Guardian*. The *Daily News* bought hand-fed Hoe machines in 1868, and in 1873 bought Walter presses, made by *The Times*. These were in due course replaced, but not until 1892.[6] The *Manchester Guardian* bought two Hoe eight-feeders in 1858 and replaced them with Victory machines in 1879.[7] The *Daily Telegraph* acquired the American Bullock presses in 1870, but replaced them with reel-fed Hoe machines in 1874 at a cost believed to be £80,000.[8] Similar accounts could be given of a number of the more important provincial papers.

The £10,000 which the *Manchester Guardian*'s new machines cost in 1858 represented nearly a year's usual profits.[9] Sometimes old machines could be sold second-hand; for example the *Glasgow Herald* managed to sell its six-feeders to the *Manchester*

[4] Ibid.
[5] Ibid. July 1878.
[6] Justin McCarthy and John Robinson, *The Daily News Jubilee*, 1896, 140–1.
[7] David Ayerst, *Guardian, Biography of a Newspaper*, 1971, 131, 224.
[8] *Printer's Register*, Jan. 1870 and Dec. 1873. The *Daily Telegraph* kept a duplicate printing installation in being in case of fire. The *Glasgow Herald* did the same.
[9] Ayerst, 131; *Guardian* archives, Manchester University Library.

Courier. But the eight- and ten-feeders were real dinosaurs, of no use except to those relatively few large papers who would inevitably opt for the new machines: the *Glasgow Herald*'s eight-feeders, which had been bought for £9,000 in 1868, were sold back to Hoes as scrap for £600 in 1876.[10] The cost of re-equipment might not be a crippling expense if it were spread over a number of years, but it inevitably brought proprieters actively into the management of their papers. Where a paper was well-established, had been producing a good return to its proprietor, and particularly where a family's fortunes and status had grown up with its family newspaper, re-equipment might present little difficulty. In Manchester, the Taylors and the Garnetts found the cash for the operation, so did the Levy-Lawsons of the *Daily Telegraph*, and the Walters of *The Times*. But where a proprietor was less closely involved, this need to re-equip might prove the critical moment which opened the door to trouble. In a later period, Yates Thompson's decision in 1892 to get rid of the *Pall Mall Gazette* came when he was faced with the need to replace the machines.[11] In the history of the *Morning Post*, we can quote the bitter letter that Algernon Borthwick, at that time editor, wrote to Rideout, the proprietor:

The world has forgotten Palmerston and the days when from being the last I worked the *Post* up to the second place of London journalism. We ought then to have become the first penny paper, and we should then have taken a higher ground and obtained a better place than the *Telegraph*. Your uncle would not listen to it, contented to receive back his debt with interest and profits.[12]

The *Morning Post* had been mortgaged in 1842 to Crompton, a paper manufacturer, the uncle in this quotation, and his nephew and heir refused to sell it until 1876. The letter serves to demonstrate that the transition from a small high-priced paper to a mass-circulation one was not automatic. The realization that a similar decision was needed may have provided the occasion when a consortium of business men,

[10] A. Sinclair, *Fifty Years of Newspaper Life, 1845–1895; being chiefly Reminiscences of that Time*, Glasgow, privately printed, [1895?], 147.

[11] Stephen Koss, *The Rise and Fall of the Political Press in Britain*, vol. I, *The Nineteenth Century*, 1981, 321–2.

[12] R. Lucas, *Lord Glenesk and the Morning Post*, 1910, 235.

backing a party, or supporting a particular interest of some kind, might move in or be asked to help. It might also be the occasion when a person building up a chain of newspapers, like H. G. Reid in the 1880s, would acquire further titles.[13] In such ways the question of machinery may be of great relevance to questions of editorial policy. And while histories of individual newspapers may merely state that capital was raised 'within the family', or from among the proprietors, there is no a priori reason why these people should not also have entered into private arrangements with lenders of capital who expected some sort of reciprocal benefit.

The introduction of mechanical typesetting would also raise similar problems, since it involved capital expenditure to be offset by great reductions in labour costs. It is, however, a question which only became important at the end of the period under discussion here: Linotype machines were being intro-duced into newspaper offices in the 1890s. Throughout the 1870s and 1880s there was active experimentation. In June, 1874, reporting the Annual General Meeting of the Provincial Newspaper Society, the *Printer's Register* stated that they had discussed giving official encouragement to the invention of typesetting machines. In the following month it reported news of the Patent Type Foundry Company who had invented a machine using hot metal, 'it being an ascertained fact that casting of new type is cheaper than distributing and re-setting old type'.[14] However they were not yet in use.

The problems which were connected with the supply of paper were also common to all countries, and were the consequence of the fast-growing circulations of newspapers in the 1850s and 1860s. In Britain the paper duties, charged at $1\frac{1}{2}d.$ a pound, shifted the blame for high prices on to the government, but, as a tax, it was not as heavy as the other 'taxes on knowledge'. The *Glasgow Herald*, paying $6\frac{1}{2}d.$ a pound in 1860, on the eve of the repeal of the duty, would have saved 23 per cent of the cost of paper.[15] This can be compared with a charge of 1s 9d. on an

[13] For Reid see Alan Lee, *The Origins of the Popular Press, 1855–1914*, 1976, 168–9.
[14] July 1874.
[15] Sinclair, 28.

advertisement which otherwise might perhaps cost 6*d*. to 1*s*., or a penny stamp tax on a newspaper otherwise costing a penny. As these taxes went, it was a low one.

Apart from any taxation questions, raw material supplies— that is cotton rags—could not keep pace with demand. Esparto was used in the middle of the century, and it is an example of the anxieties about shortage that Edward Lloyd established his own esparto estate in Algeria, and his own paper mill in 1861 at Bow on the river Lea, to maintain supplies for *Lloyd's Weekly Newspaper*.[16] The *Printer's Register* records experiments on jute fibre in 1874 when the *Warrington Guardian* was printed on paper made from it. Shortly after this appeared the first references to wood pulp: the floating of the International Pulp and Paper Company in June 1874 and in June 1875 a report that the *Eastern Morning News* of Hull had been printed on Swedish paper. By the mid-1880s the imports of wood pulp were about half those of esparto—98 and 201 thousand tons respectively. Ten years later the comparable figures were 297,000 tons for wood pulp and 186,000 for esparto. The boom years to 1874 were, however, a time for threatened shortage: the price of paper rose, there were complaints that the paper-makers were fixing prices in a ring, and there were fears that the members of the Provincial Newspaper Society would raise the price of penny papers to $1\frac{1}{2}d$.[17]

Over the long term, however, paper prices were falling, and the fears of the early 1870s proved groundless. Two series of prices actually paid show a similar trend,[18] for *The Times* and for the *Glasgow Herald*, shown in Table 1.1.

This fall in prices, sustained over many years, underlies the development of the cheap press. The halfpenny paper, which in 1870 was a small evening sheet, of columns lifted from morning publications, by the end of the century was a self-supporting and profitable institution: the *Daily Mail* was sold at a halfpenny, and other national dailies were shortly to follow suit. Where papers were not reduced in price, the cheapening

---

[16] [Edward Lloyd] *A Glimpse into Paper-making and Journalism*, [1895] 3. The Sittingbourne mill opened in 1877.

[17] *Printer's Register*, June 1874, reporting the Annual General Meeting of the Provincial Newspaper Society.

[18] *The Times* archives; Sinclair, 28.

Table 1.1

The Times price per ream		Glasgow Herald price per pound	
1867	40s.	1845	8½d.
1871	38s.	1855	7d.
1877	31s. 8d.	1860	6½d.
1880	28s. 6d.	1870	4d.
1884	25s. 4d.	1873	4½d.
1888	22s. 2d.	1879	2½d.
1890	20s. 7d.	1886	2d.
		1895	1¼d.

of paper opened up a variety of opportunities—to increase size without an increase of price, to improve or expand the coverage of news, to be less dependent on advertisements, perhaps to adopt less overcrowded layouts: the closely-packed columns of Victorian papers were a survival from the high paper prices of the middle of the century.

The history of telegraphy charges provides a rather similar account of falling costs. Whereas reductions in paper prices were affecting papers of all kinds in the same sort of way, the cost of telegraphy was a matter of much greater concern to the largest papers. For the small provincial paper the supply of news was revolutionized, and cheaply. The Act which transferred the telegraph companies to the Post Office in 1870 also specified charges—presumably, as a monopoly was being set up, it was seen as a necessary precaution. A normal rate of twenty words for a shilling acted as a brake on private users: 'I cannot recall to mind any workman in England who has risen to the dignity of sending or receiving telegrams, but I found several in America who spoke of the wire with as much familiarity as we do of the penny post.'[19] A reduction in the standard charge, to twelve words for sixpence in 1885, produced a jump in sales. Press telegrams however enjoyed much lower rates, of a shilling for seventy-five words and a night rate of a shilling for 100 words. Duplicate messages were charged at 2d. a message. This concession opened the door wide to the Press Association and to the other news agencies which were set

[19] *Printer's Register*, Sept. 1869.

up in the next few years. In the last thirty years of the century the Post Office's receipts from press telegrams steadily rose, doubling between 1879 and 1899. The average number of words transmitted weekly rose from 4.2 million in 1874 to 15.7 million in 1899.[20] These figures are hard to interpret, since they do not make it clear how much they include, and they probably exclude the material transmitted by the papers' private wires. On any calculation, however, the volume of telegraphy was increasing, and for a subscriber to the Press Association or the Central News the supply of news was cheap. For a small provincial evening paper, such as was projected by H. J. Wilson, the Sheffield Radical, in 1874, an adequate supply of telegraphed news could be obtained for £10 a year.[21] The rates for press telegrams did not go down: they were at rock bottom already.

For the large daily paper the situation was different. Such a paper had its own foreign staff, and was building a reputation for its exclusive information. It gained enormously from the excitement generated—especially before the novelty wore off—of instant communication, 'The news of a cricket match in Melbourne is presented to evening newspaper readers while they sit down at tea only a few hours after the removal of the wickets.'[22] The price however was heavy. The rates for international telegrams were controlled by an international convention: in 1885 the ordinary rates were reduced from 18 centimes a word to 10½ centimes. The rates for long distance submarine cables were considerably higher. By the end of the century , after a further round of reductions in 1895, press rates varied from 2d. a word in Europe to 2s. 3d. to South Africa and 7s. 1d. to China.[23] Thus the *Manchester Guardian*, which maintained a solid coverage of foreign news, but did not get involved in extravagant feats of foreign or war reporting, was spending about £2,000 a year on telegraphy of all kinds out of a total

[20] *Statistique générale de la Télégraphie*, Berne, pub. annually by Bureau Internationale des Administrations Télégraphiques. There is much information on press telegraphy in the report and evidence of the *Select Committee on the Post Office (Telegraph Department)*, Parliamentary Papers, 1876, XIII.

[21] H. J. Wilson MSS, Sheffield Central Library, MD 5998.

[22] *Printer's Register*, Feb. 1874.

[23] G. A. Codding, *The International Telecommunications Union*, Leiden, 1952, 58; George Scott, *Reporter Anonymous; the Story of the Press Association*, 1968, 120.

expenditure of about £73,000 in 1888, and £103,000 in 1897.[24] At the extreme, *The Times*'s expenditure on its foreign news services fluctuated around £40,000 a year in the 1870s. A breakdown of these figures for 1879 shows that a lion's share went on cables from remote places—£7,500 to the Indo-European Telegraph Company, £8,100 to the Brazilian Telegraph Company, £1,600 to the Eastern Telegraph Company, and a further £3,100 spent on the American service which, it is fair to guess will have partly gone on Atlantic cables.[25] The year 1879 was one of foreign adventures, in Cabul and Natal, and these massive bills reflect the fact: the bill to the Brazilian Telegraph Company is explained by the fact that there was no direct submarine cable to South Africa, the news being taken by sea to Cape Verde and telegraphed from there. It seems that the belief that newspapers gain from foreign wars should be revised; the telegraph companies were the chief beneficiaries at this time.

Newspapers and newspaper advertising had grown up together during the eighteenth century—the names *General Advertiser*, *Daily Advertiser*, *Hull Advertiser*, proclaim the fact. Some papers, particularly the *Morning Chronicle* under James Perry, had made great fortunes for their proprietors.[26] In calculations and projections of new publications, it was assumed that advertising would account for a large proportion of the revenue, and that a sufficient volume of such advertisements would in fact arrive. Such accounts of actual papers as exist show that a proportionately large advertising revenue could be obtained by widely different publications. For example, at the bottom of the scale, the *Bucks Herald*, a poor little weekly published in support of Disraeli, with, in 1848–9, a mere 220 subscribers, had an income from sales of £4 a week and of £13 a week from advertisements.[27] Rather larger was a projected halfpenny daily in Sheffield, for which a careful estimate was made for

[24] *Guardian* archives.
[25] *The Times* archives.
[26] Ivon Asquith, 'Advertising and the press in the late 18th and early 19th centuries: James Perry and the *Morning Chronicle*, 1790–1921', *Historical Journal*, xviii, 1975, 703–24.
[27] Disraeli MSS, Bodleian Library, box 88.

H. J. Wilson in 1874. With a total weekly sale of 50,000 copies and
£48 weekly from advertisements, it would leave Wilson, who
was anxious to promote a radical temperance newspaper,
paying a weekly subsidy of about £20.[28] The accounts of *The
Times* for the second half of 1867—a normal year—show an
income from sales of £94,463, and from advertisements of
£104,766.[29] In 1888 the *Manchester Guardian* made £35,866
from sales and £54,208 from advertisements.[30] Both these
papers made big profits in the years in question.

A similar ratio—half news and editorial matter, half advertising—held good in the allocation of space. The *Printer's
Register* published a table showing that on 20 June 1882, the
proportion of space given to advertisements was as follows:[31]

Morning Post	46 per cent
Daily News	47 per cent
Daily Chronicle	45 per cent
Daily Telegraph	63 per cent
Standard	50 per cent

In provincial papers, down to the smallest halfpenny evening
papers, this 50:50 ratio held good. It is a reasonable suspicion
that a rule of thumb may have been in use: a paper was on a
sound footing if this 50:50 ratio was preserved, though the
production costs of these various papers would have been very
differently composed. The excessive quantity of advertising
carried by the *Daily Telegraph* contributed to its reputation as a
not wholly serious newspaper. A comparison with modern
practice suggests that the potentialities of advertising were not
fully explored by the Victorian proprietors: a table of the
proportions of space and revenue devoted to advertising by
different classes of newspaper in 1960 shows, among other
variations, the national quality morning papers getting 73 per
cent of their revenue from advertising and giving 41 per cent of
their space to it, while for the popular mornings the comparable figures were 45 per cent of the revenue and 34 per cent of
the space.[31a] The ideas that advertising rates could be finely

[28] H. J. Wilson papers, MD 5998.
[29] *The Times* archives.
[30] *Guardian* archives.
[31] *Printer's Register*, Aug. 1882.
[31a] *Royal Commission on the Press*, XXI, 1961–2, 23.

tuned to the progress of the circulation, and to the age and spending power of the readers, may have been acted upon instinctively but were not articulate. There were also some anomalous situations. In the first few years of publication, when *Tit-Bits* was breaking through to a wholly unprecedented circulation, it contained no advertisements at all. Equally surprisingly, the popular Sunday papers, *Reynolds's* and *Lloyd's*, with far larger circulations than the dailies, had smaller proportions of advertising, and smaller revenues from them.[32] Wareham Smith, who became advertising manager of the *Daily Mail* some twenty years later, has described how North-cliffe took little interest in developing the advertising content of his paper.[33]

Advertising, occupying about half the space and bringing in about half the revenue of the Victorian newspaper (in those few examples where we have firm information), therefore deserves a place in the present study. It is necessary to ask what kind of needs were being answered, and what sort of pressure, if any, was likely to be exerted by the advertisers.

'Advertising', as anyone who handles Victorian papers knows, meant a vast number of small advertisements. A current issues of *The Times*[34] has ten advertisements in the main body of the paper and three pages of small advertisements, only one of which is, to a modified extent, set out in the Victorian way. By contrast, the *Daily Telegraph* of May 1889 could print 60 to 70 such advertisements to a column, and in a sample fortnight, 13–25 May, printed $183\frac{1}{2}$ such columns, giving a weekly average of 5,841 advertisements.[35] In appearance all these advertisements were similar, but their origins and target areas were different. Advertisers included private citizens, commercial organizations, and public authorities. Analysis of these advertisements, while by no mean straightforward, could offer clues to the circulation and readership of individual papers.

Advertising for domestic servants was an important part of

[32] Virginia Berridge, 'Popular Sunday papers and mid-Victorian society' in *Newspaper History*, ed. George Boyce *et al.* 1978, 250–1.

[33] *Spilt Ink*, 1932, 28–33.

[34] 19 Jan. 1983.

[35] The number of columns varied considerably from day to day, Mondays and Thursdays being the busiest days.

the whole. In *The Times* and the *Morning Post*, in particular, employers advertised for servants, and in shorter sections at lower rates and in smaller print, servants sought situations. Since both these papers circulated among the nobility and gentry this needs no explanation: both papers satisfied the advertiser's criterion that they reached a large proportion of the households in the class involved. Advertisements for servants also appeared in the penny morning dailies: it seems likely that there were separate markets—specialized servants for the households of the nobility and gentry on one hand, while the cook-generals of middle-class households were recruited more locally and in less fashionable papers. Apart from this most penny papers, and *The Times*, carried large numbers of advertisements of other situations vacant, which provide useful indications of readership, since employers learn, by trial and error, where the right response may be found. The remaining private advertisements were of an infinite variety: houses, pianos, ponies and traps, lost dogs, singing birds, and many other things. In the present context it is important to notice that these private advertisers were trying to transact a single bargain: they would be satisfied with some serious inquiries and a suitable and trouble-free sale. Many of these goods, the pianos for example, would be better sold to someone near at hand. In general these advertisers would be uninterested in circulation: provided they got a sale, that would be good enough.

We may distinguish these from two distinct kinds of public advertisements, some of which appeared because they were required by law. Included among these would be formal invitations to tender for workhouse contracts, notices of public meetings, and advertisements of concerts. There would also be more clearly commercial advertisements, notices of auctions, shipping information, and regular advertisements of the high street shops. All these would aim at a wider audience than the private advertisers, though they were still local in their interests: they might prefer the 'leading local journal' or the one they believed would reach their customers, but for most of them 'circulation' in itself would not mean very much.

Secondly there was a class of advertising which needed a more than local distribution: this included the prospectuses of

new companies, announcements of annual general meetings, company reports, and so on. These appeared in the London morning dailies, and in a few provincial papers, such as the *Manchester Guardian* or the *Glasgow Herald*, which had a following among business men. Opinions among contemporary writers on the press varied on the relative values of these different kinds of advertisements. Company reports were very large and expensive, especially as many papers had differential tariffs—one rate for private insertions, another for business ones, and a third for public authorities who could stand the expense. It was held by Massingham in 1892 that the *Standard* was short of money because company advertising had fallen off in the depression.[36] Alexander Sinclair, manager of the *Glasgow Herald*, held a different view; 'Generally newspaper owners do not covet large advertisements if they can get equal revenue from comparatively small ones, on the ground that the latter are of more interest to readers.'[37] The only available evidence of the comparative values of private and other advertising comes from the accounts of the *Manchester Guardian*: in both of the years analysed 'business' advertisement revenue accounted for 58 per cent of the total revenue in 1888 and 62 per cent in 1897.[38]

There is much to suggest that the papers went to some lengths to cultivate the advertising public and indeed to create it among those who might find the business of dealing with a newspaper office daunting. It has already been shown that they do not seem to have related rates to circulation. On the contrary rates were kept simple. Some actual examples are:

1874	*East Lancashire Echo*	16 words 6*d*.
1876	*Midlands Counties Evening Express*	18 words 6*d*.
1879	*Derby Telegraph*	18 words for 6 days 18*d*.
1879	*Daily Chronicle*	2 lines 6*d*.
1879	*Standard*	3 lines 2*s*.
1879	*Daily News*	4 lines 1*s*.
1885	*Ashton Evening Reporter*	2 lines 6*d*.
1885	*Devon Evening Express*	10–14 words 6*d*.

[36] H. W. Massingham, *The London Daily Press*, 1892, 92.
[37] Sinclair, 8.
[38] *Guardian* archives.

| 1885 | *Oldham Chronicle* | 2 lines 6*d.* |
| 1886 | *Northampton Daily Chronicle* | 16 words 6*d.* |

Thus sixpence, after 1885 the price of a standard twelve-word telegram, a conventionally affordable amount, would buy an advertisement in most provincial papers and in the London *Daily Chronicle*. In the *Daily News* in the 1870s the system was explained every day in simple terms.

In descriptions of newspaper offices there was much emphasis on the halls designed for the receipt of advertisements. Like hotel foyers and banks, they were large marble halls: those at the *Standard* and *Daily Telegraph* offices were illustrated by Massingham in 1892: in Joseph Cowen's rebuilt office of the *Newcastle Daily Chronicle* it was equally grand. It had 'mahogany counters of elaborate and useful horseshoe design' and was 'replete in every respect, with departmental sections of glass, giving quiet and comparative privacy to each person in his business with the office'. (It is satisfactory to know that on more than one occasion news was crowded out of the paper by pressure of advertising.[39]) In these places the advertiser could get help and advice (possibly even help in writing), and in Newcastle, where current publications included a morning, an evening, and a weekly paper, presumably advice on where advertising would get the best results. It was part of the process whereby newspapers were cemented into the life of their communities.

There remains one kind of advertisement, which is the one most usually involved in discussions on advertising and of the mass media of the present day, that is the advertisement of branded goods, nationally marketed and intended for mass consumption. Such goods need to catch the attention of the largest possible audience, and it is in relation to them that advertising skills have developed: here, unlike the categories already discussed, sophisticated professionals are trying to persuade the uninformed. Before the 1890s the sale of goods under brand names was still in its infancy: it had appeared in tea and cocoa, soap and tobacco, and some patent medicines. (Patent medicines appear in early eighteenth-century advertisements; they were perhaps the oldest hands in the business.)

---

[39] Massingham, 119; Cowen MSS, Tyne and Wear Record Office, D 415, 350, 404.

There were also a number of patented machines, agricultural machinery and Singer sewing machines for example, which were advertised by the manufacturers rather than by retail tradesmen. For such things (except for farm machinery which obviously had a limited market), advertising rates related to circulation figures obviously made sense, or could be made to do so. By 1897 the *Daily Mail* included a good number.[40] But in general terms this sort of advertising was a late development in the nineteenth century. The increasing range of branded goods, and the increasing numbers of newspaper readers, were both phenomena of the Great Depression: the former seeking a way of increasing their share of the market, the latter benefiting from improving working-class real incomes. Once one firm began to sell under its own name, then rival firms were pushed into similar action. All needed to establish their identities and particular virtues in the minds of consumers. Nevertheless the advertising of soap, cocoa, and the rest was slow to take root in the daily press.

That this should have been so can largely be explained by the complicated contemporary reactions to display advertising. Large business notices might be welcomed, but illustrations of any kind, or large or unusual types, were 'vulgar' and to be excluded. This distaste was expressed as strongly as by anyone else by Northcliffe, who in the end contributed much to their acceptance:

... he eventually agreed to my having display type on the entire [front] page on Mondays and Fridays, but with no illustration. But from the time he gave me permission for the greater use of display type the Chief was never happy about it. The type was a constant irritation to him. I think he realised the importance of the work I was doing, but "type" offended him. And yet he plastered the sides of houses and railway bridges and the sky with hideous advertisements of the *Daily Mail*. He hated it, however, in his newspapers.[41]

In the nineteenth century newspapers did not have a

---

[40] In January 1987 *Daily Mail* advertisements included Player's Navy Cut (with the picture of the sailor), Cuticura soap, Cadbury's cocoa, Apollinaris, H. Samuel's watches, Taddy and Co's Myrtle Grove Tobacco, Adams's furniture polish, Owbridge's lung tonic, Richmond Gem, Allen Foster clothes, Gaiety Girl cigarettes, Dunlop tyres, Dr. Tibbles' Vi-Cocoa, Beecham's Pills, Spratt's dog biscuits, Scott's Emulsion, California Syrup of Figs, and Atora suet.

[41] Wareham Smith, 35.

satisfactory technique for reproducing photographs, and illustrations were restricted to occasional maps and very occasional woodcuts of subjects of outstanding importance (the ruins of the Tay Bridge in 1879 are an example). A page of a newspaper was seen as a page of letterpress and not, as today, as a complicated layout in which letterpress, pictures, headlines, and advertisements counterbalance each other. The advertisements were printed in the same style as the news and were identifiable by their content. Branded goods cannot establish their image (the word is significant) without a trademark, or illustration, signature, or 'logo' of some kind. The advertisement 'Dog owners beware! See your dog cakes are stamped "Spratt's Patent" and an X' illustrates the difficulty. The refusal by quality papers to print display advertisements could to a certain extent be circumvented by the device of printing one long advertisement so as to look like a series of small ones—for example by using the brand name as the initials of an acrostic—but in general branded goods found themselves restricted to the obscurer weekly papers. In 1885 *Deacon's Newspaper Handbook* stated that 'Experienced advertisers have generally agreed that a short advertisement constantly repeated is the right principle to act upon', and recommended 'high class county papers for the purpose'.[42]

It seems strange that advertisements which could have paid well, been cheap to reproduce, and which, to a modern eye, would have enlivened the closely-packed pages, were felt to be objectionable. This is particularly so when one remembers that the second half of the nineteenth century was a classic period for the illustrated book, with its decorated margins and elaborate title-page and binding. Nineteenth-century newspapers show a tendency—easily perceptible but harder to demonstrate—towards social climbing, writing as if their natural habitat was the chancelleries of Europe. Display advertisements were not 'art', and the goods they sold did not belong in such society: cough cures and underwear were for the servants' hall and terraced suburb. It is significant that the one paper which accepted them was the *Daily News*, where Labouchere was a powerful part-proprietor and was ostentatiously indifferent to such conventionalities.

[42] p. 23.

This account of advertising suggests a number of impli-
cations for the general development of the newspaper press. It
must be asked to what extent it circumscribed the newspapers'
freedom of action. Their advertisers, taken as a whole, were
more numerous and less sophisticated than the clients of a
modern advertising agency. They took their business to a
particular paper because they read it, or because they knew
that other people read it, or perhaps because they saw it lying
about in the public house. If a newspaper declined in competition with a newcomer, advertising would automatically drift
towards the successful rival. Examples have been quoted where
local interests might influence editorial policy, as where
brewers might object to the full reporting of temperance
meetings, and there was a persistent suspicion of some City
pages.[43] There are also two well-known occasions when newspapers lost advertising to an alarming extent as a consequence
of the policies they had supported. In January 1886 W. T.
Stead apologized to the proprietor, Yates Thompson, that the
Pall Mall Gazette's advertising revenue had fallen by £2,500 in
the previous six months, compared with the same period of
1884, as a result of the 'Maiden Tribute' case.[44] Also in 1886
the *Daily News* lost advertising on account of its support of
Home Rule.[45] But both these last two examples are of a general
sense of outrage, rather than of an attempt to protect their own
commercial interests by forcing a change of policy.

It is also important to notice that for much Victorian
advertising circulation was of limited relevance: the interests of
many private advertisers and of many businesses were purely
local. Alternatively, given the very restricted market for many
goods, the class of readers might matter more than total
circulation. According to Macdonald, manager of *The Times*,
'The truth is that newspapers pay by Advertisements and not
by circulation and that Advertisers are attracted by the classes
of readers rather than by their numbers.'[46] At the other end of
the market the manufacturers of branded goods took their
work to the small and humble local papers because display

---

[43] Expressed particularly in Labouchere's *Truth*.
[44] J. W. Robertson Scott, *The Life and Death of a Newspaper*, 1952, 144.
[45] H. W. Lucy, *Sixty Years in the Wilderness*, 1909, 132.
[46] *The Times* archives, letter dated 26 Nov. 1884 (to F. Scarborough).

advertisements were not acceptable in the leading dailies: Mitchell's and Deacon's directories, with their thumb-nail sketches of the characteristics of various provincial papers, were designed for the guidance of the non-local advertiser. What is important is that the London-based papers, with their national circulations, had, for many purposes, no intrinsic advantage.

A further point arises from the economics of Victorian newspaper printing. The cost of newsprint was a large part of the total cost of a paper, and it increased proportionately with circulation. Advertising revenue was an important part of the whole, and rates, hovering round a conventional sixpence, would not increase automatically with circulation. In these circumstances, to sell more copies could increase their unit cost: one of the estimates prepared in the 1850s, for a projected publication by Abel Heywood, actually envisaged such a situation.[47]

These production conditions, taken as a whole, cannot be said to have favoured one particular sector of the press more than another. The rotary presses gave an advantage to the larger circulation papers: but this advantage was enjoyed, as well as by the big London dailies, by the successful provincial dailies against their smaller rivals. The cost of typesetting was obviously proportionately less to the larger newspapers. Advertisements, it has been shown, did not work clearly to the benefit of any particular sector. Their value was probably affected more by the class of readers and their spending power than by circulation. It is noticeable that provincial evening papers, probably directed to a working-class readership, did not attract a large volume of advertising in their early years; at the other extreme, the *Morning Post*, with a small circulation among the gentry, did.

A very important feature of the economic history of newspapers was the continued cheapening of the processes of production. In the 1860s and 1870s the cost of printing came down, and was followed by the conspicuous fall in newsprint prices from about 1875 to 1895. Different sections of the press might stagnate, but the business as a whole was buoyant, and,

[47] A. H. Burgess's letter-book, Manchester Central Library. The letter is dated 20 Mar. 1855, when the price of paper had not begun its long fall.

as later chapters will show, it was not difficult to attract investment from some unlikely quarters.[48] On the other hand, the easy access for all to the latest news posed a threat to the London dailies. They retained their natural advantage, in being published in the centre of the large London public, and in being close to the centres of government and business. Nevertheless, if they were to retain their dominant position, they would need to print material which could be called exclusive.

[48] See p. 70 below.

II

Distribution and Circulation

THE processes of newspaper production are not difficult to describe: the information may be scanty but it is possible to generalize from it. What was likely to happen to a paper once it came off the production line is far more a matter of guesswork and controversy. The stamp tax on newspapers had provided a means of statistical measurement, which had many difficulties in interpretation—such as the fact that some stamps were bought and not used, or were handed over to other publications.[1] Once it had been abolished, however, information had to come from the newspapers themselves. A few published 'certified' figures, though these in turn were occasionally the subject of dispute.[2] Many avoided any mention of circulation figures, or resorted to such encouraging pieces of information as that 'Two Victory presses at 44,000 per hour are now in use', or '400 specially appointed agents distribute it', or even that '400,000 people live within 12 miles of it'.[3] Such circulation figures as have been collected during the preparation of the present study which seem to be trustworthy are included in an appendix to this chapter. While they come, piecemeal, from very different places and dates, they have the merit of fitting, like surviving fragments of sculpture, into an intelligible structure. Further research might well produce further reliable figures, but the distribution, and even more the readership, of newspapers are likely to remain shadowy subjects.

Information was difficult to get even for contemporaries who had an active need to find out. H. J. Wilson, anxious to take over a Sheffield paper in order to propagate his Liberal-

---

[1] T. R. Nevett, *Advertising in Britain*, 1982, 42–3.

[2] For example the *Leeds Daily News* claimed that it had a circulation of 75,578, certified by the official auditor of the Great Northern Railway, and the *Leeds Express* offered £500 to local charities if anyone could prove it (*Mitchell's Newspaper Press Directory*, 1894).

[3] Ibid. 1892 edn. These claims refer to the *Bradford Daily Telegraph*, *Lancashire Daily Express and Standard*, and *Staffordshire Daily Sentinel* respectively.

Radical views, commissioned what would now be termed 'feasi-bility studies' in 1874. One expert estimated that the *Sheffield Daily Telegraph* sold 8–9,000 on weekdays and 16,000 on Saturdays, while the *Sheffield Independent* sold 6–7,000 on week-days and 25,000 on Saturdays. The second expert held that the *Sheffield Daily Telegraph*, though a Conservative paper in a Liberal town, had far the larger circulation.[4] A more striking example of the lack of information in the newspaper world comes from a much later time: in November 1920 the *Daily Mail* made a series of house-to-house surveys in Blackburn and a number of other provincial towns, and Northcliffe com-mented, astonishingly, 'This is the first time I have learned from a basic accurate explanation what is the foundation of our sale and the kinds of people who read the Paper.'[5] He published his circulation figures, but his knowledge of his readers was apparently intuitive.

The general expansion of newspaper production and its phases are sufficiently well known. In the 1850s there were half a dozen daily papers in London, of which *The Times* had by far the largest circulation. Outside London daily papers were very rare, twice- or thrice-weekly publication being normal. There were many weekly local papers. And an important develop-ment of the 1850s and 1860s had been the mass-circulation Sunday papers, *Reynolds's Newspaper*, *Lloyd's Weekly Newspaper*, and the *News of the World*. All were originally printed on rag paper; they were clearly printed and physically tough. They could stand up to hard usage.

Generally speaking, it was believed that their circulation continued long after they had been sold to the customer. A few specific examples will illustrate the process. In 1829 Charlotte Brontë wrote,

Papa and Branwell are gone to Keighley ... for the newspaper, the *Leeds Intelligencer* ... We take two and see three newspapers a week. We take the *Leeds Intelligencer*, Tory, and the *Leeds Mercury*, Whig, ... We see the *John Bull*; it is a high Tory, very violent. Mr. Driver lends

---

[4] H. J. Wilson MSS MD 5998, letters from Fillingham, n.d., and H. C. Ellis, 12 Sept. 1874.

[5] Northcliffe papers, BL Add. MS 62203, Northcliffe to Beattie (night editor) 17 Nov. 1920.

us it, as likewise *Blackwood's Magazine*, the most able periodical there is.[6]

With their enthusiasm for the Duke of Wellington, then the Prime Minister, and in the year of Catholic Emancipation, the Brontës had exceptionally lively political interests. The wildness of the Haworth landscape should not obscure the fact that they were living in one of the fastest-growing industrial areas of the country. They could get hold of an impressive range of publications: even so, some they borrowed, others had to be fetched three or four miles.

A second example comes from a far more remote area. In Danby Dale, in the North Riding, according to the Revd J. C. Atkinson writing in 1891,

forty-five years ago there were, I believe, about three newspapers brought into the Dale, fifty years ago, certainly not more. I myself remember the *Yorkshire Gazette* passing on from one farmer to another, and its circulation hardly ceasing until it was three or four weeks old. But all that is strangely altered now. Newspapers abound, and comprising those statedly taken, and those of more casual introduction, all classes of opinion, religious, non-religious, agnostic in a greater or less degree, sectarian and unsectarian and of many different shades of political opinion, are to be met with . . . though the qualified readers may be by some assumed to be few, still the fact remains that there are some, and they not the least thoughtful or the worst informed in the parish.[7]

The third example comes from a sleepy parliamentary borough. G. L. Browne, proprietor of the *Bucks Herald*, wrote in November 1850 to Disraeli:

The circulation I keep up to 500. This is a heavy drag, but it would be suicidal to reduce the free list. For example in one part of the Borough of Aylesbury, *Ten* are sent free. The Duke [of Buckingham?] used to pay, now no one pays—so it falls on me, if I were to drop it, in would step the Whig Chronicle backed by the Lord Lieutenant.[8]

It is noticeable that in none of these examples, except

---

[6] Mrs Gaskell's *Life of Charlotte Brontë*, 1857, Everyman edn., 55. (The fifth paper was not mentioned.)

[7] J. C. Atkinson, *Forty Years in a Moorland Parish*, 1891, 16.

[8] Disraeli MSS, box 88, letter dated 11 Nov. 1850.

possibly the first, is a newspaper being distributed automatically to a household to become part of its general provisioning. But it is also clear that these conditions were no impediment to the circulation of news.

The expansion of circulations in the middle of the century required as a precondition a change in newspaper habits. Reductions in price would certainly lead to some increase in sales, but it did not necessarily follow that this increase would be such as to make the re-circulation of newspapers obsolete. A number of different developments can be suggested, all of which would help to create a buy-your-own mentality. Of these the first would be the increasing flimsiness of newsprint. The newsprint of the 1880s, which has deteriorated so badly in libraries, would not have stood up to the treatment given to newspapers in Danby Dale. Better standards of household lighting also must have helped to enlarge the demand for reading-matter in the home. Most towns of any size were supplied with gas by the 1860s, and kerosene lamps were coming into general use. (John Cassell, the publisher, had begun his career as a temperance lecturer, and by 1850 was publishing reading-matter for the working man, and ten years later, having become, as a consequence, interested in oil lamps, established a refinery in Hanwell, Middlesex.)[9] The enforced idleness of railway travellers, also, was a stimulus to reading. W. H. Smith, with his dominant position in the distribution of London papers, and his chain of railway bookstalls, built up his fortune in the 1850s and 1860s. From his entry into the House of Commons in 1868, he was rich enough to live a life largely detached from the day to day running of the business.[10] Both careers illustrate the great expansion of printing and publishing in the middle of the century.

The increased scale of newspaper operations after 1870 has often been linked to an increase in literacy after the introduction of a national system of education. This seems an unlikely explanation—not on account of any estimates of the proportion of illiterates in the country, but for reasons which emerge from the study of the industry. In all the contemporary discussions, on the reasons for the success of this publication or

[9] G. Holden Pike, *John Cassell*, 1894, 124.
[10] Lord Chilston, *W. H. Smith*, 1965, chapters 2 and 3.

the failure of that, of lower prices, possible changes in demand, and the rest, illiteracy is never mentioned as a factor to be considered. Newspapers made no attempt, as will be shown later, to adjust their presentation of the news to people of limited education. More particularly, they did not try to enlarge the range of their readers by the use of illustrations. It may be replied that techniques for reproducing pictures were expensive or slow, but popular cartoons and broadsides had a long tradition by the nineteenth century, stretching back to the earliest days of printing.[11] Had there developed a group of publications describing, say, the doings of the House of Commons in comic-strip form, it would have been evidence of the existence of an illiterate public. *Illustrated Police News* had plenty of woodcuts, and might be classed as a publication of this sort, but the great illustrated news magazine of the time, *Illustrated London News*, appears to be directed at an educated readership—for example in its archaeological reports. The clinching arguments in support of the thesis that literacy has little to do with the growth of newspaper circulations comes from the enormously increased sales achieved on occasions of exceptional public interest. For example, the *Printer's Register* claimed that the London *Echo* printed and sold 124,000 copies on the day of the verdict in the Mordaunt trial, a sensational divorce case. A better example, since it might be argued that the *Echo* was being bought by those who already had a morning paper, was in September, 1875. The Prince of Wales visited Sheffield; the *Sheffield Telegraph* employed twenty-seven additional reporters, sold 100,000 copies 'and could have sold more'. In view of the normal size of the Sheffield newspaper readership, most of these must have gone to people who did not normally buy a paper.[12] It seems that there was, at the time of the 1870 Education Act, a massive casual demand from people who either could not afford to buy a paper regularly, or did not choose to do so.

These general considerations suggest that the main emphasis, in explaining the progress of circulations, should be on price. Working people, in the 1850s and 1860s, bought Sunday

[11] J.-P. Seguin, *Nouvelles à sensation; canards du XIXe siècle*, Paris, 1959, 9 ff. An English example is the series, *The Political Drama* of the 1830s.
[12] *Printer's Register*, Mar. 1870, Sept. 1875.

papers (at a total cost of a penny or two a week), and a daily paper at the time of a royal visit or an execution, but a penny daily was too expensive. A daily costing 6*d.* a week must be compared with a labourer's wage of about 21/-, or a ton of coal at about 20/-. The penny, which, as in the Penny Post or the Penny Bank, was so often treated by Victorian propagandists as something universally affordable, was in fact a substantial sum to spend on something of casual interest. In the last thirty years of the century the fall in the price of newsprint was greater than the fall, say, in the prices of wheat or coal.[13] From the purchaser's point of view the fall could hardly be more conspicuous if a daily paper, which would once have cost a penny, could now be got for a halfpenny. In the 1880s the halfpenny papers began to cater for a wider range of interests, in their sports pages and weekend serials,[14] thus finding new sectors of the population to whom a regular newspaper would appear as an indispensable part of life.

It seems, from the circulation figures that are available, that total newspaper sales grew in a series of jumps. The transition from the first to the second stage has often been discussed, and linked to the abolition of the taxes on knowledge. Before 1855 *The Times* dominated over a handful of very small-circulation London dailies, and the major provisional papers typically appeared two or three times a week. The repeal of the stamp duties made the penny daily practicable, and the consequence was a dramatic rise in circulations, with the *Daily Telegraph* leading the way. The increase in the *Standard*'s circulation from 30–46,000 in 1860 to 160–170,000 in 1874,[15] at a time when it showed no particular editorial merit, shows how easily new penny readers could be recruited. Thereafter the increase levelled off: between 1882 and the end of the century the circulations of the *Daily Telegraph* and the *Standard* appear to have remained stationary. The circulation of the *Daily News* sank from over 93,000 in 1890 to 61,000 in 1900, even though it supported the Boer War.[16] If the increase in the population is

[13] See the figures in S. B. Saul, *The Myth of the Great Depression*, 1969, 11–15.
[14] See chapters V and XI.
[15] See appendix to this chapter.
[16] J. Saxon Mills, *Sir Edward Cook, K.B.E.; a Biography*, 1921, 191.

remembered it is clear that they were holding on to a smaller proportion of it.

In the provinces the penny dailies grew in numbers and in circulation after 1855. We may quote three important ones as examples. The *Manchester Guardian* became a daily at 2*d.* in 1855, and the price was reduced to 1*d.* in 1858. The circulation rose at that time to 23,000, then to 30,000 in 1870, and 43,000 by the end of the century. This increase took place a decade later, but was of the same order of magnitude as the London *Daily Telegraph*. The second is the old *Leeds Intelligencer*, bought up by the Yorkshire Conservative Newspaper Company in 1866 and re-launched as the penny daily *Yorkshire Post*.[17] The circulation rose to nearly 16,000 in 1870 and to 46,500 by 1885. A third is the *Sheffield Daily Telegraph*, with a circulation of (perhaps) less than 10,000 in 1874, rising to 30,000 in 1881, and about 40,000 in the 1890s.[18] These three are representative of a fairly large group—others with less well-recorded circulation figures would be the *Newcastle Daily Chronicle*, Liverpool *Daily Post*, *Birmingham Daily Post*, or *Glasgow Herald*. As prominent members of the Provincial Newspaper Society, they, the leading papers of the largest provincial towns, had been the chief promoters of the Press Association in 1868, and they gained massive benefits from it. Receiving telegraphed news, they could bring out breakfast-time editions before the London papers could physically arrive—the further they were from London the stronger their position. In many accounts of the press the period roughly from 1870 to 1914 appears as their golden age, when they successfully pushed back the circulation areas of the London press and reduced the political domination of the Capital. In about 1895 Alexander Sinclair, manager of the *Glasgow Herald*, claimed that the number of London newspapers being sent to Scotland had been much reduced, which seems possible, and that the number of Scottish papers being sent to London had increased, a much less likely situation, which might be explained by some special circumstances, such as the subscriptions of Scots in exile, or the particular business news provided by the City pages.[19] Down to 1886 the

---

[17] Mildred A. Gibb and Frank Beckwith, *The Yorkshire Post: Two Centuries*, 1954, 45.
[18] See appendix to this chapter.
[19] Sinclair, 62.

major provincial papers were Liberal, and a number of figures notable in politics and journalism were associated with them— C. P. Scott, Wemyss Reid of the *Leeds Mercury*, or William Saunders of the *Eastern Morning News* of Hull and the *Western Morning News* of Plymouth. The fact that their editorial columns are of historical interest and value has led to an exaggeration of their general prosperity.

There is reason to think that, by the end of the century, they were past their peak. Their circulations had grown to a certain level and then more or less stuck there. The lists of newspapers given in the press directories provide the basis for an explanation. The total number of daily papers in the United Kingdom, outside London, rose from 91 in 1872 to 159 twenty years later. But, within these figures of overall growth, there was a sharp distinction between morning and evening papers: there were 69 morning papers in 1872 and 74 in 1892. Evening papers however had multiplied nearly fourfold, from 22 in 1872 to 85 in 1892. By 1913 the number of provincial morning dailies was beginning to drop noticeably, from 74 in 1892 to 64 in 1913. But the number of evenings had increased again, from 84 to 104.[20]

This growth of the provincial evening papers was also largely a change from penny to halfpenny papers. With a few exceptions, notably W. T. Stead's *Northern Echo*, a halfpenny morning paper, the morning papers sold for a penny and the evenings for a halfpenny. By 1913 the success of the *Daily Mail* at a halfpenny had forced a number of morning papers down to a halfpenny also—including seventeen of the provincial dailies—but in the 1870s and 1880s the distinction was almost complete.[21]

It seems that a halfpenny paper could enter the mass market: according to Ellis, a former editor of the *Northern Echo*, 'In all times of local excitement, or on occasions of great general interest the price of a $\frac{1}{2}d$. paper would be no obstacle to the poorest person indulging in curiosity, and on many occasions the sale of a $\frac{1}{2}d$ paper is only limited by the power of production and supply.'[22] Circulations often bounded forward in an

[20] *Mitchell's Newspaper Press Directory.*
[21] Ibid.
[22] *H. J. Wilson MSS MD 5999, Ellis to Wilson, 12 Sept. 1873.*

impressive way: the prospectus of a proposed Sheffield Newspaper Company in 1887 stated that a $\frac{1}{2}d$. evening paper in the
district had reached a '59,068 circulation on one afternoon
after only being established fourteen weeks'.[23] Reliable figures
are, as usual, scanty, but the *Manchester Evening News* is
recorded as having a circulation ranging between 48,800 and
79,900 in 1879, and in 1891 of 152,000.[24] *The North-East Daily
Gazette* of Middlesbrough had one of 40,000 in 1885 and 60,500
in 1894—far greater than the *Manchester Guardian* or the *Yorkshire Post*. The Glasgow *Evening Times*, run by the same firm as
the *Glasgow Herald*, produced an 'athletic edition' in the 1890s
on Saturdays which often ran to 150,000 copies.[25]

There are occasional suggestions that these papers were
unprofitable, and that, where they were run in conjunction
with penny morning papers, they were to a greater or lesser
extent parasitic on them. They were commonly half the size of
the penny papers, and carried a similar proportion of advertising. Their paper and typesetting costs, and their advertising
revenue, could be expected to be halved also; their editorial
costs would depend on individual circumstances. Nevertheless,
the balance of the evidence must be that they were a commercial success. New papers were established as halfpenny evenings, like the *Bradford Daily Telegraph*; the *North-East Daily
Gazette*, previously a penny morning, went over to halfpenny
evening production in 1876; a well-established weekly, the
Oldham Chronicle, decided in 1880 to come out daily, but as a
halfpenny evening paper. There is always the possibility of
political subsidy for newspapers at this period, and there is
always the possibility that proprieters might have found themselves forced into evening production by local circulation wars,
or by the existence, mentioned by Sinclair of the *Glasgow Herald*,
of pirated versions of their own news columns of the preceding
morning.[26] But, while such reasons may have operated here
and there, it is impossible to believe that so many of these
papers would have been started and survived—in many cases
to the present day—if they had not been profitable. And if they
were profitable, at fourpence a dozen, it is also reasonable to

[23] Ibid., *MD 6000*.
[24] Ayerst, 324.
[25] *Deacon's Newspaper Handbook*; Sinclair, 191.
[26] Sinclair, 185.

suppose that they sold in considerable numbers. It is relevant to quote Sir Robert Ensor, a member of the Royal Commission on the Press of 1947–9. Looking back on his own years with the *Manchester Guardian* he said to one witness: 'You are aware that Mr. Scott was able to run the *Manchester Guardian*, both for the greater part of his editorship, and when he was proprietor, because he owned the *Evening News*, which was a gold mine, and made good his losses on the *Guardian*.'[27] This remark applies to the early twentieth century, but a similar trend may have been setting in elsewhere before that time.

The development of the cheap end of the provincial press had no real counterpart in London. London had its halfpenny evening papers, beginning with the *Echo* of 1868, followed by the *Evening News* of 1881, and the Liberal-Radical *Star* of 1887. (These must be seen as quite different from the Clubland evening papers, the *Pall Mall Gazette*, the *St. James's Gazette*, and the *Westminster Gazette*, which were aimed at a narrow political public and were primarily journals of comment.) Evidence of their success is conflicting. In 1875 the retiring editor of the *Echo*, Arthur Arnold, wrote to Gladstone saying that its circulation in 1870 had reached 200,000, which is probably explained by the excitements of the Franco-Prussian war.[28] The *Star* also claimed an immediate success, in sales of over 250,000 soon after it was launched.[29] On the other hand, in 1892 H. W. Massingham estimated the combined circulations of the *Echo*, the *Evening News*, and the *Star* at about 300,000.[30] There are no firm facts to go on, but it seems reasonable to deduce that the London evening papers had a volatile readership. The fact that the business history of all three is of changes of ownership or financial difficulties suggests that they were not gold mines.

It is difficult to find a fully satisfactory explanation of this difference. One, expressed in a number of places, lies in the distribution difficulties incurred. The London trade was in the hands of W. H. Smith and of other distributors. In provincial towns the newspapers themselves usually arranged long-

[27] *Royal Commission on the Press*, 1947–9, question 3370.
[28] BL Add. MS. 44182 f. 437.
[29] Paul Thompson, *Socialists, Liberals and Labour, the Struggle for London*, 1967, 97.
[30] *The London Daily Press*, 1892, 178.

distance distribution with the railway companies, and, within their home territories, sold newspapers to the sellers over the counter or through their own systems. The distribution of halfpenny papers was resisted by the London distributors, partly because they would receive half the margin for the same amount of work, and also because they foresaw, correctly, that halfpenny evening papers would undermine the penny morning trade. Evening papers were distributed by the publishers' own carts in London, and this system, being in use by the *Star*, made it in the end possible for the *Morning Leader*, using the same system, to be launched at a halfpenny.[31]

Another reason is that the London evening papers had a less compelling range of news to offer. The provincial papers contained, particularly at the beginning of the period, large amounts of material reprinted from the same day's London morning papers. In London itself that news was already stale. On the other hand the Londoner, just as much as his provincial counterpart, might want racing results, and sports news, or an account of the day's court hearings. Another possible reason may be that the London artisan had already acquired the newspaper-buying habit, and had his own *Daily Chronicle* or *Daily Telegraph*. It is clear from the advertisements in the former that the paper was at least seen by working-class people: it carried a very large number of classified advertisements, among which one may find advertisements for potmen and bottle-washers, assistants to cats-meat men, and accommodation offering 'bed to himself'.[32] Possibly the morning papers were sufficiently well established as to inhibit the expansion of the evening papers.

These differences illustrate the distinctive environment of the capital. It had millions of inhabitants—over four in 1891—and many different communities (often with their own weekly local papers).[33] There were traditional areas for certain crafts, but the size of the city, and the distance between one centre and the next, were such as to make it worth while to advertise in a newspaper jobs that could often be menial. Thus the *Daily*

---

[31] *The Times* archives: letter from Macdonald, dated 26 Nov. 1884, the clearest description of the handicap under which halfpenny papers in central London laboured. H. Simonis, *Street of Ink*, 1917, 9, explains the position of the *Morning Leader*.

[32] These items are taken from the issue of 20 Dec. 1879.

[33] There were 43 of these in 1870. Alan Lee, 280.

Telegraph and the *Daily Chronicle* could be described by Mass-ingham as 'daily labour exchanges'.[34] In the capital there may also have been a greater political awareness, particularly an awareness of foreign events. A revealing example of this is given in the history of the *Manchester Guardian*, where a London correspondent, writing of the revolutions of 1848, noticed that the 'Cockney John Bull, meaning nearly two millions of people, makes fearful efforts in his attempts to pronounce Windisch-graetz and Jellachich: but nevertheless has some idea of who those personages are and what they are about.'[35] These circumstances—the perceived usefulness of advertising, and an active interest in world affairs—may have helped to overcome consumer resistance to penny daily papers in the middle years of the century.

It must next be asked whether it is possible to measure the relative growth of the London and the provincial press. It is possible to deduce something, but not very much, from the occupational tables of the Census, by taking the numbers in a group of occupations related to printing and publishing. Authors, editors, and journalists, reporters, and shorthand writers will be predominantly concerned with newspapers, though employment in London will be partly on behalf of the London offices, of provincial papers or the agencies, and partly of monthly periodicals, trade papers, religious magazines, and other publications, which cannot properly be classed as 'news-papers'. Few if any journalists outside London would have been working wholly for London papers. Bookbinders are concerned with books, but they are included to give some clue to the relative increases in the number of printers engaged in bookwork in different areas. Printers need no particular expla-nation. Newsagents and newsroom keepers are concerned with newspapers, though provincial newsagents might be selling London papers and vice versa. The figures bristle with difficul-ties: for example they take no account of the different manning levels needed for different kinds of printing work. Newsagents also may involve difficulties of definition: nineteenth-century cartoons show newsboys as very small urchins running along the streets as they cry their wares—were they self-employed

[34] p. 91.   [35] Ayerst, 106.

Table 2.1. *Numbers employed in printing and related industries* (1871 = 100)

	1871	1881	1891

a. authors, editors, journalists: reporters and shorthand writers (in the censuses of 1881 and 1891 reporters and shorthand writers entered separately)

	1871	1881	1891
England and Wales	2,403	3,434 / 2,662 (254)	5,771 / 2,374 (339)
London	1,285	1,722 / 1,005 (212)	2,485 / 726 (250)
Lancashire	134	256 / 295 (411)	431 / 343 (578)
West Riding	84	101 / 151 (300)	219 / 158 (449)

b. bookbinders

	1871	1881	1891
England and Wales	15,474	20,097 (130)	25,736 (166)
London	9,880	12,932 (131)	15,852 (160)
Lancashire	1,568	2,114 (135)	2,507 (160)
West Riding	706	894 (127)	1,219 (173)

c. printers

	1871	1881	1891
England and Wales	44,814	61,290 (137)	86,486 (193)
London	20,052	26,226 (131)	35,009 (175)
Lancashire	5,193	7,460 (144)	10,247 (197)
West Riding	2,237	3,362 (150)	5,197 (232)

d. newsagents, newsroom keepers

	1871	1881	1891
England and Wales	4,416	5,515 (125)	9,708 (220)
London	1,733	1,773 (102)	3,098 (179)
Lancashire	603	894 (148)	1,598 (265)
West Riding	337	471 (140)	933 (277)

Population in 1891 (thousands)

England and Wales	29,002	Lancashire	3,958
London	4,212	West Riding	2,464

and regular sellers, stating their occupations to the Census enumerators, or was it a casual occupation, when times were hard? Equally important, was practice uniform all over the country? The figures in Table 2.1 are given for London and for Lancashire and the West Riding, as two densely populated areas, each with a vigorous regional press.

The figures in Table 2.1 tell a consistent story. In all these occupations, the proportionate increase between 1871 and 1891 was less in London than elsewhere, though with book-binding the difference in rates of growth was slight. But the

greatest disparity was in occupations specifically associated with the newspaper press: for example, the number of journalists and shorthand writers grew nearly sixfold in Lancashire and just over threefold in London—the provinces were catching up with London. This, however, is merely to say that London's position was a little less dominant than it had been before. In 1891 it was still true that nearly 40 per cent of the authors, journalists, and reporters in the country lived in London. As far as newspaper readers were concerned, by 1891 there was one newsagent or newsroom proprietor for every 1,360 inhabitants in London and for 2,477 and 2,641 in Lancashire and the West Riding respectively.

Another source of evidence, which is tantalizingly substantial, but extremely hard to use convincingly, is the London Daily Papers Number Book, kept by Messrs W. H. Smith and Son, which has survived for the years 1852–7, 1876–7, and 1887–93.[36] It records, daily, the number of quires of each of the main London dailies distributed from the head office, Strand House, and the numbers dispatched by rail. (Except for the years 1852–7 it also distinguishes the number going by each main line.) In general it is impossible to say what proportion of the trade was in W. H. Smith's hands, though in 1877, where there are available circulation figures for the *Daily Telegraph*, and the *Standard*, and *The Times*, it seems that over one third of the circulation was involved. It is also impossible to tell how far the papers sent by train actually went: what proportion stayed in the Home Counties and what was directly competing with provincial papers. Smith's records show little change between 1876 and 1887, but a decline, for all papers except the much newer *Daily Chronicle*, between 1887 and 1892.

The decline between 1887 and 1892, spread evenly across different papers and across both the London and provincial trade, could hardly support a thesis that London papers were being pushed back by the growth of the provincial press; it suggests, rather, that they were stagnating. The much lower percentage of *Daily Chronicles* dispatched supports the belief that it was far more of a Londoner's paper than the others. Another feature of these figures is that they changed little from one period to another. In the records themselves the number of

---

[36] W. H. Smith's archives, A.17, A.68, A.69.

quires fluctuates by a very narrow margin daily. This is consistent with a newspaper-reading public with regular buying habits.

To these generalizations the figures for 1 September 1877 form a striking exception. In less than a year the number of *Daily News* had gone up by 23 per cent, and of *Telegraphs* by 46 per cent. This can be linked to the Turkish crisis. The number of both papers jumped between July and August 1876, July being the month in which the *Daily News* published its celebrated reports of the Bulgarian massacres. They dropped back to their previous level in the spring of 1877. With the Russian declaration of war against Turkey at the end of April they began to climb steadily. (The Number Book ends in September, so the story cannot be taken further.) Nevertheless, it provides a good illustration of the public excitement about this question and the way in which the popular papers—the *Daily News* on the Russian side and the *Daily Telegraph* on the Turkish—were involved.

Table 2.2. *The total number of quires distributed in London and the provinces*

	The Times	Daily News	Daily Telegraph	Standard	Daily Chronicle
1 December 1876	1,012	1,598	2,770	2,066	—
1 September 1877	993	1,967	4,031	2,397	—
1 December 1887	706	1,504	2,775	2,889	839
1 December 1892	700	1,222	2,486	2,588	952
Proportions dispatched by train (%)					
1 December 1887	57	63	61	62	44
1 December 1892	60	64	59	61	45

We may supplement these figures with two small but precise pieces of evidence, the solitary surviving sales records of Smith's railway bookstalls for the period, from Bradford (probably Exchange) in 1868, and Hatfield, Hertfordshire in 1876. The Bradford record, and possibly the Hatfield also, may exaggerate the usual range of reading-matter available: more titles would be on sale at the station than in the average back-street newsagents. Had these records, which were kept every year for every bookstall, and showed the publications bought

Table 2.3. *Bradford 1868 (total population, 1871: 145,830)*

	Description (Penny daily unless otherwise stated)	Daily average sale			
		March	June	September	December
The Times	3*d.*	30	27	25	26
Morning Post	3*d.*	0	0	0	0
*Daily News**	3*d.*	2	43	55	60
Daily Telegraph		99	94	74	72
Standard		87	90	64	67
Manchester Examiner	Cobdenite-Liberal	55	51	49	39
Manchester Guardian	Whig-Liberal	16	18	18	14
Manchester Courier	Conservative	8	8	6	8
Yorkshire Post	Conservative	39	36	52	52
Leeds Mercury	Liberal	95	95	92	79
*Bradford Daily Telegraph***	Liberal, ½*d.* evening	–	–	60	62
		Weekly average sale			
Bradford Observer†	Liberal	102	118	110	91 (daily)
Bradford Times	Liberal	36	37	40	46
[Liverpool]*Albion*	Whig-Liberal	0	2	2	2

* Price reduced to 1*d.* 8 June 1868.

and returned unsold every day, survived in greater numbers, they would have been an invaluable source. As it is, these two have some significant information to offer, and are summarized here in Tables 2.3 and 2.4.[37]

In Bradford in 1868 the London papers, the *Daily Telegraph* and the *Standard*, sold more than any other, except the *Leeds Mercury* and, at the end of the year, the *Bradford Observer*. There were no papers, other than a couple of Liverpool *Albions*, from any provincial town other than Manchester. The small steady sale of the *Manchester Guardian* is probably due to its excellent business news. With its market reports and raw material prices, from a wide range of places, it was the *Financial Times* of the north. The substantial sales of the *Manchester Examiner* may well have been exceptional. It was a straightforward party paper, the organ of Cobdenite principles in Manchester. The general

[37] W. H. Smith's archives, A.38 and 490.

Table 2.4. *Hatfield, 1876 (total population, 1871: 6,359)*

	Description (Penny daily unless otherwise stated)	Daily average sale	
		March	September
The Times	3*d.*	15	15
Morning Post	3*d.*	0	1
Daily News		25	34
Daily Telegraph		48	63
Standard		33	43
Globe	Evening	5	6
Pall Mall Gazette	Evening, 2*d.* Conservative		
Evening Standard		4	4
Echo	Evening, ½*d.*	8	11
		Weekly average sale	
News of the World	Sunday, 2*d.*	7	6
Lloyd's Weekly Newspaper	Sunday	95	96
Reynolds's News	Sunday	16	16
Weekly Times	Saturday	27	29
Weekly Dispatch	Saturday	21	20

No provincial papers other than Hertfordshire weekly papers

election of 1868 took place at the end of November. It was bitterly contested in Bradford, in a feud between the voluntaryist Liberals, whose candidate was Edward Miall, and the followers of W. E. Forster. The *Manchester Examiner* may have been widely read in the absence of a suitable locally produced paper. In the second half of 1868 two Bradford papers appeared, the new halfpenny *Bradford Daily Telegraph* on the radical side in August, followed by the decision of the old-established *Bradford Observer* to come out daily at a penny in October. Both immediately found a good sale on the bookstall—the *Bradford Observer* beating the *Daily Telegraph* into second place. The London papers, the *Manchester Examiner*, and indeed the *Leeds Mercury*, all declined in popularity once the strictly local papers appeared. The political infighting, between different sects of Liberals, which has parallels in many northern towns, continued into the 1880s. Both Bradford papers prospered, and one may guess that the sale of the outsiders was restricted.[38]

[38] Alan Lee, 137–8, for the *Bradford Observer*. The election of 1868 in Bradford is described in T. Wemyss Reid *Life of . . . William Edward Forster*, 2 vols 1888. 447–9.

At Hatfield, not very surprisingly, no provincial papers appear in the list at all, other than Hertfordshire weekly local papers. Evening papers had a small sale, presumably because Hatfield, though on the main Great Northern line, was too far from London. The figures are of interest as giving an illustration in detail of the effects on circulations of the Bulgarian atrocities question. All had risen: the popular papers, the *Standard*, the *Daily News*, the *Daily Telegraph*, and the *Echo* rose by about a third.

The detailed figures of daily sales show that in both Bradford and Hatfield there was little fluctuation from day to day in the numbers of each title sold, which suggests again that we are dealing with a regular body of readers. Similarly the ratio of sales of the *Daily News*, *Daily Telegraph*, and *Standard* remain roughly the same, in both places, and were similar to those in the Daily Number Book. The table also shows the totally derisory circulation of the *Morning Post*: one would not expect it to be read in Bradford, but would expect more support in the Tory borough of Hatfield, where one copy only was sold daily in September, perhaps to Lord Salisbury.

Another series of clues to circulation areas can be found, and used with caution, in the advertisement columns. Businesses may misjudge their markets, but the advertisements of births, marriages, and deaths, inserted by readers, say something about their geographical distribution. No attempt has been made in this book to study the figures on an adequate scale, but a series of sample counts made for fortnightly periods in the years 1874, 1879, and 1883 shows that between a third and a half of these advertisements inserted in the *Daily News*, *Standard*, and *Daily Telegraph* came from places outside London or the Home Counties—they are certainly enough to show that the readership had not retreated to the south-east of England.

How far afield did provincial newspapers circulate, in the sense of being easily and regularly obtainable? It can certainly be shown that they did not circulate in any regular way in London, and they would hardly have been expected to. They were obtainable, as they would be today, at the railway termini, and sometimes from special agents; the Cowen papers contain (among other evidence of vigorous local competition) a complaint that the 'Chronicle reaches Smith's bookstall at

King's Cross later than both the Journal and Leader . . . and it is consequently very seldom at the stall before the 10 o'clock express for Newcastle leaves King's Cross.'[39] When the *Manchester Guardian* wished to publicize its opposition to the Boer War it tried to organize a team of direct sellers—boys on bicycles in uniform—in the suburbs; previously it had only been available in a few places in the City and on the Inner Circle.[40]

To keep in touch with the provincial press in London needed initiative. A politician anxious to know how his public image was appearing might take in a variety of provincial papers—Dilke is a good example. The Library of the House of Commons had a selection of provincial papers, but by no means the full range: in a debate on the subject in 1887 Labouchere complained 'It really is a monstrous thing that the officers of this House should have the power of saying what literature we shall read and what literature we shall not read.'[41] (The absences actually complained of were *United Ireland* and, not a provincial paper and most surprisingly, *Reynolds's Newspaper* 'the only democratic paper I am acquainted with', according to another member.) The records of the National Liberal Club show that in 1892 they took in two copies each of the most important provincial papers: the *Manchester Guardian, Sussex Daily News, Freeman's Journal, Scotsman, Scottish Leader, Glasgow Herald, North British Daily Mail, Birmingham Post, Leeds Mercury, Liverpool Mercury,* Liverpool *Daily Post, National Press, Newcastle Daily Chronicle, Western Morning News,* and *Western Daily Mercury.*[42] Even this list has notable gaps—there is nothing from the Eastern counties, or from Bristol or Sheffield. The most important Conservative provincial paper, the *Yorkshire Post*, is not there, nor is there a single example of the flourishing evening press. As in the House of Commons, members would not be hearing a full range of provincial opinion.

This failure to be heard in London may hardly have mattered to the provincial newspapers and their owners from

[39] Cowen MSS, D 392; letter dated 6 May 1888.
[40] Ayerst, 292.
[41] *Hansard,* 13 July 1887.
[42] Archives of the National Liberal Club, Bristol University Library, (minutes of the newspaper committee).

an economic point of view. Nor would it reduce their capacity to articulate and stimulate opinion in their home territories. It would certainly make a very great difference to a provincial paper's influence: every MP would see the *Standard*, or the *Pall Mall Gazette*—or even a scurrilous gossip sheet like *The World*—but only the exceptionally enterprising Liberal would know the editorial opinions of the *Yorkshire Post*, and be able to assess how much popular support they enjoyed. It was one of the things contributing to London's ignorance of the provincial scene.

This kind of evidence which has been produced gives a picture of newspapers operating profitably within their own defined catchment areas. Several might, and did, compete in any given place, but they were unlikely to attempt to sell papers further afield. How far is this in fact true? H. J. Hanham has sketched an outline of newspaper development in the 1870s and 1880s, which suggests that the most successful provincial papers were themselves expanding their areas so as to dominate whole regions.[43] Some evidence can be produced in support of this view. Some papers could expand their circulation areas because they offered particular features or had a scarcity value: the *Manchester Guardian*'s business news has already been mentioned; the rarity of Conservative papers in the North gave the *Yorkshire Post* a scarcity value. The regional circulation of the *Manchester Guardian* is suggested by the sums quoted in the paper's accounts which were spent on railway contracts—£1,411 in 1888, and £3,189 in 1897.[44] In a number of cases a daily paper published in a big town would produce a weekly edition which would sell further afield—this was a likely arrangement in places where a large town had a rural hinterland; for example, the weekly edition of the Liverpool *Daily Post* circulated in North Wales.

The further the place of publication was from London, the better the chances for a regional role of this kind. In the Cowen papers we read that competition with London papers in Middlesbrough, Stockton, and Darlington was defeated in 1883 by sending the *Newcastle Daily Chronicle* south by a train which arrived earlier, and that this edition accounted for 'a

[43] H. J. Hanham, *Elections and Party Management: Politics in the Time of Disraeli and Gladstone*, 1959, 110–111.
[44] *Guardian* archives.

good many' of the papers printed.[45] Similarly in central
Scotland, many hours away from London, the Scottish papers
could circulate in surrounding districts in the morning without
opposition. In the 1890s the first edition of the *Glasgow Herald*
was destined for Dundee and Aberdeen, and the second for
Dumfries and the south-west, and for Edinburgh and the east
coast.[46] In the same way the *Scotsman* developed its sales to the
north-east coast and the Highlands from 1865 onwards.[47] A
town which was a railway centre was also a good place for
newspapers. One example is York, with a population of about
50,000 in 1881: it had two morning dailies and one evening
paper. Another striking example is Darlington, where Stead's
Northern Echo was published: it had a population of only 35,000
in 1881, but had good railway connections. In Yeovil, away
from the manufacturing areas, there was a population of
17,000 and two weekly papers.

Nevertheless this picture of territorial expansion is somewhat
misleading: the norm was the town newspaper, with a political
affiliation—how close is another matter. The town needed to
be of a certain size; the *Printer's Register* held that a population
of 50,000 was the minimum necessary to support a daily paper.
In what might be called a typical two-member borough one
might have, by the mid-1880s, two rival dailies, each in
association with an evening and a weekly edition. Larger places
might have more: there were two rival Liberal papers in
Newcastle, the *Leader* and the *Chronicle*, and in Manchester
there were the Tory *Courier*, the Liberal-Radical *Examiner*, and
the more Whiggish *Guardian*. Places the size of Nottingham,
Ipswich, and Southampton conform to the model. There were
also daily papers in more unlikely places; for example Scarborough, with a population of about 35,000 in the 1880s, but
isolated, had two evening papers but no morning paper. These,
the *Scarborough Daily Post* (Conservative) and the *Scarborough
Evening News and Daily Mercury* (Liberal) turn out on inspection
to be minimal productions, containing some agency news,
advertisements, and lists of summer visitors. Equally unpromis-

---

[45] Cowen MSS, D 381; Mark Noble, *Short Sketches of the Eminent Men of the North of
England*, Newcastle, 1885, 55.
[46] Sinclair, 90.
[47] Charles A. Cooper, *An Editor's Retrospect*, 1896, 165, 210.

ing was the location of the Penzance *Evening Tidings* (neutral).

The provincial newspaper, as an agency for political instruction and the dissemination of news, needs to be seen in relation to such a model. It was something with strong local roots and interests, professionally run, whose news coverage was applicable to a strictly defined neighbourhood. If it achieved a wider sale, that was a bonus. Circulations grew, but no newspaper advanced from a provincial base to swamp the country. There is no a priori reason why this should not have happened. The area of Lancashire and the West Riding would seem to be a suitable place for such a development: in 1891 its combined population was 50 per cent greater than London's, the distances between towns were not great, and the railway communications were excellent. Elsewhere there were attempts at the syndication of newspapers,[48] but these were attempts to use common news services, or syndicated articles for topographically separate publications. No megalomaniacs are famous among the provincial proprietors. The reasons for this style of development are open to discussion: it may be a matter of accident—one press baron, if he appears, may provoke the entry of others of similar mind into the arena. But it must lie also in the character of the nineteenth-century English provinces. These places, separate and largely self-governing single-industry towns, or industrialized rural areas where all the villages were involved in the same occupation, such as the Northamptonshire boot and shoe districts, or the mining areas, had limited news interests in common. It is hard to imagine a line of editorial comment which, except in times of national excitement, would have held different districts' loyalty equally, other than the vaguely democratic sentiments of *Lloyd's* or *Reynolds's*. There would have been many places where there would have been a population interested for their own livelihood in, say, the American South, or in the Baltic provinces, and in the behaviour of the local Board of Guardians, but not very much in other things. It may perhaps be argued that the First World War established the national newspaper decisively because for four years it provided an overriding national focus of interest which the London papers, with their much bigger resources, could better satisfy. Whatever the reason, the ab-

[48] See chapter VI.

sence of really vigorous competition between one area and another was the basis on which the provincial daily press grew; the system of news provision through the Press Association, established and owned by the common action of the provincial proprietors, depended on it.

It is harder to find out how many newspapers were bought by various classes of reader than it is to make assessments of their regional distribution. We can, however, be confident that by the end of the nineteenth century they were being generally read, and afforded, even by the poorest. For example, the budgets annexed by Seebohm Rowntree to his study of poverty in York include an entry for 'papers' in a number of cases, and these are the budgets of his 'Class 1' where total weekly earnings were under 26s. a week. Rowntree specifically referred to inability to buy a halfpenny newspaper as an example of real privation.[49] A variety of evidence can be adduced to suggest that the newspapers were regarded by those in authority as a normal and necessary feature of British life well before that time. A Treasury return of 1881/2 shows that the Admiralty had spent £835 on a total of just under 100,000 items for the use of HM Ships abroad.[50] A good proportion of these were periodicals of the popular but improving variety, the *Leisure Hour, Band of Hope Review, Home Words on the Waters*, and the like, but there were also large numbers of Hampshire local papers, and a very large number of *Lloyd's Weekly Newspaper*. A similar return shows the provision, at £317 much less generous but nevertheless spent, of reading-matter for HM Prisons.[51] Once again the choice was bland and improving, the cruelly-named *Leisure Hour* was bought in the largest numbers, but the Home Office was sufficiently broad-minded to include the *Irish Monthly*, and *Catholic Progress*. It is possible that newspapers additional to those listed may have been bought, as the return is stated to be incomplete. Ten years later another, privately-organized, return was made by W. T. Stead in the *Review of Reviews* in pursuit of his idiosyncratic view of a periodical as a 'church' in which the editor preached and the

[49] B. Seebohm Rowntree, *Poverty, a Study of Town Life*, 4th edn., 1902, 133, 263 ff.
[50] PRO T 1/13802.
[51] Ibid.

readers listened, and in which the editor conducted a band of willing helpers. In March 1890 he directed his church to find out what provision of reading-matter, and toys, was available in workhouses, and published the results.[52] As a celebrated ex-inmate of Coldbath Fields Prison, he was anxious to ensure that conditions for the aged and for workhouse children should not fall below those for prisoners. The inquiry produced results from helpers who had visited 127 workhouses. The reports varied greatly. In some places, near Waterloo Station for example, collections were made of commuters' discarded papers; in many places visitors brought bundles of old papers and magazines; in Irish workhouses Protestant reading only was apt to be supplied; in a number of places inmates ordered and received their own newspapers; in many nothing whatever was available; and in Kirkwall, Orkney the six inmates received the *Scotsman* daily—further evidence of that paper's circulation area. In these interesting and sometimes obscure reports one or two points stand out. The first point was that 'there is practical unanimity as to the eagerness of the old people for reading', for example in East London there were visitors who 'never can keep any old numbers by them, because whenever we show our face, the question comes, 'Have you brought us any books?' Or in Liverpool where 'Newspapers of any description are much appreciated by the inmates even if past date by days; also disused books and magazines. Any paper or printed matter will be accepted with thanks. The fault lies with the people who keep papers and periodicals lying about for weeks, for no earthly use.' A second point is that the case for providing reading-matter was endorsed by Ritchie, the President of the Local Government Board, who wrote to Stead that he was considering the issue of a circular letter to Boards of Guardians on the subject.

These returns are of interest in that they are concerned with three populations who cannot by any stretch of the imagination be regarded as a labour aristocracy, superior in tastes, education, or income to the general run of the working classes. One of them, the workhouse aged, represents a cross-section of the working class that had been in its prime and forming its reading habits in the 1860s or earlier.

[52] *Review of Reviews*, 1890, 269–75, 380–4, 472–3.

The growth of the newspaper reading public seems to have taken place in a series of catching-up operations. In the 1850s the readers of the *Daily Telegraph*, commonly believed to come predominantly from the London tradesmen and clerks, were added to the prosperous readers of the threepenny *Times*. In the next twenty years the readers of the *Daily Chronicle*, believed to be the London artisans, joined them. The provincial morning dailies introduced habits already established in London into the provinces, and the halfpenny evening papers extended them to the provincial working classes. The evidence of the workhouse readers, and the popularity of special editions in the middle of the century suggest, however, that the limiting factor on circulations was not illiteracy or lack of interest in the news, but price and availability.

A number of other reflections are suggested by consideration of a mass readership. How long did the recirculation of newspapers survive? The use of wood-pulp by itself would have restricted the practice. Nevertheless it continued for *The Times*, which was still printed on good quality paper. A recent letter to *The Times* quoted a bookseller's advertisement from Teignmouth in the 1870s offering the summer visitors, among other benefits, the loan of the 'London *Times* by the hour'.[53] The memoirs of one of W. H. Smith's employees described how in the 1860s he was employed in Birmingham, as part of his job, in collecting *The Times* from hotels and restaurants which had hired it for the earlier part of the day, for posting to country customers. It was a regular commercial operation and not the kind of private arrangement which is found in common-rooms at the present day.[54]

How far and for how long did the old habit of reading papers aloud in public houses survive? It was sufficiently common in Sheffield in the 1870s for it to be a factor in H. J. Wilson's calculations. The decline of public reading could probably be illustrated by examination of the literary style of the papers themselves. A newspaper such as the Chartist *Northern Star* was clearly designed for public reading. One can

[53] *The Times*, 11 Apr. 1983.

[54] J. E. Hall, 'Reminiscences of the Birmingham house' in *Newsbasket. The monthly journal of the staff of W. H. Smith and Son*, vol III, 1910, 131–3. Copy in Messrs W. H. Smith's archives.

sense this in the manner in which it makes its political points. The reference in H. J. Wilson's papers deserves quotation: the *Sheffield Independent* was an inferior paper, among other reasons because it introduced 'topics and language that should only be publicly met with in meetings for religious or benevolent purposes and which, when read in public houses and places of general resort not only offend, but give occasion for derisive ribaldry'.[55]

The difference between hearing or seeing a newspaper in a public house, or hearing a town crier in the market square, or indeed seeing or hearing the BBC, and having a newspaper of one's own, seems fundamental. The purchaser can choose what to read and what to skip, however restricted the selection of news and comment may be. He can read and reread till he has has understood and formulated his criticism. He can refer back to previous issues, or follow his particular interests from one day to the next. With public reading, it is a fair guess that interest will concentrate on the main stories of the day. The impact on feelings and opinions may well be stronger and quicker to take effect. The propaganda effect may well be greater: the range of tastes and interests catered for is bound to be narrower.

Other questions remain, some of which are probably incapable of a categorical answer. Were newspapers bought by working-class women? Was it usual for people to develop a strong attachment and fixed habits where their normal reading was concerned? All the anecdotes and memories that the present writer has heard suggest that they did, but the memories of those now living do not go back to the period of this study. In 1917 someone from the *Daily News* told H. Simonis, 'It is remarkable how frequently we still hear from people whose families have subscribed from 1864, or who have themselves subscribed from 1870.'[56] How far was newspaper reading a matter of social norms? Did families in suburban villas lose face if they did not take in a newspaper, or if they merely read a low-class one? Conversely were families in back street terraces putting on airs if they read penny papers, or London papers if they lived in the provinces?

[55] H. J. Wilson papers, MD 5998, letter from Ellis dated 12 Sept. 1874.
[56] *Street of Ink*, 1917, 54.

CIRCULATION FIGURES

The most commonly used source for newspaper circulations is A. P. Wadworth's 'Newspaper circulations, 1800–1954' in *Transactions of the Manchester Statistical Society*, 1954–5, which appear to be often derived from figures given by the *Printer's Register*. Two other sources are the advertisements in *Mitchell's Newspaper Press Directory*, which sometimes refer to certified figures, and *Deacon's Newspaper Handbook* which between 1885 and 1895 distinguished those figures which it believed to be reliable. There are also occasional references in private correspondence.

	Date	Circulation	Source
a. London papers			
Daily Chronicle	1886	130,000	Deacon
	1893	155,000	,,
Daily News	1868	50,000	Wadsworth
	1871	150,000	,,
Daily Telegraph	1861	141,700	,,
	1871	190,855	*Printer's Register*
	1873–4	176,174	,, 'audited, over year'
	1876 (July–Dec.)	200,317	,,
	1877 (May–June)	242,215	,,
	1882	241,201	,, 'audited'
	1885	214,900	Deacon
	1888	300,000	Wadsworth
Echo (½*d.* evening)	1870	200,000	A. Arnold, editor, see p. 35 (peak figure)
	1881	100,000	Deacon
Lloyd's Weekly Newspaper	1879 May	612,902	*Printer's Register*
	1893	910,000	Deacon
Standard, morning and *Evening* combined	1860	30–46,000	Philip Rose in Carnarvon MSS, see p. 62 below
	1874 (Jan.)	163–176,000	*Printer's Register*
	1877	171,400	,, 'certified'
	1882	242,062	,, ,,
	1889	255,000	Wadsworth
	1893	255,300	Deacon
The Times (3*d.*)	1861	65,000	*History of The Times*
	1871 (22 March)	67,806	,, ,,

	Date	Circulation	Source
The Times (3*d.*)	1877 (average)	60,886	*History of The Times*

b. Provincial papers

	Date	Circulation	Source
Barnsley Chronicle	1874	10,230 weekly	*Printer's Register*
Bradford Daily Telegraph	1881	13,000	,, ,, 'certified'
(½*d.* evening)	1886	22,500	,, ,, ,,
Bury and Suffolk Standard	1881	3,509 weekly	,,
	1886	13,800 ,,	,,
[Cardiff] *Western Mail*	1871	11,667 daily	*Printer's Register*
		7,941 weekly ed.	,,
Glasgow Herald	1870	30,000	Wadsworth
Kentish Express (Ashford)	1874	20,000 weekly	*Printer's Register*
Leeds Daily News	1888	28,600	Mitchell, 'certified'
(½*d.* evening)	1890	50,000	,, ,,
	1892	73,000	,, ,,
	1894	75,578	,, but see p. 26 above
[Liverpool] *Daily Post* *Weekly Post* }	1882	428,600	} Mitchell; audited weekly total for three papers
Liverpool Echo (½*d.* evening)	1892	805,425	
Liverpool Echo	1881	35–50,000	E. R. Russell MSS BL Add. MS 62993
Manchester Guardian	1880	30,000	Wadsworth
	1888	38,000	*Guardian* archives
	1897	43,000	,, ,,
Newcastle Daily Chronicle	1871	28,539	*Printer's Register*
	1873 (March–June)	35,534 (daily)	,, 'audited'
		31,531 (weekly ed.)	,, ,,
Newcastle Daily Chronicle	1893	120,000	Deacon
North-East Daily Gazette	1885	40,000	,,
(Middlesbrough)	1894	60,500	,,
Northern Echo (Darlington)	1875	13,000	Robertson Scott, p. 103
Preston Guardian	1873	14–20,000 twice weekly	*Printer's Register*
Scotsman	1864	17,000	C. Cooper, editor,
	1870	30,000	autobiography, p. 165
	1877	50,000	
Sheffield Daily Telegraph	1881	30,000	Deacon
	1886	40,000	,,
	1894	'about 40,000'	Wilson MSS
Western Gazette (Yeovil)	1881	31,000 weekly	Deacon
	1886	35,000	,,
West Sussex Gazette (Arundel)	1868	24,000 weekly	*Printer's Register*
	1871	28–30,000	,, ,,
Yorkshire Post (Leeds)	1870	15,000	Wadsworth
	1881	41,165	Gibb and Beckwith's
	1886	46,637	history

III

Party Politics

In recent years there has been much academic discussion of the relationship between the nineteenth-century press and party politics. It is clear that party organizations were a main force in the expansion of the press, whether we are talking of new publications, more frequent publications, or cheaper ones. It is also clear that politicians had their 'mouthpieces' in the press. The effects of the latter on the way in which news was formed and communicated is to be discussed later in this book. Here the objective is to try and assess in general terms what effect party politics had on the shape of the newspaper press as it developed in the later nineteenth century.

It is important to look at 'politics and the press' over a fairly long time-scale. The newspapers of the eighteenth century had been closely linked to party politics. John Brewer has shown how politicians in the 1760s entered into public controversy in pamphlets, and placed inspired contributions in the *Gazette* and the *Public Advertiser*. It comes as no surprise to read of a contemporary who says 'I am very apt to believe that Mr Pitt is greatly owing his Popularity at home, and his Reputation abroad to Pamphlets and News Papers wrote under his Direction and that of his Admirers.'[1] It is more remarkable that Bute, the Scotch favourite, 'should also be the politician who, more than any other, made covert attempts to shape public opinion by using the press.'[2] No mention is made in this context of the use of political funds, public or private, to establish newspapers, but it is plain that the frontiers between journalism, pamphleteering, and government and party propaganda, were hazy in the middle of the eighteenth century.

Aspinall's work, dealing with events a generation later, describes a press very closely integrated into the political system, by subsidies, pressure on editors, the giving of exclusive

---

[1] John Brewer, *Party Ideology and Popular Politics at the Accession of George III*, Cambridge, 1976, 228.
[2] Ibid., 221.

news, or advertising preferences. It is not perhaps sufficiently emphasized how exceptional the conditions were: over twenty years of war with the largest and most dangerous European power were followed by the nervous anxieties of the 1820s and 1830s. It would have been surprising if the press had not been under political control. Aspinall brought his book to an end in the middle of the century, with the belief that nineteenth-century conditions would loosen the links, not least by the greatly increased prosperity of the press which would therefore be less susceptible to bribes and threats.[3] The effects of recent writing by Alan Lee and Stephen Koss has been to modify the picture:[4] political intervention continued. It is important, nevertheless, to remember what went before: if we take, say 1760 or 1800 as a base line it would be hard to draw a graph showing a 'rise' of the political press.

Some of the old connections disappeared, such as the imprisoning of journalists for writing critically of the government, or (as far as we know) the payment of government subsidies. One connection at least survived: the list of papers friendly to the government to be used for official advertising. According to Aspinall, the use of such a list does not go back to the eighteenth century. It was first clearly seen when *The Times* turned against the government in 1805 and temporarily lost its advertising, but we do not know how much revenue the paper lost as a result.[5] Advertising would have consisted of such matters as government contracts: it might have been important to the finances of papers in such places as the dockyard towns, but the growth in wealth and prestige of *The Times* would be scarcely affected. The government list survived, in the teeth of the wind of change, and to the annoyance of civil servants, to the end of the nineteenth century: the fact that it did so suggests the partiality and self-interest of the agitation for a free press in the middle of the century. The 'taxes on knowledge' put up costs and were evil, but the government list, in a period of predominantly Liberal administrations, attracted no attention.

The list appears from time to time in the historical record. In

---

[3] A. Aspinall, *Politics and the Press c. 1780–1850*, 1949, 379 ff.
[4] See chapter I note 11 and note 13.
[5] Ibid., 127–8.

1874 E. A. Fitzroy, the proprietor of the Conservative *John Bull*, complained that he was getting no advertisements, despite being on the government's list, and received a snub from the officials (about which he complained again, this time to Disraeli's secretary): 'I may remark that the John Bull is scarcely likely to be read by the class of people who tender for Admiralty contracts.'[6] In August 1879 a parliamentary question established that current spending on government advertising was a little over £10,000, the War Office, Admiralty, and Inland Revenue each spending three or four thousand pounds, and the Customs a mere £150.[7] The following year, when the Liberal government took office, the President of the Press Association made a complaint against the new government's proposal to discontinue the advertising of the names of bank shareholders: newspaper proprietors 'having been kept from the (comparatively small) patronage of the late government for more then six years, a re-deprivation of that to which they had reasonably looked forward is not pleasant to contemplate.'[8]

In June 1880 a copy of the list was sent from the Treasury to the Board of Trade by Lord Richard Grosvenor, the Liberal Whip, with the instruction 'I should be obliged if you would give intimation for having the list strictly adhered to.' The list in question excluded the *Daily Telegraph* and *Morning Post*. Chamberlain, President of the Board, inquired what the departmental practice was, and was told 'We do it cheaply and well and we use the best papers for our purpose irrespective of Politics.' The writer added, contradicting himself, 'I object very strongly to these political lists but for peace and to save worry and letters often use them when otherwise I should not.'[9]

In January 1893, again with an incoming Liberal government, the subject once more came to the surface, in the Home Office. Herbert Gladstone, parliamentary secretary, explained to Asquith, the Home Secretary, the current practice: 'Whether good or bad, in every department so far as I know excepting the Home Office and the Foreign Office, which I don't suppose

[6] Disraeli MSS, box 88, B XX/A.
[7] *Hansard*, vol 249, 12 Aug. col. 814.
[8] Herbert Gladstone MSS, BL Add. MS 46048, ff. 123–4.
[9] PRO BT 13/11, letters dated 21 June and 7 July 1880.

ever advertise (or very seldom) it is the custom to transfer advertisements according to the politics of governments.'[10]

These examples show that the practice was still normal, and not seriously questioned. In some cases it had been relaxed: technical advertising of the Board of Trade's Marine Department, and the advertising of the Prison Commissioners, escaped the system. It must in practice have caused the newspaper readers more inconvenience than the excluded journals suffered. For example, the competitive examinations of the Civil Service were advertised, and the lists, excluding the *Daily Telegraph* in 1880, and the *Yorkshire Post* in 1893, cut off advertising in papers likely to be read by the sort of people interested in clerical work. These lists are a curious survival from Namier's political world, and illustrate the way in which archaic arrangements can survive simply through the lack of any drive to remove them.

The major significance of party politics to the development of the press derives from the propensity of party organizations to establish fresh papers in order to organize different sections of the voting public. The total extent of this would be hard to measure. H. J. Wilson of Sheffield received a letter from J. H. Bell, the former editor of the *Northern Echo* of Darlington, concerning a political paper which Wilson was anxious to establish

... if there is to be a limited liability company then the *Investors Guardian* will publish the names and any person can at any time see the articles of association. I counsel the avoidance of that publicity if possible in the interests of the proprietors of the paper, and the placing of the manager as the only ostensible proprietor before the public as Mr. Bell is in relation to the *Northern Echo*.[11]

In this case the power in the background was the Pease family of Darlington, and J. H. Bell, who already had other newspaper interests, remained the ostensible proprietor. It is not known how long this continued.[12]

One cannot tell how often a similar obscurity cloaked the real moving force. But it must be suspected wherever an

[10] PRO H.O.45 9864/ 13734. Letter dated 15 Feb. 1893.
[11] H. J. Wilson MSS, MD 5999, Ellis to Wilson, 21 Oct.1874.
[12] Alan Lee, 136.

apparently penniless journalist started a successful paper, or where a small and previously obscure newspaper ventured into daily or (even more) evening halfpenny publication, and did this at a politically significant time. The newspaper history of Oldham, about which fairly full details are available, can serve as an example. Oldham was a new industrial town, enfranchised in 1832, and incorporated in 1849, with no eighteenth-century publications on which to build. The list of Oldham papers contains a large number of short-lived publications from the first half of the century, until, in 1852, a general election year, there was a burst of journalistic activity. Eleven different publications were produced during the election campaign, by three people, John Hirst, Thomas Hayes, and T. Dornan, on behalf of W. J. Fox and the Liberals. A month later, there appeared the *Borough of Oldham Vindicator, and Lancashire Ten Hours Advocate*, the main local issue being Liberal attack on the Factory Acts and Tory defence of them. In May 1854, the (weekly) *Oldham Chronicle*, the first paper to survive for more than a short time began, ostensibly on a non-party footing. A few months later it was sold to R. L. Gerrie, a young man of twenty-four, and in the summer of 1857, when he died of consumption, to Jonathan Hirst and Wallace Rennie, two young journalists who borrowed the money to buy the paper. At the same time, to quote the *Oldham Evening Chronicle*'s *Centenary Supplement*, 'After 1852 the Oldham Liberal Party, as distinct from the wilder Radical and Chartist movements, emerged, and attracted sane and balanced progressives of both the working and middle classes. This new Liberalism found its voice in the *Oldham Chronicle*.' While this was happening the *Oldham Standard*, a weekly (at 1½d.) on the Conservative side, was established in August 1859, shortly after the General Election. In April 1869 came an evening paper, the halfpenny *Oldham Evening Express*, which lasted until 1889. The *Oldham Chronicle* began to come out twice weekly in 1877, on the eve of a local by-election, and on 17 March 1880, a week after the announcement of the dissolution of Parliament, the halfpenny evening *Oldham Chronicle* was launched, 'so that its readers can rely upon being adequately advised of the advancing and ever-changing position of affairs'. As the *Evening Chronicle*'s *Centenary Special* comments, readers could not rely on being 'adequately'

informed by the two already existing evening papers. This sequence of events suggests that the sane and balanced progressives of Oldham were giving an active support to the paper (and that the local Conservatives were doing the same for the *Standard*).[13] Financial risks were taken in 1857 and 1880, and perhaps also in 1859, not because there were good commercial opportunities for the circulation of a new paper (such as a long-running foreign crisis), but at the moments of importance in local party politics, in a town where both parties had a substantial following.

The history of Sheffield provides another example of the way in which things might actually happen. Sheffield Liberalism was divided in the 1870s, between rival camps and on policy questions. The Radical militant Nonconformists were led by H. J. Wilson, and the moderates by the Leaders of the *Sheffield Independent*. In the General Election of 1874 two Radical candidates came forward, A. J. Mundella and Joseph Chamberlain. Robert Leader wanted to run his own candidate, H. Allott, against them, whereupon his son, J. D. Leader, wrote to him:

It is the duty of the *Independent* to serve the Liberal party and not to split it up. The newspaper ought to be in accord with the advanced Liberals of the day, not fomenting disruption, which but for our support would never be able to show its head. . . . There is more than this. Chamberlain in the field without the support of an existing newspaper means a new daily opponent, throwing away hundreds of pounds, and entailing years of vexatious competition. Mr. Allott and his friends will not vindicate their views by a new newspaper, while nothing is more likely than that Chamberlain will do so.[14]

This quotation, coming from correspondence between people who had spent their lives in the newspaper business, shows better than anything the almost casual way in which newspapers were embarked upon: where a modern candidate might

---

[13] This paragraph is based on information kindly provided by Messrs Hirst, Kidd, and Rennie, proprietors of the modern *Evening Chronicle*, and particularly from the *Centenary Supplement* of 8 May 1954, and the *Evening Chronicle Centenary Special* of 17 Mar. 1980. John Foster, *Class Struggle and the Industrial Revolution* [1974] shows that there was a substantial popular following for both parties in Oldham at this time.

[14] Leader MSS, Sheffield Central Library, J. D. Leader to Robert Leader, 3 Jan. 1874, L.C.188.

be expected to produce an election address, Chamberlain was expected to start a newspaper.

The newspaper directories suggest that Oldham and Sheffield were not abnormal. The *Bradford Daily Telegraph*, also started by an outsider, Thomas Shields, appeared providentially a few weeks before the 1868 General Election, and it was reported that one of the election committees had ordered 30,000 copies of it as a way of circulating their candidate's election address.[15] In October the *Bradford Observer* began to come out daily. Two years earlier there had been a major development in the same part of the country, when the old *Leeds Intelligencer* was remodelled and began to come out daily as the *Yorkshire Post*. For once the proprietorship was not concealed: it lay with the Yorkshire Conservative Newspaper Company, with a capital of £50,000 and a board of directors which included prominent local politicians.[16]

It is instructive to study the dates at which new provincial dailies emerged, particularly the halfpenny papers at the bottom of the market. Sometimes they appear to be inspired by public events: a group date from 1870–1, the time of the Franco-Prussian war, and another from 1876–7 when agitation over the Eastern Question was at its height. In both periods the circulation of newspapers can be shown to have risen.[17] But they were also bunched, as in Oldham, round dates which are significant in local politics, when commercial advantages would seem to have been strictly temporary. Thus, between 1867 and 1869 daily halfpenny papers appeared in Leeds (the *Evening Express*), Bolton (the *Evening News*), Bradford, Manchester (the *Evening News*) and Sheffield (the *Evening Star*). In 1874 another batch appeared—in Manchester (the *Evening Mail*), Leicester (*Daily Mercury*), the Potteries (the *Staffordshire Daily Sentinel*), Wolverhampton (the *Midland Counties Evening Express*), Bolton, again (the *Evening Guardian*), and in 1879–80 another—the *Tyneside Daily Echo, Liverpool Echo, Derby Telegraph, Oldham Chronicle*, Brighton *Argus, Worcester Daily Times, Gloucestershire Echo* of Cheltenham, and two in Northampton on the eve of the famous candidature of Bradlaugh and Labouchere,

---

[15] *Printer's Register*, Sept. 1868.

[16] Mildred A. Gibb and Frank Beckwith, *The Yorkshire Post: Two Centuries*, 1954, 107–9. The list includes members of the Lascelles, Duncombe, and Beckett families.

[17] See chapter II.

the *Northampton Daily Chronicle* and the *Northampton Daily Reporter*, the former Conservative, the latter Liberal. The papers in this list are halfpenny papers, nearly all evening ones, some offshoots of existing papers, others entirely new. They went on to become substantial institutions in these places, many surviving down to the 1930s, when a process of amalgamations and take-overs will have left one only in each place. As in Oldham, it seems likely that party politics will have influenced the decision to begin them, though this is not proven.

These enterprises appear to be locally initiated and related to local political considerations. A good deal also is known about the organization and subsidizing of newspapers from central sources. The subject appears fitfully in collections of political archives and has been discussed by Lee and Koss. It is accepted that most of the metropolitan papers of the 1850s and 1860s, with the exception of *The Times*, the *Daily Telegraph*, and the as yet obscure *Clerkenwell News*, (later the *Daily Chronicle*), were indebted in one way or another to political groups. The *Morning Post* was Palmerston's organ. The *Morning Chronicle* had been bought by the Peelites in 1848 and sold again in 1854. Disraeli established his paper, *The Press*, in 1853 and sold it again in 1858. The Adullamites failed disastrously to get their mouthpiece *The Day* into running order in 1867.[18] With the opening up of the market for penny papers after 1855 political interruption continued, though the problem was changing in character. The penny papers were, or were likely to become, much bigger undertakings, making much bigger demands on capital, and the audience they were hoping to reach was much larger and further removed from the centres of parliamentary power. The *Daily Telegraph* was developed by the Levy-Lawson family as a straight commercial enterprise, and was too successful to be in the market for subsidies. Nevertheless Gladstone worked hard to maintain political contacts with it.[19] The *Standard* and the *Daily News* were both linked to Parliamentary parties, though there are obscurities in the story of each. The

[18] Stephen Koss, *The Rise and Fall of the Political Press in Britain*, I *The Nineteenth Century*, 1981, 179–80.
[19] See chapter IX

Daily Telegraph set off a competitive round when it cut its price
to a penny in September 1855, and used its expanding circulation to preach radical-populist doctrines. The need was felt for
an equally popular paper on the Conservative side, aimed at
'artisans, farmers and small tradesmen,' a 'class of persons
difficult to approach by any new organ'.[20] The *Standard*, an old
Tory paper, was bought in 1857 by James Johnstone, an
accountant and a Conservative supporter. He seems, though
there is no definite evidence on the subject, to have been
working there as a business manager for an enterprise in which
some Conservatives had invested funds, though it is also clear
that the responsibility for employing a staff and bringing out
the paper was his. The cover price was reduced to 2*d.* in 1857,
and 1*d.* in 1858. Such price-cutting carried a big risk with it: a
very large increase in circulation was needed to offset the
reduction in price; such a large circulation would require large
and expensive machinery installations. The *Daily Telegraph*,
owned and managed by a highly shrewd firm of printers,
succeeded in making the change. The *Standard* ran into debt.
The figures given to Disraeli in 1862 show a deficit of £2,785
for 1875 and £8,510 for 1858.[21] The financial collapse in the
City in the winter of 1857/8, which would entail the loss of the
advertising revenue normally received from company prospectuses, could have contributed to these losses. In 1858 the
Standard received a loan from the Conservatives. It took the
form of a mortgage on the premises and plant, the funds being
put up by prominent figures in the party and organized by the
party agent, Philip Rose. It was expected that the paper should
follow guidance given by party leaders. To quote Rose's
report, the 'political director' was George Hamilton,[22] MP for
Dublin University, who had to give up the post on appointment as Financial Secretary to the Treasury in the Derby
administration of 1858–9. He was succeeded by George Townsend, a journalist who 'became almost exclusively the medium
of communication between the heads of the Party and the
Newspaper'. Then Johnstone got rid of him 'and there

[20] Carnarvon MSS, BL Add. MS 60779, Philip Rose to Malmesbury, 30 Dec. 1859.
[21] Disraeli MSS, box 88.
[22] Carnarvon MSS, loc cit., Hamilton was a genuine character, not, as Koss
suggests, the Editor, Hamber, using a pseudonym when seeing politicians (p. 135).

is no political channel which subscribers can legally require'. Johnstone's 'most reprehensible conduct' in asserting his independence was explained by the improvement of advertising revenue that had taken place: in 1859 the deficit was a mere £295. But in 1860 and 1861 the losses rose again, to £1,152 and £1,677, and there was again talk of a loan, or of floating a public company to run the paper. But in April 1863 Johnstone repaid the mortgage—one reason, according to Koss, being the popularity of the paper on account of its support of the South in the American Civil War. This might mean a dramatic rise in circulation, but it could equally be possible that it had been offered a retainer by some interest anxious to put forward the Southern case. In April 1862 Henry Hotze, a Confederate agent in London, wrote home,

Two more newspapers, the 'Herald', Lord Derby's organ, and the 'Standard' ... have voluntarily placed themselves at my disposal. The editor in chief of both called on me, and offered the use of the columns of both, including the editorial columns, of which offer I have, though guardedly, availed myself.[23]

By the end of the 1860s the position of the *Standard* had not essentially changed. Since the Reform Act of 1867 the need for a paper speaking to artisans and small tradesmen was greater than ever, and Gorst, who had become party agent, was acting as part-time editor. In the early 1870s the existing editor, 'Captain' Hamber, was dismissed and replaced by William Mudford, son of an early nineteenth-century Tory journalist, and the great figure who finally established the viability of the *Standard*.[24] There is no evidence to show whether by the 1870s the paper was still in some way financially dependent on the Conservative party. By the time that Mudford was installed, the circulation had risen a great deal from the 30–46,000 reported by Philip Rose: figures were published for January 1874, after the boost to circulations provided by the Franco-Prussian War, and at the height of a commercial boom, showing a circulation varying between 163,000 and 176,000.[25]

[23] Basil L. Crapster, 'Thomas Hamber, 1828–1902, Tory journalist', in *Victorian Periodicals Newsletter*, 1978–80, 117, quoting Hotze MSS in the Library of Congress.
[24] Koss, 154. The exact chronology is obscure: Koss suggests that Hamber left in 1871, and that Mudford took office a year later.
[25] *Printer's Register*, Feb. 1874.

It is hard to believe that they still needed contributions from the Conservatives. The subsequent history of the paper suggests that there had been long-standing tension between the politicians' desire for control and the wishes of the proprietor to be master in his own house. When Johnstone died in 1878 he left a will giving Mudford in effect the editorship for as long as he wished it—and he remained there till the end of the century.[26] The legends of Mudford's independence, of his refusing to see politicians, probably have something to do with the conditions under which the paper had been run in the 1860s. The ambitions of politicians had not been slight: in 1859 Rose had written 'A complete and an entire control of the Policy of the Paper—a power of insertion and a right of prohibition are all that the party can require'—this in a report modestly arguing that a successful paper could not be directly run by the party, but needed to be conducted by a 'speculator' with a financial interest in it.[27]

On the Liberal side there was also apparently a politically-motivated drive to get a daily paper of mass circulation on to its feet. The *Morning Star*, a daily of Cobdenite principles, ceased publication in 1869. The year before the *Daily News* was reconstructed.[28] Its price was reduced to 1*d.*, and it was re-equipped with new printing machinery. The ownership passed to a syndicate of Liberals: three of them were distinguished by being immensely rich—Samuel Morley, the hosiery maufacturer, Henry Labouchere, who had recently inherited a share of the family banking business, and Henry Oppenheim. The paper began to make its mark in the Franco-Prussian war: one element in its success was its willingness to spend liberally on telegraphy. Substantial funds, it would seem, were being put into the reorganized paper.

These two histories are similar to those of the provincial papers already discussed: political intervention proceeds by a

[26] See the account in Koss, loc. cit.

[27] It is fair to add that Northcote expressed far more liberal sentiments on this subject 'a Conservative paper ought to make its own way ... but they ought to do so independently of "the party". There ought to be perfect freedom of criticism, praise or blame ... and no affectation of exclusive intelligence ... The Liberals look upon the Times or the Daily News or the Economist with respect as having in some sense opinions of their own which it is important to conciliate.' Carnarvon MSS, loc. cit.

[28] Koss, 192–3.

process of rivalry—one side has a penny paper and the other has to take counter-measures. Then political money, with strings attached, is available for investment. Secondly, the move into the mass market required investment in machines, and larger offices, constructed to take heavy machinery, situated in city centres. Thirdly—which in the long run is the important point—party backing was not in itself a recipe for commercial success. In all cases the paper gained a start in life through political funding, but established itself more slowly, with a general growth in its reading public, and especially through normal journalistic processes—by finding a share of the market, by developing specialities, or by particular journalistic successes. We can cite Labouchere's *Diary of a besieged resident* in Paris in 1870–1, or Mudford's successful penetration of the secrets of the Gladstone cabinet after 1880, both of which had little or nothing to do with party politics, but attracted readers' attention.[29]

In discussing the establishment of party papers, we are dealing with something more closely related to the constitutional organization of the parties than was implied by the personal links between politicians and particular political journalists. Both the *Standard* and the *Daily News* were connected with the party machines as they were developing in the 1860s and 1870s, the connections being closer on the Conservative side. There, there was already a long tradition of intervention stretching back to the 1830s (and probably back to the time of Pitt). In 1832–3, immediately after the party's crash in 1830–2, the Carlton Club was supposed to have given Alaric Watts, editor or ex-editor of the *Standard*, £10,000 to spend on the development of provincial Conservative papers. These were prepared in London and distributed, with additional local matter, in the various districts.[30] Disraeli's papers contain a trickle of begging letters from newspaper proprietors— mostly in small country towns—saying that they will close, with dire results to the party at the next election, unless they receive a subvention.[31] After 1867, as the party began once

---

[29] See p. 186 below.
[30] Alaric Alfred Watts, *Alaric Watts, a Narrative of his Life*, 2 vols., 1884, ch. XIV. He lists eleven; the *DNB* believes there were 21 of them.
[31] Disraeli MSS, box 88.

again to be an effective alternative to the Liberals, their activity in promoting press enterprises increased. They were not weak in the country districts from which Disraeli's begging letters had come: their problems were with the industrial areas and town artisans where they might be able to find latent Conservative support. The total extent of newspaper promotion is not known, and further research could well uncover more; for example the *Printer's Register*, in an article of 1870 quotes four: the *Conservative Journal* (1836–43), the *Weekly Mail* (October 1858–October 1860), the *Imperial Review* (January 1867–December 1868), and the *Blue Budget* (December 1868–January 1869).[32] We can also include the *British Lion* (9 May–11 July 1868) and the *Sun*, published directly by the Conservative Central Office at a farthing, which ran from 1 January 1874 to 24 December 1875.[33] The launching of the *Yorkshire Post* as a daily, and the campaign, by a consortium of Scottish politicians, to bring out a rival to the *Glasgow Herald* in central Scotland, were more substantial undertakings with the same general objective. The difficulty of making the Conservative *Glasgow News* pay its way is a good example of the problems involved. The *Glasgow Herald* was not merely a Liberal paper, but one with a solid organization behind it: it had a distributive network, a shared news service with the *Standard*, and (the sort of thing that historians rarely take sufficient account of), an elaborate system for reporting amateur sporting fixtures every weekend.[34]

Another area of concern was the London artisans and small tradesmen: the need to get through to them had been mentioned by Philip Rose in 1859. To do this it was necessary to enter the evening or popular Sunday field. Here also the Liberals dominated the scene. *Lloyd's* and *Reynolds's*, the most widely read, were both Liberal-Radical as far as they were political. So was the *Echo*, which came out as the first halfpenny evening paper in 1868. The *Globe* had been a Conservative evening paper since the beginning of the century, and was one of those which lost money in the 1860s. In July 1869 its price

[32] *Printer's Register*, Feb. 1870.

[33] For the *Sun* see Koss, 206. According to *Mitchell's Newspaper Press Directory*, the *British Lion* was particularly directed towards the working man. The dates given are of the files at Colindale.

[34] Sinclair, 191.

was reduced to a penny and its history then followed that of the
Standard ten years before. Charles Wescomb, the proprietor,
like Johnstone was part party nominee, part 'speculator' with
his own money in the concern. He lost money with the
reduction in price and handed over to three politicians, Hart
Dyke, the Conservative Whip, George Cubitt, an active Conservative in the Westminster Association, and Marwood
Tucker. In 1871 a new manager came forward in George
Armstrong. Armstrong had been agent for W. H. Smith in the
Westminster constituency, where their outstanding achieve-
ment had been to mobilize a vast electorate and unseat John
Stuart Mill in 1868. Armstrong apparently understood the
kind of people he needed to cater for, but he had no money of
his own, and it must be presumed that he too was helped with
political funds.[35] Like Mudford however he was a successful
editor/proprietor: the *Globe* continued in his control and he
became proprietor in 1875. On his moving to larger premises in
1881 he expanded into the popular Sunday business, with the
starting of the *People*. The Liberal victory of 1880, and the fears
of growing Radicalism which the Bradlaugh case expresses,
had sparked off another round of Conservative newspaper-
making, which also brought the London *Evening News* into
existence.[36] The *People*, at its inception, was very different from
what it was ultimately to become. It had as its first editor
Sebastian Evans (uncle of Arthur Evans of Knossos), and was
written in the spirit of *Sybil* and the Disraelian legend: it spoke
of the reconciliation of capital and labour and carried a
regular column by 'One from the Forge'. Within a few years it
had become a sensational Sunday paper, specializing in full
reports from the police courts in general and the divorce court
in particular. There is no evidence that has come to light so far
to show how this change in tone happened, or whether the
early idealistic paper would not sell. But Armstrong retained
control of both the *Globe* and the *People* until his death in 1907.
There is no evidence of the size of its circulation in its early
years.

This account by no means exhausts the range of infiltration

---

[35] Hambleden MSS, PS 2/56; Armstrong to Smith, n.d. 1867. The history of
Armstrong, the *Globe* and the *People* is given by Koss, 178–82, 248.
[36] Koss, 246.

of the parties into the press. It says nothing about the smart
Clubland evening papers, such as the *St. James's Gazette* or the
Pall Mall Gazette, nor about periodicals. It is intended to show
the range of papers which were substantially helped into
existence by political funds. The politicians' activities in the
promotion of papers directed at the working classes deserves
special mention, as it has not received much attention from
historians. Far more than the Education Act, the suitably
controlled and developed newspaper press offered a way of
educating our masters. A newspaper could provide, as well as a
medium for explanation, a magnet for party loyalty, which
was in continuous existence, and would lead the political
faithful from one election to the next. A reading of W. H.
Smith's correspondence, in particular, brings out the continuous sense of anxiety at the problems of coping with the
unprecedented numbers enfranchised by the Second Reform
Act. The Act is known to the student as being limited in its
effects, but nevertheless it posed the problem of moving from
electorates of perhaps up to 1,000, to electorates which might
run to 10–20,000. As well as this, the case for the Act had been
built on the idea of the thinking artisan, with his intelligent
understanding of savings banks and foreign policy, and such a
person's loyalty was naturally enlisted through reasoned argument on the printed page. Something of this interest in the
working man is shown in *Mitchell's Newspaper Press Directory*. It
is necessary to look at the advertisement pages in which we see
descriptions of each paper as its proprietors liked to imagine it.
The appendix to this chapter lists examples of papers which
specially claimed a working-class readership, together with
advertisements for the same papers ten years later. The papers
fall into two groups. There are the old Radical papers, of which
very few would describe themselves in a way which would
specify any class in opposition to another: they are much more
likely to define their programme in terms of a drastic extension
of political rights. There are also papers which display care for
the interests of the working classes, or for their readers among
the working classes. Sometimes they are Conservative, sometimes their politics are unstated. Sometimes they may be
independent publications clambering aboard the bandwagon
of 1870. In the second group as a whole the fall-out rate is high:

by 1880 most had either changed their advertisement to a more conventional one, or had disappeared. But we can see here more evidence of the Conservative recognition of their need to strengthen their popular base.

Thus party politicians were heavily involved with the promotion of new newspapers. On the Conservative side the list seems endless. In the 1830s Alaric Watts had been described by Dr Maginn, joint-editor of the *Standard* of that time, as 'head nurse of a hospital of rickety newspaperlings, which breathe but to die',[37] and the flow of patients had continued, a handful of them—such as the *Standard*—growing up eventually into vigorous life. On the Liberal side there appears to have been no exact counterpart. The Reform Club was not the headquarters for similar operations (as far as we know, for these moves were always made with discretion). For most of the nineteenth century the Liberals had hardly needed them: they already possessed most of the leading provincial papers—the Liverpool *Daily Post*, the *Birmingham Daily Post*, the *Scotsman*, the *Glasgow Herald*, the *Manchester Guardian*, and the *Leeds Mercury* among them. Their strength was in the large towns, where the concentration of population favoured newspaper enterprise anyway. Whether the ideology of free speech and an untaxed press had anything to do with it or not, the Liberals had a goodly number of intelligent, efficient, and independent proprietors on their side, who might have been expected to object to the kind of news management which Philip Rose had proposed for the *Standard*. The politics of these people and their papers might vary widely, from the Whiggish to the Radical and near-Republican (the *Staffordshire Daily Sentinel* is an example of this), and they might well be critical of Mr Gladstone on specific issues. Nevertheless, down to the Home Rule crisis, Liberal candidates, and in general terms Liberal Governments, were not short of press support, especially in the provinces. In 1886 there were a great many defections from the Liberal party among newspapers[38]—the *Birmingham Daily Post* and the *Scotsman* being two of them—and the Conservatives had no longer the same need for further rickety newspaperlings. In any case the scope for such activity was now limited: few places

[37] Alaric Alfred Watts, vol. 2, 175.
[38] They are discussed in detail by Koss, ch. 8.

of any size now lacked a daily paper, and the scale of subsidy needed was much greater. As James Annand, editor of the *Newcastle Daily Leader*, and lamenting the situation, put it, it took 'as much or nearly as much to establish a new newspaper as it did to build an ironclad'.[39]

It must be asked what the effect of these party actions was on the way in which the press developed, since the subject of the present book is the newspaper and not party politics. The general effect must have been to increase the resources put into the newspaper industry: the constant references to papers in need of subvention, or to failed schemes, suggest that plans were over-ambitious and running well ahead of the size of purchasing public which could be reasonably expected. Newspaper proprietorship was a very speculative business, which might not have attracted so much investment without the additional lure of political influence, whether local or national. Success would probably depend on the ability with which it was conducted, and, unless we are thinking of the expansion of a well-established paper, we are talking of people risking their money on a body of journalists whose skills they could not really assess. Such involvement needed political commitment. Among politicians the putting of money into political newspapers could easily be assimilated into an old tradition. The nobility and gentry had always spent money on elections, and industrial leaders had adopted the same habits. From the middle of the century such spending was coming under legislative control, and support for a local newspaper was an alternative. Thus there is nothing inappropriate in the Duke of Buccleuch putting £2,500 into the *Glasgow News*, or the Hon. Mark Rolle organizing a group of north Devon gentlemen to establish a newspaper in Barnstaple.[40] The *Printer's Register* believed that Lord Bute's solicitors had sunk £30,000 in the *Western Mail* of Cardiff—a far greater investment, though it may not have had a specific party objective.[41] The nobility and gentry may have been a normal source of newspaper finance: as late as the Royal Commission of 1947–8 it was stated that

[39] J. L. M'Callum, *James Annand M.P., a Tribute*, 1908, 205.
[40] Koss, 207; Iddesleigh MSS, BL Add. MS 50038 f. 36.
[41] Apr. 1873.

successive Dukes of Devonshire were the owners of the *Buxton Advertiser*.[42]

A second consequence of party involvement was that a competition between newspapers became the norm in provincial Britain, and was organized and articulated through comment on the party struggle. There is no commercial reason why a town the size of Scarborough with a population of about 35,000 in the 1880s should have had two daily papers of its own. A main reason for the appointment of the Royal Commission on the Press in 1947 was to examine the reasons for the decline in competition, and it was treated as almost axiomatic that a variety of voices reporting different things and expressing contrasting opinions was the good end to be aimed at. In Victorian conditions local editors found themselves the chief expounders, not merely of local political issues, but of rival views of world affairs, social problems, and anything which came before Parliament.

It also seems true that party political considerations influenced the shape of the newspaper press. Thanks to the conservative nature of the first and second Reform Acts, the bulk of parliamentary constituencies were also towns: the same area was, usually, at one and the same time a shopping centre, a Poor Law union or unions, a parliamentary borough, the seat of a law court, and was perhaps heavily concentrated on some particular kind of manufacture. The variety of these features gave common news interests which reinforced each other and provided a continuing flow of subject-matter for a local paper. The nature of this influence is suggested if we speculate on the kind of political press that might have come into existence had there been equal electoral districts or proportional representation.

How far did the newspapers thus brought into existence remain politically slanted? The fact that political funds had gone into them does not by itself mean very much: owners can grow old and moderate their views, and what begins as a crusade can very well continue as a business. A well-documented example is Joseph Cowen and the *Newcastle Daily Chronicle*. Cowen is one of the few nineteenth-century Liberals who can legitimately be described as 'left-wing': in the 1850s he

[42] Question 351.

was a rich man whose wealth was inherited, but he nevertheless cultivated the friendship of the revolutionary exiles Mazzini and Herzen, and organized the spectacular visit of Garibaldi to Newcastle in 1864. He acquired the *Chronicle* in 1858, and it developed greatly under his proprietorship: by the 1880s it had morning, evening, and weekly editions. On the great issue of the Eastern Question he enforced his strong anti-Russian views, sacking the Gladstonian editor, James Annand, in 1877. Very occasionally, also, his correspondence suggests the particular slant of his mind: for example he organized a fact-finding expedition to go to the South-West of Ireland to visit the Land League and 'report on the state of the peasantry. Mr Bryson of the Northumberland Miners, Mr Patterson of the Durham Miners' Association, Mr Birkett, a Newcastle engineer, along with a reporter, will be the deputation.'[43] On another occasion he was able to reject a report of an anarchist congress as bogus, through being able to check it with Kropotkin, whom he knew.[44] But these are entirely exceptional: the bulk of his correspondence related to the *Chronicle* reveals concerns no different from any other proprietor's: he follows up news items of local interest, or is anxious to provide a better service than his rival, the *Leader*. The same sort of evolution is probably true of the *People*. The *Manchester Guardian* moved in the opposite direction. In the middle of the century it had been Whiggish, the paper of the Manchester business élite. The *Manchester Examiner* had been the paper for the doctrinaire Liberal. Under C. P. Scott's editorship the *Guardian* became the Radical paper.

When the political initiative rested, not with a working proprietor, but in a body such as the Conservative Central Office or the Yorkshire Conservative Newspaper Company, the significance of the party label would have been much more uncertain. Parties were loosely associated, without, for much of the time, a continuing official party policy formulated and accepted by all, and on the occasions when they spoke with a unified voice, how could their line be imposed on a newspaper? But where a paper was being run by a 'speculator' mostly with his own finance, but with some party help, the party was

[43] Cowen MSS, F 41 4A—there is no date for this expedition: presumably it was some time in 1879–81.
[44] Kropotkin to Cowen, 25 June 1889, ibid. D 409.

hardly in a position to ask very much. A policy of demanding control over contents or editorial opinions was likely to be self-defeating. A successful paper with a large circulation, and at least the appearance of independence, was the most useful ally. The strongest influence in the 1870s and after, when a good variety of papers were in this independent position, was therefore exerted by informal means.

Advertisements in Mitchell's Newspaper Press Directory *claiming a working-class readership*

	1870 advertisement	*1880 advertisement*
Blackburn Patriot	Conservative, for the large body of the working class	Disappeared
Bradford Review	Chartist, for the six points and the United Kingdom Alliance	Disappeared
Bucks Advertiser	Supports extended suffrage and ballot. Against game laws	Non-political
Congleton and Macclesfield Mercury	Advocates the interests of the working classes	No change
Derby Gazette	Elevation of the working classes is sought	A Liberal-Radical $\frac{1}{2}d$. evening paper
Derbyshire Chronicle	Pays special attention to the interests of the working classes	Disappeared
Doncaster Reporter	Circulates extensively, notably among Great Northern Railway workmen	No reference to railway men
East Anglian Echo	Conservative. News of the week arranged in comprehensive form for working classes	Disappeared
Eastern Weekly Press	Liberal. All measures for the benefit of the working classes	No reference to working classes
Essex Examiner	Cobdenite	Disappeared
Gateshead Observer	Free trade and universal suffrage	No change
Halifax Courier	For liberal extension of the suffrage	No such programme mentioned
Huddersfield Chronicle	Cobdenite	Thoroughly independent
Leeds Times	Free trade, complete suffrage, repeal of all obnoxious laws, voluntary principle	No change

	1870 advertisement	*1880 advertisement*
Liverpool Mail	Tory, an especial Tory organ, highly appreciated by the working classes	No reference to working classes
Manchester Examiner	Cobdenite; amelioration of the working classes	No change
Norfolk Herald	Independent. Seeks the elevation of the working class	Disappeared
North Cheshire Herald	Improvement of the middle and working classes	No change
Oldham Standard	Advocates the claims of labour against the encroachments of capital	No change
Peterborough Times	Advanced Liberal	Disappeared
Preston Herald	Advocates the true interests of the working classes	No reference to the working classes
Rochdale Observer	Radical	No change
Runcorn and Widnes Examiner	Advocates liberty in all things	Best and cheapest facilities for advertisers
[North] *Shields Daily News*	Cobdenite	No change
Wakefield Free Press	In favour of the advancement of the working classes	No change

IV

Journalists

THERE is no difficulty in finding out about the life of Victorian journalists and newspaper offices. It was a favourite subject for articles in the reviews. A great deal of information also exists in journalists' memoirs. They were people who wrote quickly and easily, and possibly finding themselves short of money in their old age they wrote the story of their lives. These are usually of very poor quality, rambling, and anecdotal, and have certain characteristics. They are always inaccurate on political facts and dates: they remember the Phoenix Park murders and the reaction of the office, but not the year. They are usually vague about the papers they work for, that is about circulation, profitability, and ownership; they know if the paper is going downhill, or if it changes hands, but a new proprietor is likely to be merely a 'mysterious personage'. On the other hand on their own lives they are specific and unlikely to be wrong. Certain regularities emerge.

Victorian journalists were drawn from a very wide social range. At one extreme the newspaper would provide a route by which the intelligent self-taught working man could rise to a position of social weight and influence. Of these the most spectacular was Sir Henry Lucy, author of *Peeps at Parliament* and *Behind the Speakers' Chair*, who had a long career as Parliamentary correspondent of the *Daily News*, who had been born in Crosby, Lancashire, the son of a turner in the watch making industry.[1] One can also cite the example of Thomas Frost, who began as a printer working on various struggling early socialist publications, and by the 1860s was writing leading articles for the Liverpool *Albion*; and W. E. Adams, son of a plasterer, who also began work on Chartist and Republican papers in the 1840s and ended his career as editor of the successful Newcastle *Evening Chronicle*.[2]

[1] *D.NB.*

[2] Thomas Frost, *Reminiscences of a Country Journalist*, 1886; W. E. Adams, *Memoirs of a Social Atom*, 2 vols., 1902.

More commonly journalists were recruited from the more insecure and impoverished sections of the middle classes; they were people who had more formal education than Frost or Adams, but who knew from an early age that they were dependent on their own wits and industry. Wallace Rennie, one of the original promoters of the *Oldham Chronicle*, was a graduate of Aberdeen University; Duncan Campbell, editor in the 1860s of the *Bradford Advertiser*, had been a schoolmaster; Hartley Aspden, who worked on the *Manchester Examiner*, had begun life as a solicitor's clerk.[3] There was also a steady flow of Irishmen into British journalism, of whom Justin McCarthy is probably the best known.[4] Another important group of journalists came from the families of nonconformist ministers: Wemyss Reid was the son of a Presbyterian minister in Newcastle; W. T. Stead was the son of a Congregational minister, also in Newcastle; Sir John Robinson, for many years manager of the *Daily News*, was also the son of a Congregational minister, in Halesworth, Suffolk.[5] It is easy to see how such an upbringing would provide a training for a Liberal journalist. Beyond this, journalism, with its wide scope for part-time and freelance work, offered a refuge for all sorts of people who had a capacity to write and needed money. Morley, down from Oxford and refusing to enter the Church of England, found his first employment as editor of a short-lived *Literary Gazette*. George Meredith wrote a weekly summary of events for the *Ipswich Journal* in the 1860s, and then got additional work on the *Morning Post*. The young Thomas Hardy, before he had begun to write novels, was advised by his friend and mentor, Horace Moule, that he might be able to supplement his income by writing a London Letter for a provincial weekly such as the *Dorset County Chronicle*.[6] In much grander circles of society the same forces might be in operation. Lord Salisbury, Sir William Harcourt, and G. C. Brodrick had all written regularly for the press in the 1860s. Herbert Paul, a leader-

[3] For Rennie see p. oo above; Duncan Campbell, *Reminiscences of an Octogenarian Highlander*, Inverness, 1910, 320; Hartley Aspden, *Fifty Years a Journalist*, n.d., 1–7.

[4] Alan Lee, 113.

[5] *DNB*.

[6] J. W. Robertson Scott, *The Life and Death of a Newspaper*, 1952, 15; C.L. Cline, ed., *Letters of George Meredith*, 3 vols., Oxford, 1970, vol. 1 *passim*; Robert Gittings, *Young Thomas Hardy*, Penguin edn., 1978, 108.

writer on the *Daily News* in the 1890s, was heir to a landed estate in Northamptonshire.[7] To many of these literary and political figures journalism remained a part-time stop-gap occupation: they were not concerned with the daily business of collecting news or putting a paper together.

To others, however, journalism was an overriding ambition. Sir Edward Cook and J. A. Spender both began their careers by contributing, the former to *Temple Bar* and *Truth*, the latter to the *Pall Mall Gazette*, while they were still at Oxford.[8] Wemyss Reid began, at the age of fourteen, by writing a letter, signed 'A Bedesman', criticizing the appointment of a High Church vicar in Newcastle. J. L. Garvin, similarly, was a contributor to the *Eastern Morning News* of Hull at the age of sixteen.[9]

Journalism was exceptional and noteworthy in its employment of women. Harriet Martineau and Frances Power Cobbe both wrote leading articles for the *Daily News* at different times, and Miss Cobbe also acted as their correspondent in Italy for a short time.[10] Mrs Lynn Linton claimed that she had acted as Paris correspondent for the *Morning Chronicle* from 1851 to 1854, though it seems that she can have done little more than write letters descriptive of the social scene.[11] Mrs Emily Crawford, Paris correspondent of the *Daily News* in the 1880s and 1890s, carried out a far more substantial job.[12] Another woman, whose expedition seems to have been more of a stunt than anything else, was Lady Florence Dixie, daughter of the Marquess of Queensberry and wife of Sir Beaumont Dixie, who had been ruined by gambling and the turf. She succeeded in being sent as war correspondent of the *Morning Post* to the Zulu war of 1879.[13] There were women journalists, sometimes in key positions, before there were women's pages. Their

[7] Humphrey Paul 'Random Northamptonshire reminiscences' *Northamptonshire Past and Present*, II, 1955, 91.

[8] J. Saxon Mills, *Sir Edward Cook K.B.E., a Biography*, 1921, 37; J. A. Spender, *Life, Journalism and Politics*, 2 vols., 1927, I, 25.

[9] Stuart J. Reid, ed., *Memoirs of Sir Wemyss Reid*, 1905, 34–5; J. A. Spender, 39.

[10] *DNB*; Frances Power Cobbe, *Life of ... by Herself*, 2 vols., 1894 II, 37 and ch. XVI, *passim*.

[11] *DNB*.

[12] H. W. Massingham, 60.

[13] Leonard E. Naylor, *The Irrepressible Victorian: the Story of Thomas Gibson Bowles*, 1965, 88.

careers are the best demonstrations of the openness of journalism as an occupation, in comparison with the more organized professions which were developing.

How far did the proprietors and editors show a preference for university-educated men? It is difficult to establish a definite trend. The list of contributors to *The Times*, given as an appendix to Dasent's life of Delane,[14] shows strong links with Oxford, and there is no reason to suggest any change after Delane's retirement. Lord Burnham emphasized the high academic qualifications of men appointed to the *Daily Telegraph* (and it was in fact always anxious to appear as equivalent in style and content to *The Times*).[15] The *Manchester Guardian* similarly appointed a number of university graduates from 1871, when C. P. Scott joined the paper on leaving Oxford. Graduates might be expected to write better, and have a better ability to understand and expound questions of economic and social policy. They might also be able to develop, and exploit usefully, contacts among the political and administrative world—E. T. Cook, for example, had been a friend of Rosebery at Oxford.[16] More simply, they would give a paper a better image: a writer in *Cassell's Magazine*, reprinted in the *Printer's Register*, contrasting the brisk new world of the telegraph and the rotary press with olden days, described the change thus:

...The other day I went back to the old office. What a change in twenty years!... No longer the sleepy old weekly paper with its stale news, its dead-alive Tory leaders, its tiresome reports of the dinners and the comings of age; no longer the dull drowsy concoctions of dull old tradesmen for leaders. No, a smart daily paper now, quite up to the mark of the day; a staff of three reporters with a room of their own. The editor is an Oxford man, a gentleman and a scholar. In the evening telegraph boys come running in every moment with telegrams, leaders arrived from London, intelligence carefully posted up from all parts of England, and the latest betting. The editor, no longer a mere agent of the lawyer of his party, associates as a gentleman with gentlemen, and visits the commercial room and the public meetings of the city as an equal with the best. He is entirely

---

[14] 2 vols., 1908, II, 347–50.
[15] *Peterborough Court*, 1955, 9–10.
[16] Saxon Mills, 16.

independent, and attacks any abuse of the day boldly and fear-lessly.[17]

How far this picture was true, even at the time of writing, is open to question, but the idea of the 'Oxford man, a gentleman and a scholar' remained attractive. According to the evidence presented by the National Union of Journalists to the Royal Commission on the Press in 1947, Beaverbrook had also initially favoured graduates, but had changed his ideas. By 1947 it was generally agreed that they should not have a privileged mode of entry. 'University men had not come from the Universities merely to write, but had trained themselves as technicians.'[18] In the 1870s people such as Morley or Brodrick had not begun with all-round training as technicians'–on the other hand Spender or Cook had done so. It can be shown that graduates were going increasingly into journalism in the 1860s and 1870s. According to Francis Hirst:

... among Morley's contemporaries, and in the succeeding gene-ration, a number of remarkable men, after taking their degrees at Oxford or Cambridge, won distinction as editors or leader writers on the daily or weekly press or as contributors to the magazines. Leonard Courtney, Sir James Fitzjames Stephen and his brother Leslie, C. P. Scott, Herbert Paul, J. A. Hobson, E. T. Cook, Henry Nevinson, J. A. Spender, L. T. Hobhouse and J. L. Hammond are among the names that might be quoted. Most of them had won reputations at College, and all had made their mark as editors, assistant editors, or leader writers.[19]

These people, however, gravitated to a relatively limited range of newspapers and periodicals in London: how often graduates were preferred by provincial papers is not clear. It may also be that they were looking for employment in journa-lism, rather than that employers sought them out: a reason for the rise of the highly educated journalist of this period being the atmosphere of Liberal reformism in the Oxford and Cambridge of the time. When J. A. Spender went to the *Pall Mall Gazette* in 1892, under Cook's editorship, he wrote that he had 'not only security of tenure, but the place which, of all others, had been most envied by the young Oxford men of my

[17] *Printer's Register*, Sep. 1872, quoting from *Cassell's Magazine*.
[18] Questions 170, 168.
[19] F. W. Hirst, *Early Life and Letters of John Morley*, 2 vols., 1927, I, 35.

own time who dreamed of journalism'.[20] On the other hand
the *Life* of Samuel Jeyes, assistant editor of the *Standard*, shows
the same sort of process at work in a Conservative setting.[21]

It can be shown that, apart from such people as drama
critics and City editors, who needed particular kinds of experience or contacts, most journalists had begun their careers in
their teens, or as soon as they left the University. Journalism
was seen as a specialized craft. The discipline of writing, to a
specified theme, at a fixed length, to a precise deadline, is
probably one that can only be acquired when young. This
early entry alone gave journalists a distinct identity, separat-
ing them from politicians on the one hand and 'men of letters'
on the other. That separateness was reinforced by their unso-
cial hours, and by their constantly renewing old acquaintances
at the agricultural dinners and annual general meetings they
were sent to report. Their consciousness of themselves as a
Fourth Estate is shown in the way in which their memoirs are
peppered with anecdotes boring to anyone other than fellow-
journalists. W. E. Adams's description of a night in Fleet Street
in the 1860s gives an impression of their style of reminiscence:

When we had completed our work it was proposed that we should go
and see how the debaters finished up their proceedings. Discussion by
that time had degenerated into a noisy and general hubbub, in which
everybody seemed to be talking at once. All manner of strange
characters, most of them more or less muzzy and muddled, were
holding forth to each other. Political orators, writers for the *Standard*,
subeditors of the *Family Herald* and the *London Journal*, contributors to
other popular periodicals, waiters on Providence, hirelings of the
press and of the platform, were among the men of light and leading
who were enjoying a midnight revel in Shoe Lane. Instead of reeling
home when the tavern closed its doors, most of them adjourned to a
'night house' in Farringdon Street, where, being joined by other
sweepings from the streets and the newspaper offices, they continued
their noisy drinkings and disputations till far into the morning.

Adams, at that time working on Bradlaugh's *National Reformer*,
added 'The spectacle, so far from being impressive or elevat-

[20] J. A. Spender, *Life, Journalism, and Politics*, 2 vols. n.d., I, 48.
[21] Sidney Low and W. P. Ker, *Samuel Henry Jeyes, his Personality and Work*, 1915,
22–3.

ing, was calculated to take the heart out of a young and ardent propagandist.'[22]

Another common feature of journalistic careers, which has some general historical significance, was their extreme mobility, in a fast-expanding market. Many men moved from job to job at bewilderingly frequent intervals, and were able to find work at considerable distances from their existing employment. Here is, for example, the *curriculum vitae* of H. C. Ellis:[23]

1852–4 *Border Advertiser* (Galashiels)
1854–6 *Berwick Advertiser*
1857–9 *Sunderland Times*
1859   *Sunderland Times*, as leader-writer, also working
        for *Newcastle Daily Chronicle*
1859   *Star of Gwent* (South Wales)
1860   Established his own *Featherstone Observer*,
        (W. Riding), sold, 1869[24]
1872–3 *Northern Echo*
1873–4 *Newcastle Courant*

By 1878 he was working as editor of the *Bucks Advertiser* in Aylesbury. This sounds like the life story of a rolling stone, of someone with a quarrelsome temperament or a drink problem; but it is the career of someone who was acting as confidential adviser to H. J. Wilson, in his attempts to establish a serious Radical paper in Sheffield. An even more restless career was that of H. F. Bussey, who went, between the mid-1840s and 1868, to the *Cumberland Pacquet*, the *Carlisle Journal*, the Liverpool *Albion*, the *Herts County Chronicle*, the *Brighton Guardian*, the *Wakefield Express*, the *Brighton Examiner*, then back to the *Brighton Guardian*, to the *Manchester Examiner* in the Crimean period, to the Manchester *Telegraphic News*, to the *Plymouth Mail*, the *Preston Guardian*, the *Sunderland Times*, the *Shields Advocate*, the *Taunton Courier*, and the *Norwich Mercury*. He then went to London with a job on the parliamentary staff of the *Morning Post*, and finished his career with eighteen years working for the Press Association.[25] Hugh Gilzean Reid, who had become the owner of a number of provincial evening papers by the 1880s,

[22] p. 318–9.
[23] H. J. Wilson papers, MD 6000, dated 23 Oct. 1874.
[24] Not in BL catalogue.
[25] H. F. Bussey, *Sixty Years of Journalism*, Bristol, 1906.

had gone from Edinburgh to Peterhead then to Middlesbrough between 1861 and 1865.[26]

These roving careers suggest that in the middle decades of the century there was some sort of national organization— formal or informal—linking the newspaper press in different areas together. These journalists were in contact with new jobs in remote areas, whether through advertisement or personal contacts. (One would guess that, by contrast, there were few careers of minor officials in local government in the nineteenth century that moved round the country in this way.) It also illustrates that the promoters of new or expanded papers looked for professional and experienced people to run them, rather than for people with local connections. The *Printer's Register* in 1872 described how the *Barrow Times* was now improving in both circulation and tone with the appointment of an editor from outside, Francis Leach (a BA of Cambridge). Such a person, it was believed, would develop an interest in local affairs and history.[27] To a modern reader Victorian provincial papers express, more eloquently than anything else, the particular character of the places where they circulated, but in fact they would have been put together by professional experts who would have been gathered from all the corners of the kingdom.

What sort of staff would have been employed in a newspaper office? The gap between the big London daily and the small provincial weekly was too wide to make a general answer to the question possible. The weekly local paper was likely to be run by a man and a boy, as part of a jobbing printer's establishment. Richard Jefferies in *Hodge and his Masters*, (1880), published originally as a series of letters in the *Standard* and slightly condescending in tone, described how such an editor would write the paper, correct its proofs, help illiterate customers to write out their advertisements, and do everything other than work the printing press.[28] C. S. Bundock, of the National Union of Journalists, told the Royal Commission on

[26] W. R. Nicoll, *James Macdonell, Journalist*, 1890, 84, 129.

[27] Apr. 1872. For an interesting account of the workings of small local papers in one region see P. J. Lucas 'Furness Newspapers in Mid-Victorian England' in Peter Bell, ed., *Victorian Lancashire*, Newton Abbot, 1974, 83–102.

[28] Ch. 19.

the Press in 1947 that a weekly local paper could run on 'two men and a junior'.[29] There had been no change in sixty years.

For the provincial dailies, which themselves varied greatly in their scale of operations, there was more development. Editorial staffs might still be small: in the extract from *Cassell's Magazine* just given, 'three reporters with a room of their own' represented a great advance. Wemyss Reid described how, in the late 1850s, the *Northern Daily Express*, a penny daily in Newcastle, was produced in two rooms and two cellars, one of the rooms being occupied by the compositors. The other 'was by day the counting-house and the place where the papers were sold and advertisements received, whilst at night it became the editorial office—the editor, sub-editor, and reporters all working here together at the desks occupied by the clerks during the day'.[30] The printing went on in the cellars. H. J. Wilson in Sheffield was told in 1874 that he could run a halfpenny daily with a manager, leader-writer, sub-editor, and two reporters, together with the printing and office staff. An alternative estimate thought that it could be done with one editor, one reporter, and one junior.[31]

The more notable provincial dailies were on a considerably larger scale. The *Yorkshire Post* in 1866 had an editorial staff of twenty-eight, including the editor, an Oxford man and former President of the Union.[32] The *Manchester Guardian* grew from five reporters in 1838 to seven in 1868.[33] The *Glasgow Herald* was smaller; in 1859 it had an editor, two sub-editors, and three reporters.[34] The gap between the bigger and the smaller papers is clearly indicated: those papers produced by an editor and a reporter could not hope to offer more than a few items of local news, a leading article, and a great deal of scissors and paste. Newspaper construction of this kind is suggested by a letter of 20 March 1855 from a Manchester printer, A. H. Burgess, to Abel Heywood about a new project, 'I shall want the London Times daily, half price will do except Friday. The Field or other gardening and agricultural paper, the Manchester Guardian

[29] Question 201.
[30] *Memoirs*, 39–40.
[31] H. J. Wilson papers, MD 5999.
[32] M. A. Gibb and F. Beckwith, 40.
[33] Ayerst, 81, 174.
[34] Sinclair, 41.

of Wed'y and any other papers we might exchange with. I will undertake the bringing out of the paper, make its selections, see after the local news and editing.'[35]

The staffs of the major London papers would have been very much bigger again, though there is an almost total dearth of information (other than for *The Times*). They all differed from even the largest provincial papers in the resources they put into foreign correspondence, as will be shown later.[36] *The Times*, which can be expected to have been the most lavish in its staffing, employed a total of 376 persons in 1885. The size of its editorial staff is suggested by its office bill, which did not vary much from one half-year to the next. The figures for the first six months of 1877 are:[37]

Foreign news	£16,457	19	8*d.*
Home news (salaried)	£1,500		
Office expenses, reporting, and linage	£17,018	9	6*d.*
Managing and editing	£3,398	11	4*d.*
Leaders and reviews	£5,520	17	10*d.*

a total of nearly £44,000 for the half-year. The comparable figures for the *Manchester Guardian* for 1888 (the nearest available year) is just under £29,000 for the whole year.[38] In both cases the figures include expenses on telegraphy, which could have accounted for the greater part of *The Times*'s foreign expenditure. Nevertheless, inconclusive as they are, they show that *The Times* was paying far larger salary bills, to more people. Human resources on this scale made possible a much broader range of news interests.

How were these staffs, many of which were very small, deployed to do their daily work? It seems that there was a range of specialized occupations in all but the very smallest offices. From a modern standpoint there is nothing very remarkable in this, but over the previous sixty or seventy years there had probably been an elaborate development. The generic word 'journalist' goes back to the seventeenth century. The particular divisions of work—editors, sub-editors, and reporters, were

[35] A. H. Burgess letter-book, Manchester Central Library, Misc/740.
[36] See chapter X.
[37] *The Times* archives.
[38] See next table.

of recent origin, but now firmly established. The appearance of the reporter—an uninvolved person sent to some public occasion to make a record for publication—is an event in modern history of some importance. The first reference to the word, in this sense, is given by the *Oxford Dictionary* as occurring in 1813, in relation to the Press Gallery. The history of the *Yorkshire Post* refers to reporters at Peterloo in 1819.[39] Cobbett referred in 1826 to a 'lying Irish reporter' at Preston.[40] 'Sub-editor' was a more recent introduction: it had been used by Carlyle in 1837, and by Thackeray in 1850, referring to the 'sub-editorial arrangements of a newspaper'. Sub-editors were made necessary by the use of prolix penny-a-liners, and were first recorded in 1834. 'Leader-writer' is not recorded in the *OED* till 1888, though by that time there were plenty of people employed in that capacity. More surprisingly, 'editor' for the conductor of a newspaper was first recorded, used by George Rose, in 1803, and, again by Cobbett, in 1823. These various kinds of jobs may have been in existence before these first recorded dates. From the point of view of the present study it is important that the newspaper press entered the period of the telegraph and of the wide circulation of daily papers with the established mode of conducting its business which has continued since that time. The mobility which has been described would not have been possible if, for example, a sub-editor from one paper had not been able to slip into the place of a sub-editor elsewhere without fuss.

Between the middle and the end of the century there is widespread, but patchy, evidence of development in all but the smallest concerns. The reasons can be easily deduced. The volume of information coming into the newspaper office was increasing by a natural process: there were more correspondents, in Britain and in all parts of the world, filing more stories, there had been a revolution in the speed of communication, and the Press Association had expanded its activities. If sub-editors had been needed in the mid-century, they were doubly necessary now. The copy-taster, acting as a preliminary filter to the flow of news, does not appear in the *OED* at all,

[39] Gibb and Beckwith, 8.
[40] *Rural Rides*, Everyman edn., n.d., II, 144.

though 'copy-reader', one who reads and edits the work of reporters, does, in 1903.

Enlarged staffs were also made possible, and also probably made necessary, by the falling production costs. The price of newsprint fell very substantially between *c.* 1870 and the end of the century.[41] This opened the way to the enlargement of newspapers, leading in turn to larger staffs to fill the additional space. The money saved could also, or alternatively, be spent on increasing staffs. Ultimately it made possible the reduction in price of many morning papers to a halfpenny in the early years of the twentieth century and in the wake of the *Daily Mail*. The process can be illustrated in relation to the *Manchester Guardian*, in Table 4.1, whose archives contain an elaborate comparison of the paper's finances in 1888 and 1897.[42](It increased its size from eight to twelve pages in this period.)

Table 4.1

	1888 £			1897 £			Increase or decrease %
Editorial expenses*	6,144	17	10	7,766	3	8	25.7
Literary contributions	6,364	8	10	5,956	14	3	− 6.4
London office	5,094	9	9	6,298	7	9	23.6
Salaries:							
Staffs	3,473	3	4	9,102	6	8	162.0
Clerks	1,625	16	0	2,830	16	9	74.2
Reporters	1,754	12	0	2,351	0	0	34.0
Sub-editors	1,307	4	0	1,758	17	0	34.5

* These include private wires and telegraphy

The table shows clearly the disproportionate increase in staff, that is of those who formed the policy-making, selecting, and leader-writing elements of the concern. A similar increase could be seen in the *Glasgow Herald*, which had grown by 1895 from the six persons of 1859 to an editorial staff of 15, together with 15 reporters, 6 Parliamentary reporters, and 13 others, making 49 in all.[43] A group photograph of the staff of the *Newcastle Daily Leader*, taken in 1895, shows 22 people, including one messenger.[44] Kennedy Jones, Northcliffe's associate,

[41] See chapter I.
[42] *Guardian* Archives.
[43] Sinclair, 41.
[44] Aaron Watson, *A Newspaper Man's Memories*, n.d., 180.

commented on the increase of editorial staffs at this time, saying that heads of departments, including the messengers, were being given the title of 'editor'. More editing of material was being carried out, so that more topics could appear in the papers, with less space being given to each.[45] Simonis, writing in 1917, commmented on the changes in the daily papers which had made 'the editor control in every sense the contents of all the columns except advertisements and not merely the two or more columns dealing with comment'.[46] These references, though they may be straws in the wind, all point the same way. The increased numbers of editorial staff opened the way to more thorough-going management of the news being offered, or of the tone of a paper. This management can be seen in a highly developed form in Northcliffe's well-known communiqués.[47] Newspapers and party politics were closely involved with each other, as the previous chapter has shown: it is worth asking how this affected the life and work of the journalists. Were Liberal papers staffed by Liberals, and vice-versa? It is plainly impossible to give any systematic answer to this question; if we judge by the tone of memoirs and biographies it seems that it was far more usual for them to work for their own side. Alfred Austin and G. A. Henty, who both worked for the *Standard*, were vehement Imperialists out of the office as well as in it; Massingham, Spender, Cook, Stead, and Reid were Liberal journalists, and also prominent political figures. On the occasions when the *Pall Mall Gazette* changed hands and changed its politics the staff left *en bloc*. This happened twice: when it was sold to Yates Thompson in 1880, and again when it was sold to W. W. Astor in 1894.[48] It could not be held that this was normal practice—the Liberal press was deeply divided for and against Home Rule in 1886, and there would have been mass migrations of Liberal journalists had they shown the political commitment of the staff of the *Pall Mall Gazette*. Nevertheless, the general tone of contemporary writing on newspapers suggests that journalists normally expected to be personally in sympathy with the views of the publication they

---

[45] Kennedy Jones, *Fleet Street and Downing Street*, n.d., 188, but cf. chapter XI below.
[46] H. Simonis, 250.
[47] See Tom Clarke, *My Northcliffe Diary*, 1931; and Wareham Smith. The Northcliffe MSS in the BL also contain good examples; see chapter XI.
[48] J. W. Robertson Scott, 273; and Koss, 337 ff.

worked for.[49] Those who were merely 'in it for the money', or who viewed their papers' politics with contempt, have remained silent.

The question of loyalty to particular policies was serious for leader-writers in particular, since they had constantly to expound views which they might not personally support. This was generally recognized as a problem, and is described by Brodrick, a leader-writer on *The Times* from 1860 to 1873:

> One misgiving ... was the fear that I should be expected to write strictly to order, and to advocate views opposed to my own convictions. A little reflection satisfied me that it would be wiser to put aside bugbears of this kind, since the supposed difficulty might never occur, and, if it did occur, I might rely on the good sense of the Editor to relieve me from it. This is exactly what happened ... On my appealing to Mr. Delane, he promptly substituted another subject, and placed the first in the hands of some other contributor, who no doubt honestly took a line which I could not have adopted.[50]

The same point occurs in another book of memoirs, by Aaron Watson, at one time a leader-writer on the *Newcastle Daily Chronicle*. He refers to an office discussion about the dismissal of James Macdonell from the post of leader-writer on *The Times*, after a disagreement on policy on the Eastern Question: 'and there Mr. Cowen intervened. "Macdonell was not required to write against his convictions", he said. "Mr. Walter never asks any man to make that sacrifice".' As for the *Chronicle* itself, 'Nobody was expected to write anything that was contrary to his convictions. "I make up for not paying large salaries by employing a large staff", Mr. Cowen once said to me. There was always a choice between writers where any difficulty of conscience arose.'[51]

The same impression, of scrupulousness, is shown by the memoirs of the ex-Chartist Radical, Thomas Frost. He had to struggle to make a living, and in the 1850s was writing leaders at the same time for the Radical *Birmingham Journal* and the Whig Liverpool *Albion*. He found difficulty in writing acceptably for the latter since 'Liberalism is a very elastic term'. By the

---

[49] Koss, 426–7, cites many examples of journalists whose careers were shaped by their determination to write as their conscience dictated.

[50] G. C. Brodrick, *Memories and Impressions, 1831–1900*, 1900, 130.

[51] Aaron Watson, 44–5.

late 1870s he was working as sub-editor of the *Sheffield Evening Post*, a Conservative paper: in these circumstances he felt obliged to concentrate on non-party questions—smoke abatement and sanitary reform—pursuing them so vigorously that he was believed to be in league with the Local Government Board.[52] Such anecdotes as these need to be remembered when the nineteenth-century press is searched for evidence of opinion.

Editors were in a somewhat different category from other journalists in that they were in regular contact with the proprietors. They may have included a higher proportion of 'gentlemen and scholars' than did the profession as a whole, though this was by no means universal. Charles Cooper of the *Scotsman*, Wemyss Reid of the *Leeds Mercury*, James Thackray Bunce of the *Birmingham Daily Post*, are all examples of self-made men who were conspicuously successful as editors, and who had all begun at the bottom of the ladder. In general, editors were recruited from leader-writers and political journalists. Nevertheless no generalization is watertight, and two of the most outstanding editors of the nineteenth century took on their jobs with virtually no experience: Delane was a young man of twenty-three, who had worked on *The Times* for less than a year since leaving Oxford; and C. P. Scott, nephew of the proprietor, became editor of the *Manchester Guardian* in 1872, also fresh from Oxford, at the age of twenty-five.

What is an important and unvarying generalization is that the sovereign powers of decision were exercised by the proprietors and not by the editors. A sleeping proprietor was very rare indeed. The *Morning Post* provides a solitary example: it had been acquired in the 1840s, by T. B. Crompton, a Lancashire paper manufacturer, and on his death had passed to his nephew, W. J. Rideout. Each drew a fixed interest from the paper and never put any money into it. It continued, starved of capital for development, to have a small circulation among the aristocracy until it was bought out by Borthwick in 1876.[53] The great periodicals, owned by publishing firms, may also have left the editors to manage their own affairs. The *Fortnightly Review*, which, since it was more controversial and

[52] Thomas Frost, *Reminiscences of a Country Journalist*, 1886, 133, 281.
[53] Reginald Lucas, *Lord Glenesk and the Morning Post*, 1910, 28–31, 157, 178, 254.

political than most, might have provoked comment and control, seems to have been edited by T. H. S. Escott without supervision: the very full archive which he left contains no hint of such a thing. These however were not newspapers, and their production process was too slow for them to be natural vehicles for political manœuvring. Leaving them aside, among the newspapers there are many examples of constant and close supervision, or of the taking of independent action, by proprietors. Borthwick, once in command, continued to give day-to-day supervision to the *Morning Post*. At *The Times* Delane had been an exception to the rule, and seems to have decided the policy of the paper without interference, but his successors, Chenery and Buckle, did not inherit his power. The disastrous decision to publish the Pigott forgeries in 1888 was taken, after strong encouragement from W. H. Smith on behalf of the government, by Walter, the proprietor, and Macdonald, the manager, and not by Buckle, the editor.[54]

At the *Daily Telegraph* power had never been devolved on to an editor outside the proprietor's family. Edward Levy, son of J. M. Levy, the printer who had originally acquired the paper, was actively at work as political editor. James Macdonell, who became a leader-writer on the *Daily Telegraph* in 1865, described how Levy was the real editor: 'I shall sit with Mr. Levy and be his confidential helper. Gradually I shall be brought into contact with great people—statesmen etc.—on the business of the paper'; a little later he described his evening's work 'under the control of Mr. Levy'.[55]

At the *Daily News* the manager, John Robinson, complained of the difficulties of running the paper with constant intervention from his proprietors—as these included Samuel Morley, the doctrinaire Liberal, and after his death his son, Arnold Morley, a Liberal Whip, and Labouchere, who had journalistic ambitions of his own, this is easily believed.[56] There is evidence of their influence in the conduct and sometimes in the text of the paper. At the fall of the Second Empire in 1870, Labouchere was already in Paris. He went to see Crawford, the *Daily*

[54] F. S. L. Lyons, 'Parnellism and Crime' in *Transactions of the Royal Historical Society*, 5th ser., 1974, XXIV, 123–40; *History of The Times*, III, 45–6.
[55] Nicoll, 124–5. Edward Levy assumed additional surname of Lawson in 1875.
[56] Algar Thorold, *The Life of Henry Labouchere*, 1913, 87.

News's correspondent, and reportedly said, 'A fancy seized me. ... It is to take your place as correspondent of the *Daily News*, and to send you to the provinces. As I am a proprietor of the paper, Robinson won't object to this arrangement.'[57] From this fancy sprang the celebrated *Letters of a Besieged Resident*. After the end of the war Labouchere's distinctive style can be suspected in the paper from time to time, particularly in accounts in 1874 of a fictitious place, Coaleyflat, which clearly refer to his own experience as a candidate at Nottingham in the General Election of 1874.[58] Samuel Morley's influence can perhaps be seen in the full and interesting accounts of strikes published in 1871 and 1872—trade unions being one of his interests.[59] The varied and conflicting views of the proprietors were seen most clearly in the troubles over the editorship which came to a head in 1885–6. The best account, and one which very well illustrates the relationship between proprietor and editor, was given by Labouchere to Herbert Gladstone. In it he wrote:

Last year Hill was the Editor. Almost all the Members of the Cabinet were perpetually complaining of him. We got rid of him and faute de mieux appointed Lucy. The difficulty of finding a good Editor is greater than that of finding a good Cabinet Minister. The Editor has to understand about the working of the Press—arranging news—and getting Articles upon various social topics, as well as on politics. Lucy does not know much about the matter—To meet this, I got Morley to write political Articles. His appointment in the Cabinet of course upset this, and politics have been left to Lucy. So soon as we can we will find a man— ...

It is one thing knowing what an Editor should do, and quite another making him do it, unless you never leave him.[60]

Some of the commanding tone of this letter may have been the result of the relatively unimpressive political progress that Labouchere had so far made: within the *Daily News* office he carried weight.

Many parallels can be cited in greater or lesser newspapers. At Leeds, Wemyss Reid complained that he did not have a free

[57] Ibid., 109.
[58] *Daily News*, 7 Feb. 1874.
[59] *D.NB.*
[60] Herbert Gladstone MSS BL Add. MS 46016, ff 4–5, letter dated 10 Feb. 1886; Koss, 268 ff, gives a full account. 'Lucy' is Henry Lucy, political columnist.

hand in the *Leeds Mercury* (and ironically wondered if he could be considered for Lucy's job).[61] Most people who worked for Passmore Edwards, proprietor of the *Echo*, grumbled at his constant interference: 'There was a time, not many years since, when it was a smoking-room joke in the National Liberal Club that the place seemed full of former editors of the *Echo*.'[62] In Manchester we have the testimony of R. C. K. Ensor, a member of the Royal Commission on the Press of 1947–8. He told a witness how he remembered that a leading article could be strongly influenced by C. P. Scott's remark 'Uncle would not like it', Uncle being the absentee proprietor and chief shareholder of the paper, J. E. Taylor, who was living at that time in the South of France.[63] In Hull, William Saunders was proprietor of the *Eastern Morning News*. He was a fanatical disciple of Henry George, and according to his nephew, J. A. Spender, who was editor in the mid-1880s, Saunders would search the paper daily for anything that could be construed as favourable to landlordism and unfavourable to George. This was in spite of the fact that the readers consisted 'almost entirely of local businessmen and shopkeepers' who hated it for its radicalism but needed it for its shipping news.[64] In Northampton the proprietor of the *Northampton Mercury* was A. V. Dicey, whose family had owned it since the eighteenth century. He wrote the weekly leaders.[65] Joseph Cowen's active management of the *Newcastle Daily Chronicle* and the *Evening Chronicle* has already been discussed. 'He was a coalowner, and a shipowner, and in some respects also a captain of industry; but first and foremost he was owner of the *Newcastle Chronicle*. The paper meant much more to him than all his other interests combined.'[66] Lastly we can quote the ideas of a would-be proprietor, H. J. Wilson, whose many earlier attempts to enter the business had ended in frustration of one kind or another. In

---

[61] Herbert Gladstone papers, BL Add. MS 46041, ff 81–90, Wemyss Reid to Herbert Gladstone, 26 Feb.–17 Mar. 1886.

[62] Aaron Watson, 121.

[63] Question 342.

[64] J. A. Spender, I, 33.

[65] *Royal Commission on the Press*, question 3831. (Dicey died in 1907. An interesting account of his management of the paper is given by one of their old employees, W. W. Hadley, in *Northamptonshire Past and Present*, II, (1956), 123–30.)

[66] Aaron Watson, 39. See p. 72 above.

1895 he was at last on the verge of taking over the *Sheffield Independent*. He set about finding an editor as other people might search for a nonconformist minister, and wrote to the favoured candidate, J. Derry, currently editor of the *Nottingham Express*, asking for evidence of how that paper had handled divorce reporting, the Contagious Diseases Acts, and the 'treatment of subject races'. Derry expressed great offence and insisted that he must have independence; 'If you want at Sheffield a hack writer . . . I am not the man.' He added that he was 'not altogether his own master', being obliged to use material set up in type for the evening paper of the day before (the shoe-string financing of many of these papers is too easily forgotten).[67] All these various episodes throw into relief the successfulness of the arrangement that Johnstone had made for the *Standard*: under his will the family beneficiaries could not interfere with the running of the paper, and Mudford had every incentive to stay in the job and make a success of it.[68]

These examples are not surprising. The people who went into newspaper proprietorship often went into it because they had active public interests, not necessarily party-political interests. They would have asserted the freedom of the press against intervention from government, but would hardly have accepted limitations on their own freedom to determine the opinions of their own property. In some cases, Cowen, Borthwick, and the Levy-Lawsons, the day to day conduct of their journals seems to have been their major pleasure and interest in life—like those politicians of the eighteenth century who, according to Pares, were involved in borough-mongering 'for fun'.[69]

What is strange is that this situation which, as these examples show, was widespread, should have coincided with the assertion of the principle of editorial sovereignty. That principle is well summed up in Spender's obituary of Sir Edward Cook in the *DNB*: 'He took a high view of journalism as a profession, and claimed to exercise complete independence as an editor. Though a convinced Liberal he was fearless in criticism of his

---

[67] H. J. Wilson MSS, MD 1988. Derry took the job.
[68] See p. 63 above.
[69] R. Pares, *King George III and the Politicians*, Oxford, 1953, 30.

party when he thought the public interest required it and was no respecter of persons.'

This demand for independence, which bore fruit in the present century in the trusts set up to govern a number of notable papers, was certainly not a defence of an established norm. In the hearings of the Royal Commission on the Press of 1947–8 there was discussion of the subject, and different dates were put forward as the period when the status of editors had begun to decline: Ensor suggesting that it had begun with Northcliffe, and Mr Michael Foot placing it after the First World War.[70] But in fact there is little to choose—except the size of the paper's circulation—between Saunders's attitude to Henry George and the vendettas which have been associated with the Beaverbrook press—against the British Council for example.

The journalists of the later nineteenth century, editors and the rest alike, had, as a body, none of the characteristics (paper qualifications, or membership of a self-governing body regulating admission) which are used to define a profession—quite the reverse. In a looser sense however they were professionals: there was a well-understood and long-established organization of the various tasks involved in the production of newspapers. Journalists learned these systems on the job, and usually treated the work as a lifelong career. They had their political sympathies, hoped perhaps for more independence, and aimed to work for publications of whose views they approved. But they were not all people like Cook or Stead, nor were they political pamphleteers. For most of them the day's work consisted of putting together a saleable and readable publication.

[70] Questions 1868–72.

V

The News

WHAT sort of service of news could be given by Victorian newspapers? They were far more numerous than newspapers today, but had much smaller staffs and circulations, and closer links with organized political groupings. Where did the news come from? How was it selected and put across? To answer these questions some sort of definition of 'news' must be attempted.

It is difficult to offer anything more precise than a description of the way we use the term in everyday parlance. It is a bundle of pieces of information about recent events adapted to the interests of the recipient: 'I have news for you'; 'What is your news?' News purports to be factual, and is recent. Subsequent information automatically demotes an item from being news to being background or explanatory information. The term is used of specific happenings. The discovery of a law of natural science is news, not so the law itself. News is essential to human existence: an individual is linked to his world by a network of relationships, to government, employers, and relations. 'News' can tell him of changes in his world or reassure him that the network is still holding firm. A person who returns home after having lost contact with his news has a feeling that he floats adrift until he has found it out. We can take as an example the British doctor who emerged after the lifting of the siege of Paris, urgently asking Archibald Forbes, the *Daily News* correspondent, 'Is Ireland quiet? Is Mr. Gladstone still Prime Minister? Is the Princess Louise married?'[1] Involvement in news, including the most intense and extravagant attempts to find it out, is a fact of human psychology. 'Why bother to speculate when it is already decided?' is no answer to the person who is worried. Newspapers must find ways of exploiting this anxiety in such a way as to focus it on public questions.

The news must also, somehow or other, by the artistry of its

[1] Archibald Forbes, *Memories and Studies of War and Peace*, 1895, 125.

presentation, or by constant repetition and explanation, if not by its intrinsic qualities, establish a link with the reader's experience and interests: if it deals with the remoter parts of the world it is more compelling if our nationals are concerned, or if human good or bad deeds of a kind we find intelligible are being described. The news holds our attention when we have grasped the essentials of a situation and want to know developments: the enquirer after news asks the question 'How is——getting on?' Old or irregular news, where the stages of an event are condensed in one report, has not the emotional force of news which proceeds from stage to stage, leaving the reader at any one time ignorant of the state of the situation. Continuity, with members of the cast reappearing regularly, is an important element in holding the reader's attention, and it is an element which the newspaper, like the serial story or regular private correspondence, is well fitted to supply. The newspaper reading habit is stimulated by the regular reporting of new instalments of a long running story.

The supply of a miscellaneous collection of dramas, crimes, and catastrophes, which is often supposed to be the staple diet of the popular press, lacks the element of continuity. It formed an important part of the mid-Victorian newspaper business: the major Sunday papers—*Reynolds's, Lloyd's* and *News of the World*—subsisted, essentially, on police court reporting, an attractive recipe for success, being cheap, simple to organize, and popular, and they all enjoyed massive circulations. But they were read more as fiction or entertainment than as news; a good example of the Sunday-paper mentality (though it refers in fact to *The Times*) is given by Dr Prendergast, a doctor in the Crimea. In May, 1855, he wrote home with thanks for a bundle of old newspapers, ' . . . sat down and had two hours' sound reading of the old Times. The quiet miscellaneous news-perusal really most grateful. Trevelyan's Examn, Emperor's Visit, a divorce case, and some of British wife-beating.'[2]

The appetite for news comes from different sources. The history of the Shaftesbury News Club, which is given in a printed testimonial for the Central News, provides an example:

We find the Central News very convenient. At the time of the illness

---

[2] BL Add. MS 59849 f. 86. On the Sunday papers see Virginia Berridge, op. cit.

of the Prince of Wales, we felt the want of more frequent supplies of news than the daily papers furnished. We, therefore, made an effort, and obtained subscriptions from the inhabitants of the town to enable us to subscribe to the Central News. At the end of the first year we found the townspeople so accustomed to the daily Telegrams that we continued our subscription. It is now almost a necessity.[3]

The 1860s and 1870s offered a sequence of exceptionally interesting news stories which could train and develop the public taste for news. The same kind of process may have been at work in South and East Lancashire during the cotton famine as in Shaftesbury. Businessmen may always have been conscious that their welfare depended on events afar off, but the famine brought this fact home to a large and once prosperous population, who had been working in the most advanced industrial sector of the day. It is noticeable how the dialect poetry of the 1860s in Lancashire turns again and again to descriptions of people learning to read the newspaper and learning to read the news of the American Civil War.[4] In 1862 the *Illustrated London News* carried a full page illustration of Manchester cotton workers studying the news in the public library during the cotton famine.[5] There was a spate of new halfpenny evening papers in Lancashire during the later 1860s which gained further impetus from the fact that the Franco-Prussian War followed only a few years after the American Civil War. The Franco-Prussian War was over quickly, but the siege of Paris, followed by the Commune, kept the level of public tension high until the middle of 1871. In July 1871 the *Printer's Register* reported that while several halfpenny papers had ceased publication with the ending of the 'feverish demand' for war news, 'there still remains a creditable list of journals which have, by the tremendous events of the past year, been able to secure a hold on the public'. Some of the intense interest given to the two Tichborne trials, which lasted 102 and 188 days, may perhaps be explained by the need to find an alternative focus of public attention. So perhaps can the emphasis given to the Ashanti expedition in 1874, a colonial

---

[3] H. J. Wilson MSS, MD 6002.
[4] Brian Hollingworth, *Songs of the People: Lancashire Dialect Poetry of the Industrial Revolution*, Manchester, 1977.
[5] *Illustrated London News*, 20 Nov. 1862.

war which did not have the intrinsic importance of the
Bulgarian question two years later, but which allowed the
machinery of war reporting to be brought into play.[6] At the
time of the Russo-Turkish war, in 1877, the *Bristol Evening News*
stated in its first issue (29 May) that the paper was being
started because 'The want of a mid-day report of war telegrams, legal, commercial and sporting events is greatly felt at
the present time.' The *Evening Post* of Worcester, begun a few
days later, on 4 June, wrote how 'ready information of passing
events is desirable, especially in view of the gravity of foreign
affairs at a time like the present'.

It is worth asking whether the conditions of life in Victorian
Britain were reflected in the scope and content of the news—
whether there are differences in some way related to the great
social differences between them and us. Three examples, and
no doubt more are possible, can be suggested. There was a
much higher proportion of young people in the population
than today, and as the scope of state education was growing, it
might have been expected that newspapers were being bought
by a larger proportion of the young than the old. Then, there
was massive emigration from Britain to Australia, New Zealand, and North America—it would be natural, to expect that
news from these regions would have a high news value, and
would be prominent in the papers. Another conspicuous difference is in the practice of religion: the percentages of church
attenders recorded in 1851 are incontrovertibly higher than
would be found today, and one would expect the Victorian
newspaper to provide a good source for the history of church
life. These are all areas of research where it is difficult to devise
simple ways of establishing degrees of emphasis, or of relating
the content of newspapers firmly to the demands of readers.
The existence of a young readership is perhaps suggested by
the rapid expansion of sports reporting—in particular of
football in the 1880s. Then, a number of evening papers began
to produce 'athletic editions' with match reports, plainly aimed
at those interested in the game rather than those concerned

---

[6] See Brown 'The treatment of the news in the mid-Victorian newspaper', in
Transactions of the Royal Historical Society, 5th ser., XXVII, 1977, 23–39, where this
growth is more fully discussed.

with gambling.[7] But, apart from that, the general reader of the newspaper—London or provincial—is not conscious of the presence of the young in the population (in the way that a visitor from another planet might today notice the constant reference to the aged). On the question of emigration, and the probability that many readers would have had close relations living overseas, it is possible that careful sifting through newspapers would produce printed emigrant letters. Australia, New Zealand, and America were not however prime subjects in the overseas news columns. With religion a simple test shows that much religious news was not reported. Spot checks on the Monday issues of four substantial morning papers in big towns with important Nonconformist congregations—the *Western Daily Press* of Bristol, the *Manchester Examiner*, the *Birmingham Daily Post*, and the *Leicester Daily Mercury*—show that Sunday services, at which influential preachers such as the Revd R. W. Dale of Birmingham might have spoken, were not reported.[8] Speeches by the clergy on other occasions—Sunday school anniversaries, retirement presentations, or political meetings— were. The reason is given by Joseph Cowen in reply to a complaint from a positivist lecturer:

It is the custom of provincial newspapers not to notice Sunday meetings, religious or semi-religious. If once the practice was begun every sect would ask for their special preacher to be reported. It is not out of any regard for the Sunday, but out of consideration for the reporters, who do not get many holidays.[9]

(Another reason could have been the desire to avoid the alienation of readers of other denominations.) The active church or chapel member could read his own section of the religious press, but the general picture of what was being preached about, and which were the most thriving congregations, was not offered to contemporaries, and is missing from the historical record. A closer look at Monday's papers

---

[7] Ross McKibbin, 'Working class gambling in Britain, 1880–1939', *Past and Present*, no. 82, 1979, 147–78.

[8] These were studied for Sept. and Nov. 1869; Jan. and June 1875; Jan. and May 1874; and Feb. and Apr. 1874 respectively. The Bristol paper, covering the period when Irish disestablishment was being actively canvassed, does report fully a meeting on the subject (15 Nov. 1869).

[9] Cowen MSS F 47, dated 8 Mar. 1883.

suggests that Sunday events in general were not reported.[10]

In general, therefore, it seems that the selection of news offered does not correspond closely to what we know to have been characteristics of the readers. It seems, rather, that the news was assembled from what was easily available in the office: and what that was, in turn, depends on a range of considerations which will be discussed in later chapters. Australian news was very expensive to transmit; there was not the same constant preoccupation with diplomatic events in America that there was with the Balkans. It is possible that this tendency to accept established news values uncritically came from the long professional experience of the kind of journalists who were commonly employed: they had a recognized way of doing things—often on a shoe-string—and not much imaginative insight into fresh areas.

Another general feature of nineteenth-century British newspapers was the extent to which they show common standards. *The Times* at one extreme and the *Ashton Evening Reporter* at the other would have a similar layout. Nearly all newspapers concentrated their advertisements on the first and last pages; presumably these pages were set up in type earlier in the day. Leading articles appeared on the middle page, usually on the left-hand side, and the major political questions, foreign affairs or meetings of the Cabinet, were reported on the page opposite to them. Late news, or late foreign telegrams, appeared in no very regular position. Presumably the organization of the printing programme would determined their position.

To an external critic reading these papers a hundred years later it also seems that there was a far smaller difference in style and language than there is today between the 'quality' papers and the 'down-market' ones. The latter did not try to attract readers through a simplification of thought and vocabulary, as in a modern paper where journalistic skill goes into packing the maximum implication into words of one syllable. A small provincial paper credited its readers with a reading ability to understand a complex argument in appropriate language. This can be illustrated by a couple of examples taken at random

[10] This raises the interesting question of the labour demonstrations of the 1880s and 1890s, commonly held on Sunday afternoons.

from papers about which we know something. The first comes from the *Sheffield Evening Star*, which was run in conjunction with the Leader family's *Sheffield Independent*, and was much investigated by H. J. Wilson. It was not very flourishing at the time this extract was written, but it was aimed at the Sheffield working class:

Many persons have doubtless been of opinion that spectators present at a prize fight are in point of law guilty of an assault and liable to be punished accordingly. Prize fights are direct breaches of the peace, and are consequently illegal and persons who attend and therefore encourage them are aiding and abetting the combatants in their illegal offence. This has been the dictum of more than one judge; but precedent is not necessarily binding on the learned occupants of the bench, and as human minds differ, we find one judge totally disregarding the opinion of another judge and laying down principles which differ entirely from those of his predecessors.[11]

The article went on to argue that prize-fighting needed to be abolished by law.

The second extract comes from the weekly *Barnsley Independent*, of which Thomas Frost, the self-educated ex-Chartist, was editor. The paper is full of articles about his favourite hobby-horse, municipal improvement, which was an area of reform acceptable to a Conservative newspaper.

We must congratulate the Town Council on their awakening, however tardily, to a proper sense of their duties and responsibilities towards the ratepayers in respect of the condition of the streets. When the question of repairing Tune Street was before the Council a month ago it was argued by Alderman Marshall that it was not their duty to do anything for private property, and that the owners of the property ought not to be obliged to put it into a safe and proper condition, because they could not afford the necessary outlay. How a public thoroughfare can be private property and how property owners can be held to be too poor to be able to maintain the roads they have thrown open for public use, has never been explained; and if the alleged poverty of the owners could have been proved, it would simply have been a case for the application of some such legislative remedy as the Irish Encumbered Estates Act. But it is now admitted that the owners can afford to do what is required, and the Council have been converted to the views we have always held on this point.

Tune Street is to be repaired.[12]

[11] 21 Mar. 1882. The history of the paper is summarized in Lee, 172.
[12] 23 Feb. 1884. For Frost see p. 88, and *Reminiscences*, 314.

These extracts are typical of the writing that was put out, week by week, in the hundreds of newspapers circulating in the country. It is not claimed that they show any particular literary skill: on the contrary they show, though not in a bad form, the repetitiveness which was the besetting sin of nineteenth-century journalism. But they do not talk down to their readers, either in argument or vocabulary. Apart from the joke, by 1884 somewhat dated, about the Encumbered Estates Act, there is not much to choose between them and the writing then found in *The Times*. It is often asserted that Newnes' *Tit-Bits* and Harmsworth's *Daily Mail* brought newspapers to the masses by writing simply and brightly and in short articles. It could be better argued, as Mrs Leavis did, that these popular papers were creating a cultural division which had not existed before.[13] Where *The Times* or the *Manchester Guardian* differed from the *Sheffield Evening Star* was in the range of news that they carried and the fullness with which they gave it.

A similar solidity and seriousness can be sensed in the reporting of the period. The conventions governing different types of contribution to a newspaper at that time obviously varied; Labouchere's letters from besieged Paris were personal; he chose what to write about and gave his own impressions. The foreign correspondent and even more the war correspondent gave his own summary of the situation. Between *c.* 1860 and *c.* 1900 the presentation of the news was also evolving. But the main building blocks of the newspaper at the end of the century, and even more so thirty or forty years earlier, consisted of transcripts of statements by public figures, reported with the minimum of intervention and explanation by the journalists. A single example, originating with Reuters and taken from the *Standard* and the *Daily News* of 5 April 1871, illustrates the point. Significantly the report, of the opening of the Spanish Cortes dated 3 April, appeared word for word the same in both papers. It read:

President Calatrava opened the Cortes today. There was a great crowd of spectators, among whom many ladies were present in the galleries.

[13] Q. D. Leavis, *Fiction and the Reading Public*, 1932; for example 'One is struck almost equally by two things that emerge—the ability that these barely literate working-men display to tackle serious works, and the absence of any but material difficulties in their way.' (1968 edn., 114.)

The King arrived at half-past two p.m., accompanied by the Ministers, and was received with loud cheers. His Majesty read the Speech from the Throne in a firm voice. He said:—[and there follows the text of the speech, which was short and formal. The report ended]

Cheers repeatedly interrupted the speech of the King.

The weather is splendid.

There is no explanation of the significance of the speech, and no hint of the writer's attitude, other than the faint hint of approval implied in the use of the words 'firm', 'loud', and 'splendid'.

Reporting of this austere standard provides the context of C. P. Scott's dictum 'Comment is free but facts are sacred'. It had both strength and weakness. The strength, as anyone who uses nineteenth-century reports, for example of meetings of local Boards, finds out, is that reporters produced a body of solid and coherent information. They were making a record in much the same way as law or parliamentary reporters were doing. The weakness was that they could not operate effectively outside the framework of the set speech on the special occasion: they were like the painter who can copy but cannot paint direct from nature. Reporters, as the summaries of their careers in the last chapter suggest, learned their trade on the job, and had no practised way of dealing with situations, particularly those which were unforeseen. This was partly the result of the papers' small resources: the reporters' diaries of the *Manchester Guardian*, which survive for the 1880s, show them fully booked in advance at local meetings: they were unlikely to get quickly to the scene of a disaster. But their reticence in assessing situations was also a matter of training. Their memoirs, which relive the outstanding experiences of their working lives, give us an idea of what they considered to be the real professional problems: there are anecdotes about the tricks by which a reporter transmitted the verdict in a sensational trial ahead of his rivals, and about hiring special trains, but the writer has not so far read discussions of the problem of establishing what had really happened or assessing its significance.

The limitation of such reporting is best illustrated in relation to a particular situation, the well known riot of 8 February 1886, when a meeting of the unemployed in Trafalgar Square led to a riot through Pall Mall and the West End. On 8 February, which was a Monday, *The Times* reported meetings

of the unemployed which had taken place on Sunday afternoon at Clerkenwell Green. They could not have foreseen what
would happen in the following week, but they were sufficiently
alive to the general situation to say, in the same news item, that
meetings on the same question had been held in four other
places. Clerkenwell Green was reported in greater detail, but
when faced with the problem of what to say about it, the writer
copied the mottoes embroidered on banners, gave the names of
the chairman of each meeting, and stated that the proceedings
were orderly. He offered no analysis or interpretation.

On Tuesday 9 February, the day after the disorders, all
papers printed long reports. They prove, on comparison, to
have been distributed by the Press Association and the Central
News, and reprinted without alteration of the wording. They
reported the proceedings in Trafalgar Square—the names of
the speakers and reports in full of what they said. Of the
crowd's rampage through the West End there was a detailed
report—the exact route, how many windows in which Clubs
were broken, which shops were damaged and what they lost,
for example the named butcher's shop where a number of
joints were thrown about. It appears that the reporters had
gone along in the wake of the rioters, collecting information—
facts, not the emotional responses of the shopkeepers—and still
less their estimates of what it had all been about. The only
piece of opinion in these reports was that the worst of the
damage had been done by 'roughs' who had attached themselves to the crowd. By Thursday 11 February, reactions to the
riot had crystallized: headlines referred to 'panic' in the
capital, and foreign correspondents reported reactions
abroad—where there was dismay that the British tradition of
political stability had been broken. The *Newcastle Daily Chronicle*'s London correspondent, who may have been Cowen
himself, walked along the route and, always a friend of the
unemployed, held that reports of damage were exaggerated.
Nevertheless it is hard to see how the reporters' carefully
itemized lists in the papers could have been guilty: shopkeepers
may have exaggerated, or leader-writers written alarmingly.[14]

This solidity, which gives the data and leaves the reader to

---

[14] This account is based on reports in *The Times*, the *Scotsman*, the *Yorkshire Post*, and
the *Newcastle Daily Chronicle*.

decide on its meaning, is less characteristic of the reporting of foreign affairs; in this respect the report of the opening of the Spanish Cortes is not typical. The foreign correspondent had a higher status than the reporter. Better paid and better educated, he had a responsibility for surveying and interpreting the situation, rather than for reporting specific events. He proceeded by reading the local press and talking to contacts. The war correspondent had a similar kind of job. In their work personal assessment and their personal preferences could not be avoided. Furthermore, both the foreign and the war correspondents had what was essentially a watching brief: there were long periods when nothing much was happening yet a report was expected. At these times the correspondent would send in general descriptions and personal impressions—there were endless descriptions, during the expedition for the relief of Khartoum in the autumn of 1884, of the overland transport of boats past the Nile cataracts and the troops' reactions; the expedition was going very slowly and this was all there was to say. It seems therefore to have been a convention that more latitude was enjoyed by the foreign and war correspondents: to give a specific example, two reports on the same page of *The Times* on 11 September 1885 begin 'The present condition of Servia gives grounds for believing that there may be serious troubles in that country before long,' and, from Madrid,

The situation here continues to be in a condition of the utmost uncertainty and confusion. The Government, which recklessly gave to the public and the Press the contents of the telegram from Manila announcing the German capture of Yap in the presence of two Spanish men-of-war, without taking the most ordinary precautions to protect the German Legation, when in the excited state of public opinion an explosion was almost certain to occur, has now gone to the opposite extreme, and veils all communications from the Philippines in mysterious silence, a proceeding which, while sustaining the excitement, further exasperates the people.

The first extract is a prediction of trouble; the second openly takes sides against the Spanish Government—'recklessly', 'most ordinary precautions', 'mysterious silence' are all emotive words, not strictly necessary to the sense of the report. Such phrases were not used in the descriptions of the Trafalgar Square meeting.

Another important generalization about the Victorian newspaper is that news reporting occupied a far larger proportion of the space and emphasis in a paper than would be usual today. If we take a modern issue of *The Times*, we find that out of 24 to 28 pages, three are regularly devoted to features, that the centre pages consist of leading articles, letters to the editor, and commentary of various kinds. Perhaps a total of six or seven pages will be of advertisements, and allowing for the space taken up by illustrations, and articles throughout the paper which are not strictly reports of recent events, there is a good variety of reading-matter. In comparison *The Times* in February 1886 had sixteen pages, of which six to eight would be of advertisements. Every day the leading articles covered most of one page. Otherwise, in an ordinary week in January 1886, general features were: on Tuesday 19th half a column on life in New Guinea, and another half column on a newly discovered Roman tomb, and also a review article of one and a quarter columns of books on the Sudan—a topical subject at that time. On Thursday 21st there was a three-column article on Lord Salisbury's tenure of the Foreign Office,[15] and on the following day two columns reviewing the Badminton Library of sporting books. On Monday and Wednesday there had been nothing which could be classed as a feature. In the other London dailies, which were usually of eight pages (occasionally rising to twelve), the position was similar. In the *Daily Chronicle* in the same week there was a notice of a play on Monday, of less than half a column, and another on Wednesday. On Thursday there was a column and a half from a special correspondent on distress in the west of Ireland, and on Saturday a column of book reviews. In the *Daily News* there was a little more: an interview on Monday with the ex-Communard Louise Michel, just released from prison in Paris, on Wednesday a theatre column, on Thursday a column and a half of book reviews, on Friday something on the 'Fashions', and on Saturday two columns of imaginary 'New Beaconsfield Letters'. In the *Daily Telegraph*, where more than half the space was given over to advertisements, there was a rather higher proportion of features: on Monday four columns on a visit to Rotorua, New Zealand, on Wednesday the theatre notices, and on Thursday

[15] Salisbury's government resigned the following week, on the 27th.

two columns on books, four on 'India revisited', and one and a half on 'Ireland today'.

In the provincial dailies the practice varied. In the *Scotsman*, to take the second week in February 1886, there was on Monday 8th a column on the state of the Turf, on Tuesday half a column on New Music', on Wednesday two columns on winter in Cairo—again a topical subject—on Thursday and Friday three and four columns on new books. In the *Yorkshire Post* the proportion was similar; readers were offered in the same week an article on the vintage of 1885, a report by a special commissioner on agriculture in Cambridgeshire, another on picturesque old Whitby, and on two days reviews of books and magazines. The *Newcastle Daily Chronicle* had no such features in that week. These were all normally papers with eight pages, of which on average over three would be given to advertising. While the amount of reading matter other than news might vary from time to time, and between one editor and another, the impression given overall is that the newspapers were there to provide news, and that general articles and features (a word first recorded in the *OED* in 1928) appeared at best fitfully.

This characteristic is probably to be explained by the continuing vitality of the periodical. The early nineteenth century had been the age of the great quarterlies. The *Edinburgh Review* and the *Quarterly Review* were still in being in the 1870s but more frequent publication was normal. The periodicals founded in the 1860s and 1870s, *Macmillan's Magazine* (1859), the *Cornhill* (1860), the *Contemporary Review* (1866), and the *Nineteenth Century* (1877) were all monthlies. So was the *Fortnightly Review* (1865) after the first few months. They attained massive circulation: the *Wellesley Index* records that the *Cornhill* reached 20,000 in its early years, and the *Nineteenth Century* sold more than 10,000. They specialized in different subjects; the *Contemporary Review* and the *Nineteenth Century* in metaphysical and political ideas, and the *Cornhill* and *Macmillan's* in literature, including serialized fiction. These were all independent of party politics, but the *Fortnightly*, beginning under Morley's editorship from 1867 to 1882, and continuing, but more uncertainly, under Escott until 1885, became the mouthpiece of the secular Radicalism associated with Joseph

Chamberlain. In reply Alfred Austin's *National Review* was founded with the blessing of the Conservative Central Office in 1883.[16] As well as all these there were the family magazines such as *All the Year Round* (1859–95) and *Good Words* (1869–77). As a group all these periodicals were characterized by their high quality and high price. If they are taken in conjunction with the mass of specialized publications, there would have been few serious tastes and interests which would not have been catered for to a good standard.

Periodicals also gained from the fact that the convention of anonymous publication, which was still universal in the newspaper world, was beginning to break down with them: the *Fortnightly*, the *Contemporary*, and the *Nineteenth Century* were all signed from the beginning, and the *Cornhill* adopted signed articles from about 1880.[17] The main defence of anonymity in the newspaper press had always been that anonymous articles carried more weight because they were published with the authority of the newspaper behind them.[18] But where comment and analysis were concerned this could hardly apply: a political rumour could well gain in authority if it appeared anonymously in *The Times*; on the other hand an article on the Vatican Decrees in the *Nineteenth Century* gained in interest as well as authority if it was signed by Cardinal Manning.[19]

Newspapers, particularly those directed to the educated and prosperous, were to be read in conjunction with periodicals. The contents of each month's batch of publications certainly had a news value: it was quite usual for a newspaper to publish a review article on the subject.[20] W. T. Stead's *Review of Reviews* was built on the idea of epitomizing the contents of the periodical press: that such a publication could ever have been successful is best proof of the general interest they aroused.

It was an interest, however, which limited the range of a daily paper. If we look at publications directed towards people who were unlikely to afford or to see the monthlies, we find a more varied range of contents. In the popular Sunday papers,

[16] Koss, 249.

[17] *Wellesley Index to Victorian Periodicals*, 1966–.

[18] John Morley on 'Anonymous journalism' in *Fortnightly Review*, VIII, 1867; and Lee, 107–8.

[19] Published Mar. and Apr. 1877.

[20] For example the *Yorkshire Post*, 12 Feb. 1886.

and in a number of provincial papers, there would be gardening hints as a regular feature, and many provincial papers
would have serialized fiction, especially but not exclusively on
Saturdays, and many would have columns of jokes. Much of
this would be distributed from a central source or, in the case of
gardening hints, be lifted from specialized gardening magazines. The distribution of suitable fiction by Tillotson's, the
publishers of the *Bolton Journal* and the *Bolton Evening News*, is
well known through their refusal of *Tess of the D'Urbervilles*.
The great bulk of newspaper fiction was very different, with
titles such as 'Flora the orphan' or 'Lucy the factory girl'.[21]
The halfpenny papers were designed, in a way which is much
closer to the modern newspaper, as a package for the family,
and were so advertised.

The descriptions of the news given in this chapter are more
appropriate to the middle than the end of the century. Some
lines of evolution can be seen, and will be discussed in later
chapters. Here the evolution of the periodical which concentrated on political commentary is noticed. By the 1860s the
most influential were monthlies; by the end of the century the
significant vehicles for political comment were the weekly
Spectator or the *Speaker*. The *Edinburgh* and the *Quarterly* had
been admirable vehicles for the discussion of the great struc-
tural questions—of economic policy, parliamentary reform,
church and state, and the rest—which exercised the minds of
the educated after Waterloo. Their publishing cycle was too
slow to cope with the rapidly changing political situations
which preoccupied politicians of the 1889s. The same was true
of the monthlies: the Escott papers occasionally enable one to
measure the time between the commissioning of an article
(most were initiated by the editor), and publication;
for example James Bryce offered to do an article on 'Democracy' late in October 1882. He wrote it slowly, corrected the
proofs in early January, and it appeared in February 1883.

[21] Gardening hints in the 1870s were published in the *Leicester Daily Mercury*, *Bolton
Evening Guardian*, *Evening Star of Gwent*, and *Bucks Advertiser*. Jokes may be found in the
Leeds Evening Express in 1868, *Manchester Evening News* in 1874, *Leicester Daily Mercury*,
and *Leeds Daily News*, both in 1874. Serial stories are in the *Daily Gazette* of
Middlesbrough, *Leeds Evening Express*, and *Leeds Daily News* in 1873, the *Ashton Reporter*
in 1876, and Gloucester *Citizen* in 1877, and many other locations. These are merely
quoted as examples.

'Democracy' is not a fast-changing subject: it was different when Sir Lepel Griffin, Agent-General to the Governor-General of India, wrote saying that he had an article on Afghanistan ready to appear in May, as war was imminent. By the beginning of May the crisis was over.[22] The political weeklies operated on a much shorter time-scale, and were written by journalists.

The demand for more analysis and discussion than was provided by the morning papers, which would be also more topical than that given in the periodicals, was proved by the great popularity of the evening Clubland papers, the *Pall Mall Gazette, Westminster Gazette*, and *St. James's Gazette*, all of which offered commentary, interviews with public figures, and from time to time initiated the public discussion of general questions, for example the 'Truth about the Navy' campaign. But they did not give the day's news as the average reporter would have understood it. There can be no doubt about the public interest they aroused—the excitement engendered by the 'Maiden Tribute' case is evidence of that. This interest was not solely the effect of the journalistic skill of W. T. Stead; the *Pall Mall Gazette* was much quoted in the 1870s when it was a Conservative organ, and continued to be important after Stead had left it. Between 1887 and 1889 the number of copies delivered to the National Liberal Club rose from 13 to 26 (compared with four *Globes*, three *Stars*, and one *Evening Standard*). Copies were to be put in the billiard room, the smoking room, the reading room, the grill room, and the card room—it is impossible to resist the conclusion that it was a necessary priming of the evening's conversations. When it was sold to W. W. Astor, thirty copies of the *Westminster Gazette* were substituted for it.[23] The popularity of the weekly papers of social gossip, *Truth, Vanity Fair*, and *The World*, also suggests that there was a demand for something lighter and more descriptive than the orthodox morning papers provided.

It is tempting, but ill-judged, to relate the trend towards more frequent publication and shorter articles to the speeding up of nineteenth-century life with its railways and telegraphs.

[22] BL Add. MSS 58774–796; Bryce is in 58776, Griffin is in 58780.
[23] National Liberal Club, minute-book of newspaper committee, Bristol University Library.

A weekly could react to events as they happened, and offer advice early enough in the process to have some chance of influencing the outcome. But it does not follow that the process of political decision had accelerated in sympathy with the transformation of communications: three months, or even one month, was an equally long time in the history of Catholic Emancipation or Peel's Hundred days. A more likely explanation for the demand for instant political commentary might be found in the nature of the problems being faced. The problems of the years after 1870 which constantly rise to the surface in political memoirs and in the newspapers concern the strategies needed to defend British interests in a hostile world. In the *Pall Mall Gazette*, or in, for example, Chamberlain's correspondence, the country seems beset by enemies—Turks, Russians, Egyptian and Irish nationalists, bondholders, foreign manufacturers, and foreign navies. These situations demanded swift discussion and response.

News, then, throughout this period dominated the newspapers in a way which it hardly does today. This predominance—over features, analysis, fiction, and the rest—was most pronounced in the London morning dailies, with their columns of foreign correspondence, and least in the weeklies, particularly those with a mass circulation, and in the halfpenny provincial evenings. By 'news' would have been understood serious reports of public affairs, local and national. Social events might be reported, but in a subordinate way: the standpoint of the reader was assumed to be that of someone with a serious concern for the affairs of a world power.

VI

News Agencies

THE establishment of the Press Association in 1868 is rightly
seen as a landmark in the development of the nineteenth-
century newspaper press. It was, however, only the largest and
most comprehensively organized of a whole network of co-
operative news-gathering arrangements. Such co-operation
may be a system towards which newspaper work tends at any
time, but in the later nineteenth century conditions were
particularly favourable, indeed made co-operation necessary.
There was a very large number of fairly small papers, which
individually had small resources of staff. They also had separate and defined circulation areas. Thus the same material could
appear, word for word if necessary, in different areas, without
the readers in all probability being conscious of the fact. By co-
operative arrangements the quality and range of news and
features could be vastly extended: in some fields fresh categories of news could be created. In the collection and dissemination of news economies of scale apply to a very marked degree.
In the later nineteenth century there existed a great range and
variety of arrangements, which have it in common that they all
differ from a model situation in which a newspaper collects
information, prints it, and sells it to its own customers.

There were, first of all, the activities of free-lance journalists—the penny-a-liners selling what they could where they
could—and the journalists on the staff of a particular newspaper making a little extra money on the side. There are
countless examples and variations on these types. J. A. Spender
has described how, after he had left Oxford and was looking
for work, he organized his life as a free-lance journalist, writing
notes, and small and large articles for a variety of publications.
From this he earned between seven and twelve pounds a week,
specializing in out-of-the-way topics which he knew would not
be covered by the regular newspaper staffs.[1] Spender is one

---

[1] J. A. Spender, 47; *Printer's Register*, Feb. 1873.

example out of many: another in a more humdrum walk of life is 'Fire' Fowler, the free-lance reporter who lodged with a member of the London Fire Brigade and was always the first with the news of fires. It was difficult to maintain a living wage in this way; such people were 'Always living from hand to mouth and often on the verge of destitution.'[2]

It is difficult to estimate the proportion of the news that came from such sources. The balance of comment suggests that they were viewed with suspicion. They span out their contributions; and certainly there are many examples of extreme prolixity in Victorian papers. They were believed on occasion to invent news.[3] But they could not be dispensed with: Joseph Cowen, who disliked them as a crowd of beggars might be disliked, found that he lost out to his rival '. . . the "liners" must take the news to the Leader and not to us. I suppose we so often did not use their news they won't now offer it to us & I think in future you should *pay* the liners for good news whether we use it or not.'[4] It was also argued more positively, by another writer, that they fulfilled a useful function in London: the national papers did not employ their reporters on the collection of London local news (unlike provincial papers in their localities) and the penny-a-liners filled the gap.[5]

The general tone of comment, and the course of development of the press, suggest that their share of the business was declining. H. Simonis, writing in 1917, referred to penny-a-

[2] John Oldcastle (pseud. possibly of Wilfred Meynell), *Journals and Journalism, with a Guide for Literary Beginners*, 1880, 45. Oldcastle quotes a writer on his earnings over the preceding three years, 'I had about 200 paragraphs in *The World*; a still greater number, and ten articles besides, in another society paper; thirty paragraphs in *Truth*; five articles in *The Queen*, three articles in *The Spectator*; a poem in *Good Words*; a poem in *The Quiver*; thirty five articles in different monthly magazines; fifty-two columns of London correspondence in a provincial paper (at 12s 6d a column); twenty-six London letters in a colonial paper (at 10s a letter); and a few odds and ends besides . . . they represent little more than half of that which I actually wrote—the balance having missed fire. My total proceeds were £247 13s 2d.' (Ibid., 49.) By comparison, Edwin Reardon, the hero of Gissing's *New Grub Street* (1891) thought that 'Four hundred pounds, at the rate of eighty pounds a year, meant five years of literary endeavour'; on a hundred pounds he spent 'six months travelling in the south of Europe', (Penguin edn., 1966, 92–93).
[3] *Printer's Register*, Oct. 1875. They were accused of inventing a 'Waterloo Bridge Mystery', pretending to have found a body dredged out of the Thames.
[4] Cowen MSS, D 344, letter dated 10 Nov. 1886.
[5] Alfred Barker, *The Newspaper World*, 1890, ch. 16.

liners as a feature of the Fleet Street scene in his youth.[6] Since, by definition, they could only operate at the edges and in the interstices of the usual range of news, they would have served to broaden the narrow standards of reporting which were described in the last chapter. Since it was always a lottery whether their contributions would be accepted or not, they would hardly have been a useful vehicle for the propaganda of an interest group.

As well as the true free-lance journalists, it is important to remember that it was very general for journalists to work for more then one publication. T. H. S. Escott worked simultaneously as editor of the *Fortnightly Review*, as leader-writer for the *Standard*, and as a regular contributor to *The World* and to *Lloyd's Weekly Newspaper*, and was useful in handing on the information gained in one employment to the others.[7] Henry Lucy, political correspondent of the *Daily News*, wrote a London Letter which was sold to eight provincial newspapers in different parts of the country.[8] Another well-documented example in a different field was George Saunders, who in the end became *The Times* correspondent in Berlin. He came down from Balliol in 1886 and, like Spender, looked for work in journalism. After the publication of a piece on the Irish situation he was noticed by Stead, and was employed by him as the *Pall Mall Gazette*'s correspondent in Berlin. He then got work as the correspondent of the *Morning Post* and of *Galignani's Messenger* which 'will mean five guineas a week more to me ... I have ... only to write a couple of letters a week and telegraph "when required".' These appointments overlapped in time. He also tried, apparently unsuccessfully, to organize a weekly syndicated newsletter from Berlin 'say to 6 English and Scotch papers at 2-2-0 each ...[Berlin] is the last capital in Europe which I would choose for a residence. But it is *the* place in Europe at the moment where money is to be made out of journalism.'[9]

Thus, in each of these examples, an individual was placed—

[6] pp. 16–17.

[7] His activities are documented in BL Add MSS 58774–96, and are discussed by Koss, 244 ff.

[8] *Sixty Years·in the Wilderness*, 1909, 111.

[9] Saunders collection, Churchill College, Cambridge, GS 1/44–45 letters dated 17 and 26 July 1888. He began work for *The Times* in 1896, ibid., GS 1/106–115.

through his own abilities—in a position of some potential influence, which would not, thanks to the anonymity of journalism, be obvious to the reader. Escott and Lucy were both fluent and essentially lightweight writers. It would be interesting to make an analysis, which is not attempted here, of how Saunders handled his different jobs: he was passionately anti-German, as the quotation illustrates, and he was working for two papers diametrically opposed in standpoint—the *Morning Post* was the main champion of the Turks, and the *Pall Mall Gazette* of the Russians. *The Times* was the only newspaper at this time to operate an effective prohibition on its staff from writing for other papers.[10]

A similar form of duplication was that organized for the sharing of news services by particular papers (or the sale of news by one to another). In these the benefits of exclusive news, and it would be hoped better informed news, would be shared by the parties to an arrangement, who would be geographically separated, and the costs would be more widely spread. The *Standard* entered into such an arrangement with the *Glasgow Herald*. This arrangment was in force in 1876, when it was a matter of complaint that a Conservative paper should be giving help to a strong Liberal one.[11] It was still in being in 1885 when a column or half column of news from the *Standard*'s foreign correspondents, duly acknowledged, regularly appeared in the *Glasgow Herald*. Another association existed between the *Daily News* and the *New York Tribune*, who shared the costs of foreign correspondents in the Franco-Prussian War,[12] and possibly later in Bulgaria. Joint arrangements were also made *ad hoc*, in order to allow smaller papers to have the prestige of their 'own correspondent' in time of war. In March 1887 Cowen of the *Newcastle Daily Chronicle* was invited to join with the *Manchester Guardian* and others for correspondence if war broke out in the Balkans—'But you recollect the mess we got into with the *Freeman*, *Advertiser* and *Morning Post* and are

[10] For an example see Escott MSS, BL Add MS 58777, f. 149, where Gallenga was prevented from writing for the *Fortnightly Review*.

[11] The complaint came from the *Glasgow News*, Wicks to Corry 12 Aug. 1876. Disraeli MSS B/XX/A/45.

[12] J. R. Robinson, *Fifty Years in Fleet Street*, 1904, 176. Macdonald (*The Times* archives) speaks of the alliance in 1876, but refers to the *New York Herald* (letter dated 22 Sept.).

not very anxious to join another syndicate of this kind unless I am pretty clear both of the men they send out, and the papers we combine with.'[13]

It was also common for whole columns of printed matter to be used in different publications. The invention of stereotyping, in general use by the middle of the century, whereby columns were set up in type and plates cast from them, made the transfer of news from one organization to another simple. It was popular in the 1850s and 1860s when the London papers were all struggling to compete against the domination of *The Times*. The two Conservative papers the *Morning Herald* and the *Standard*, had been produced in this way in the 1860s: the former cost fourpence and the latter a penny, but much of their contents were identical 'like the Siamese twins'. In fact each had its own foreign correspondence and leading articles. In the same way the *Daily News* had supplied stereos to the *Morning Post*, both papers being Liberal, though differing widely in political standpoint. The *Daily News* gave up the practice in 1868.[14] These arrangements are perhaps evidence of the party-political objectives behind the running of most newspapers at that time, and the abandonment of both schemes may show a belief that straightforward competition in the mass market was a better way of putting a political message across.

The same system was seen in a variety of forms in the provincial papers in the 1860s and 1870s. A sophisticated and successful attempt at the running of syndicated newspapers was that of William Saunders, who started the *Western Morning News* at Plymouth in 1860 and the *Eastern Morning News* in Hull in 1864, and a news agency, the Central News, discussed later in this chapter, in 1863. In 1865 he also acquired the Newcastle *Northern Daily Express*, at that time edited by James Macdonell, who reacted violently against Saunders' ideas of management, and left to become editorial assistant on the *Daily Telegraph*, and ultimately leader writer on *The Times*. In his attacks he left an account of what were to be Saunders's methods: 'Eight columns would reach us daily, including—the leader! Yes, the leader! Our politics would come down from London daily, sir,

[13] Cowen MSS, D 367.
[14] *Printer's Register*, Aug. 1868. See also Koss, 135–6.

by train, packed in a box. Charming, isn't it?' Then again 'Under him the *Express* will have no creed, no principles, no anything but a sneaking determination to pay.'[15] Saunders therefore had the idea of the newspaper chain, getting its politics and its leading articles from London, which was extensively discussed and attacked before the Royal Commission on the Press of 1947–8. It is not clear without further research how far he managed to implement his plans. The *Northern Daily Express* folded in 1886: the *Eastern* and *Western Morning News* survived till 1929 and the present day, respectively. J. A. Spender, who was Saunders's nephew, was editor of the *Eastern Morning News* for some years in the 1880s.[16] He did not say then that leading articles were sent down from London, nor that the paper had no creed or principles. On the contrary, his main complaint was that Saunders's doctrinaire attachment to the principles of Henry George was losing readers.

The system was exploited by the political organizers of the Press in the provinces. It could be used on a small scale and without advertisement: for example in 1875 a Conservative paper, the *Stalybridge and Dukinfield Standard* contained exactly the same material as the *Oldham Standard*, including columns of advertisements of houses in the town of Oldham. It was an Oldham paper attempting to take root in the neighbouring town of Stalybridge. It is not known how much of this sort of proliferation, which is common at the present day among advertising sheets, was going on in the country as a whole. In and around Cheshire Alexander Mackie developed a chain of local papers—the *Warrington Guardian, Altrincham Guardian, Runcorn Guardian* and so on: by 1878 there was nine in all. It was an enterprise well known to contemporaries and prominently advertised in the directories.

With these chains or groups of papers went the central political institutions to cater for them. Mackie was an active Conservative, and in 1873 he came down to London to organize the distribution of Conservative news. In August 1871 the Whips bought Saunders's Central Press, or rather thought that they did, for he continued with an agency under the same name. In 1873 they obtained an injunction obliging Saunders

---

[15] Nicoll, 107, letter dated 1 May.
[16] See p. 92 above.

to operate under another name; he changed his organization's name to Central News and the two agencies continued side by side until the Central News closed down in the 1950s.[17] In reply the Liberals set up a Liberal Press Agency early in 1873, advertising it as 'distinctly representing the Liberal cause'. In June of that year it was reconstituted as the National Press Agency, promoted by the Liberal Whips.[18] It also has survived until the present day. Both agencies were clearly political in intention, though in later advertisements there was no mention of their political activities. They offered to supply, for a charge, leading articles, parliamentary and law reports, London letters and gossip, a weekly letter for ladies, and 'original tales'. Both would supply partly printed papers to be completed with local matter.[19] The Central Press published a small farthing political news-sheet, the *Sun*, which however stopped publication at the end of 1875. Both produced a daily 'newspaper for newspaper proprietors', the *Central Press* and the *National Press Journal*, printed on one side of the paper only and designed to be cut up and pasted into position in the preparation of other publications.[20]

The evidence is lacking, without further research, as to how much they were actually used, and by whom. Through leading articles, reviews of the year, and telling extracts from other papers and periodicals, which they recirculated, they would enable the most dependent of rickety newspaperlings to present a coherent account of party policy. But whether a study of such papers would reveal identical leading articles, appearing in different parts of the country in different papers under different managements, it is impossible to forecast. It might be expected, if at all, in the weekly provincial papers or in the local papers of various London districts, which might circulate among people who were normally indifferent to public affairs, but nevertheless commanded votes. It is probably significant that both agencies came into existence during the last year of Gladstone's first administration, when there was impending the

---

[17] The law report in *The Times* of 5 May 1873 gives a reliable account of the dispute.

[18] *Printer's Register*, Feb. and June 1873.

[19] Based on the advertisements in *Mitchell's Press Directory*, 1870–1900.

[20] The *Central Press* and the *Sun* are at Colindale, but the *National Press Journal* is not catalogued.

first general election after the Second Reform Act to be fought
with a full knowledge of the new electoral conditions to be met.
It is inconceivable that the major provincial newspapers could
have been controlled in this way: the Baines family of Leeds or
the Scotts and Taylors of Manchester would have reacted with
the same horror as Macdonell to the idea of leaders from
London.

It is possible that these agencies were intended to operate
also as public relations agents, handing out information on
party policy or arrangements. For example, the issues of the
Central Press which appeared at the end of January 1874 gave
lists of candidates. The London newspapers of 1874 and 1880
were able to give, immediately on the dissolution of Parliament, lists of adopted candidates.[21] Such information would
have come from party sources. These agencies may in their
early days have represented an attempt to manipulate the news
to party advantage—as when it was proposed to make the
Central Press the link for disseminating official information
between the Conservative government of 1874 and the press.[22]
But there is no record of this happening: it is hard to believe
that such a system would not have provoked furious objection,
public or private, on the Liberal side. By 1900 the National
Press Agency was offering to write descriptive parliamentary
sketches for both Liberal and Conservative journals, which
suggests that the strict party ties had been broken.

Finally, there were the news agencies proper: those concerns
which employed people, whole time or part time, in collecting
certain kinds of information which they then sold to the
newspapers, the agencies having no part in the printing and
distribution process. Between 1870 and 1900 their number was
increasing. A number of them were small and highly specialized. *Mitchell's Newspaper Press Directory* of 1872 includes the
American and English News Agency, which supplied American
news, and of 1877, Wheeler's Press Agency in Dublin supplying
Irish news. Joseph Cowen referred in 1892 to an agency
specializing in information on new company registrations in
particular localities, and to another specializing in Australian

[21] *Central Press*, 27 and 28 Jan.; *Daily Telegraph* and *Daily News* 28 Jan. 1874; *Daily Telegraph* 8 Mar. 1880.
[22] Lee, 154.

news. His correspondence illustrates the variety of sources from which different parts of his newspaper, the *Newcastle Daily Chronicle*, was being obtained. In 1887 the London Letter was being obtained from a Mr Moore, the Parliamentary service from Central News, commercial matter from a Mr Jones, and other unspecified material from Exchange Telegraph. The mixture varied from year to year, but it certainly came from a good variety of places.[23]

The major agencies and their histories are well known: there were Havas, Wolff, and Reuters in the international field, dating from the mid-century, and the Central News and the Press Association in Britain.[24] Central News was the smaller: the foreign news it distributed was more derivative and there is no evidence that it employed its own permanent staff abroad, though it sent some war correspondents. Examination of those papers which took their news from Central News and not from the Press Association shows that they were the ones with the smaller circulations and resources.

An advertising prospectus of the Central News of 1874 gives a full picture of its activity. It had among its subscribers, not merely provincial newspapers, but a variety of other institutions, including hotels and a long list of mechanics' institutes and working men's clubs, such as the Accrington Mechanics' Institute, the Bolton Conservative Club, the Dundee Working Men's Club, the Liverpool Bowling and Billiard Saloon, and a good many others. This list suggests that one of the main functions of the agency was to provide these bodies with an up-to-the-minute service of racing results. It also had an elaborate schedule of different news services that it could provide. There was the 'Morning Express' in which the leading articles of the London morning papers were summarized and late announcements in the London papers were also reproduced. This was sent to 'Large News Rooms' and to provincial papers which went to press before the London papers arrived in the town. This cost the subscriber £1 6s. a month. An abbreviated version could be bought for 13s. a month. For 16s. 8d. a month

---

[23] Cowen MSS, D 377, D 379.
[24] Graham Storey, *Reuters Century*, 1951; George Scott, *Reporter Anonymous; the Story of the Press Association*, 1968; Michael Palmer, 'The British press and international news, 1851–99: of agencies and newspapers' in Boyce *et al.*, 205–19.

a supply of two to four telegrams daily could be sent giving the price of corn and consols, important events, and the racing news: 'No large hotel or newspaper should be without it.' A more elaborate service, suitable for a provincial newspaper, and including reports of such things as by-elections, would cost £2 5s. a month; and a full service of sporting news, which included London betting, the results of races, and descriptions of the running would cost £2 11s. This schedule shows, more clearly than anything else, how cheap and easy it would be for an enterprising provincial printer or journalist to set up in business. Most of the non-local news that he needed could be obtained for a few pounds a month; and he could supply the rest from reporting of local events.[25]

The history of the Press Association is well known. It was formed by the Provincial Newspaper Society to concert and make effective their opposition to the inadequacies of the news service provided by the old telegraph companies; and the Society then agitated for the acquisition of the telegraphs by the Post Office, which took place in 1870. This joint action by members of an industry to push for the extension of state ownership in an area as politically sensitive as the transmission of information is an important landmark in Victorian administrative history. The Press Association had something of a public character. Shareholding in the Association was restricted to newspaper proprietors, and it was formally a cooperative. Policy and the previous year's working were discussed actively at annual general meetings.

The Press Association differed from the other agencies in the scale of the service it could offer. Some of the minor agencies were concerned with the searching of foreign papers in order to supply particular wants, or they specialized in particular fields—for example sport. The Central News had its own reporting staff, as the accounts of the riot of 1885, discussed in the last chapter, show, but its foreign reporting, to judge by examples published in newspapers, was sketchy. It made part of its income by selling British news abroad, for which there was said to be 'an insatiable demand'.[26] The Press Association's services were comprehensive and were greatly enlarged

[25] H. J. Wilson MSS MD 6001.
[26] John Boon, *Victorians, Edwardians, and Georgians*, 2 vols., 1927, 17.

by its agreement with Reuters in 1868. Under this the London papers, within fifteen miles of Charing Cross, continued to be supplied direct by Reuters, but outside that area the Press Association held a monopoly: subscribers could only take Reuters news through the Press Association, and in that case might not subscribe to any other such agency. It was therefore the institution which, taking advantage of the telegraphs, made possible the development of a provincial press which could compete with London in the news it was able to offer to educated readers.

The Press Association's scale of operations increased with time. Their annual revenue grew from just under £20,000 in 1871 to just over £50,000 in 1880. By 1887 gross income was £76,000 and expenditure £74,000. It is impossible, on these figures alone, to tell how much of the increase came from an increased number of subscribers and how much from a better service.[27]

It is probably a mistake to claim that the London and provincial papers were on terms of practical equality in the foreign material which they received. A comparison of the foreign news columns of different publications makes this clear. The disparity between the short summaries of the news given by Reuters and the long explanatory columns published by the London dailies explains why, in spite of the existence of the link between Reuters and the Press Association, so much continued to be copied from the London papers in the provincial press. The tariff of the Central News in 1874 included a service designed to distribute news and comment on foreign affairs culled from the early editions of the London papers, before they could physically arrive at their provincial destinations. Joseph Cowen, who did not normally set much store by the opinions of the London papers, considered that they were essential on important occasions, and made careful and anxious arrangements that he should receive them by telegraph in time for them to be printed in the *Newcastle Daily Chronicle*. The difference between Reuters reporting, and the reporting of

---

[27] Information gained from the published accounts of Annual General Meetings, held in June every year. They were usually published in *The Times*.

the 'own correspondents' of the main London dailies is discussed in a later chapter.[28]

Was the Press Association politically biased? The active promoters in the 1860s—Jaffray of the *Birmingham Daily Post*, J. E. Taylor of the *Manchester Guardian*, Frederick Clifford of the *Sheffield Daily Telegraph*, George Harper of the *Huddersfield Chronicle*, and William Saunders were all Liberals, and the provincial press, down to the Home Rule split of 1886, continued to be predominantly Liberal. Some Liberal bias could therefore be expected. They seem, however, to have made a real attempt to achieve a political balance. A proportion of the annually elected chairmen were Conservatives, and of the seven active figures of 1880 mentioned in their history, three were proprietors of papers listed in the directories as Conservatives, two as Liberal, and two as Independent-Liberal (which presumably means Whig).[29] The examples of political bias raised at the annual general meetings of 1871 and 1889 do not appear to be serious or systematic.[30] There are hints, however, discussed in a later chapter, that Liberal administrations were friendlier to them than Conservative ones. For instance, it is stated that in 1894 they were admitted to a meeting at the Reform Club at which Gladstone's successor was to be chosen, but excluded from a meeting at the Carlton.[31]

What light do these arrangements for news sharing, article sharing, and agency work all throw on the character of the Victorian paper?

First, it is important for historians who use newspapers as evidence to remember the variety of ways in which they were compiled. If evidence of opinion is being cited it is necessary first of all to establish where and how that opinion had originated. The straight party-political paper is usually easily recognized, and would have been well-known as such in its own area. It is the paper which expresses views not its editor's,

---

[28] Cowen MSS, D 335, 357: on 6 Jan. 1887, 'Rumours of war are all important just now. The Daily Chronicle had got a good correspondent at Vienna. If we could get an early copy . . . it might be useful. The man that does the Times and the Daily News might perhaps do the Chronicle also.'

[29] Scott, 71.

[30] Ibid., 64, 80.

[31] Ibid., 75–6. See chapter IX.

supplied by an agency, and in turn written by somebody employed by them because he could be relied upon to deliver on time, and inserted in haste to fill a column without being understood, which would present problems to a textual critic. Such things, it is fair to add, are unlikely to be found in the better-known papers. The same difficulty affects the news columns, though not the leading articles, of every grade of newspaper: if a particular item was reported was it the result of selection by that journal, or had it arrived as a ready-made package from somewhere else? It is also important, though it is not clear how well this was recognized at the time, that the newspapers had even less knowledge of the original sources of agency news than they had of what was supplied by their own correspondents. Reuters representatives overseas could as easily be subject to political pressure as the correspondents of individual London papers, but it would be harder for those using their material to establish just what the nature of that influence actually was. One politician and newspaper proprietor, Labouchere, recognized the dangers and wrote a series of frenzied letters to Moberly Bell of *The Times* in 1892 'Havas . . . is such a reptile that it actually has a tariff for puffery in its news' and, a few months later, 'Reuter "exchanges" with Havas and Wolff, both of which receive subsidies from their respective Govts.'[32]

The growth of the telegraph, and of the agencies which worked through them, led to the development of kinds of news which had not been possible before. They were concerned with those topics where interest attaches not to individual facts but to accumulated details or to statistical trends. A modern newspaper reports regularly on a number of such topics: the most important are sporting results, market reports, weather and temperature reports. Telegraphy made it possible to know about situations existing simultaneously in a number of centres. The work of the agencies made it commercially practicable to collect by telegraph the results of a large number of race meetings and football matches, tabulate the results, and transmit them to many small-circulation papers across the country.

In its sporting news the Press Association used the services of

----

[32] *The Times* archives, letters dated 19 Mar. and 6 July 1892. See chapter X.

an existing agency, run by C. H. Ashley and William Wright, the proprietors of the *Sporting Times*.[33] There is no doubt that, whatever else they did or did not include, every daily paper of the later nineteenth century included columns of sporting results: tables of national results, rather than local match reports, occupied a good proportion of space in the halfpenny evening papers. The scoring system of the Football League, whereby the position of team X in the table is affected by the result of a match between teams Y and Z, presupposes the ready accessibility of tabulated results to sustain supporters' interests.

Outside the sporting world comparatively little use was made of the potentialities of concerted news gathering, and its dissemination through the news agencies. It could have been a powerful tool, able to establish facts which the state's administrative machinery at that time could not do, but, as it was, organized sport provided a bridgehead by which the daily reading of news entered into the general run of households.

A third general trend, fostered inevitably by these sharing arrangements, was to narrow the gap between the most and the least sophisticated publications. Henry Lucy does not in retrospect seem a political commentator of much distinction, but he was in constant contact with the Liberal leaders in the 1880s, and he could be read in the *Sheffield Independent*, the *South Wales Daily News*, the *Bolton Guardian*, and others in his syndicate.[34] The *Central Press* circulated extracts from the *Saturday Review* which the editors of small Conservative country papers might well not have seen or appreciated but which, if reprinted, would stiffen the quality of their comment.[35] Through the processes of copying, reviewing, re-hashing of what had been read elsewhere, and the circulation of the same agency telegrams, the news became a mix of similar ingredients in papers of very different quality and information. And, what seemed even more important, the news could be received simultaneously by all. These points were made (with particular reference to the *Northern Echo*) by John Bright, with an eloquence which brought cheers from his audience:

[33] Scott, 38.
[34] Henry Lucy, *Sixty Years*, 111.
[35] e.g. issue of 2 Feb. 1874.

This $\frac{1}{2}d$ Daily Paper comes for a whole week into the house of every pitman in that county who chooses to take it in. It comes there, bringing all the news, concisely but accurately reported, from all parts of the world, and he has it in his pitman's house just as early and as certain as the news reaches the grand ducal mansion of Raby Castle.[36]

[36] Quoted in the *Northern Echo*'s advertisement in *Mitchell's Newspaper Press Directory* for 1882, and doubtless referring to the Bulgarian atrocities.

VII

Social Contacts

'AT this dinner it was agreed that you were *the* Amphitryon as well as the Demosthenes and Tacitus of the day, and a special banquet at which you entertained the Cabinet etc. at the Garrick Club was cited in proof.'[1] This is not a quotation from a fashionable novel, nor from a play, but comes from a letter from Edmund Yates to T. H. S. Escott, describing a dinner he had had with Lord Randolph Churchill and some others. Is it a faithful picture of the political world or a fantasy? If it is true, how general was this informal intimacy between journalists and those who made policy and knew secrets of high news value? The question of status, in most professions, is fundamentally a matter of social rewards—who can the successful doctor or lawyer, or his family, mix with on terms of social equality, what public positions can he hold? With the journalist social status may well be an essential condition of his trade.

One may begin with an examination of the membership of the London clubs. These were at the height of their prestige and prosperity in the second half of the nineteenth century: they were not yet undermined by the habit of living in remote commuter suburbs, and were at the centre of a world where it was accepted that women stayed at home. Some of the largest and most influential, the Carlton, the Junior Carlton, and the Reform, were political in origin and membership; others were social or honorific. But in all of them it was assumed that easy social relations, that is conditions of practical equality, were essential to the purpose of the club, and members were elected with that in mind. There is no suggestion, in club histories, that there was a shortage of candidates, and the question arises whether there was any prejudice against journalists, or against people with known connections with the press. It has been suggested that at the beginning of the century there was a 'feeling that in some sense journalists were really spies against

[1] BL Add. MS 58796, 21 Oct. 1884.

whom "Society" should be secured'.[2] An isolated case from
1879 can be cited where this feeling was explicitly mentioned.
On 24 February Thomas Gibson Bowles, proprietor of *Vanity
Fair*, wrote to Montague Guest, asking for his support for his
election to the St James's Club: he was 'fearful that among the
Conclave of electors there may be some who will perhaps be
inclined to pluck anyone anyhow connected with the Press'. A
few days later, after the worst had happened, he wrote again,

Those who elect for Clubs appear yet to have to learn that the only
way to get any control over the Press, the only way to make sure of its
good and to avoid its ill-offices, is precisely to make members of those
who have the direction of Newspapers. No Editor could avoid
standing up on occasion for his own club, or for its members, and
occasions do arise when that may be of a certain consequence.[3]

But, as *Vanity Fair* was a magazine of social gossip, it is easy
to understand such misgivings. However the general principle,
that it is prudent to make friends of influential journalists, was
widely acted upon.

There is substantial evidence to suggest that journalists were
elected into membership on equal terms with other candidates
in a wide range of clubs. At the Athenaeum they included G.
W. Dasent of *The Times* (1854) and Delane (1862), R. H.
Hutton, joint-editor and part-proprietor of the *Spectator* (1871),
John Morley (1874), and G. E. Buckle, editor of *The Times*, in
1887[4]. Morley in 1874 had only recently arrived in London,
and would have been known as the editor of the *Fortnightly
Review* and of some volumes of the English Men of Letters
series, while Buckle had been editor of *The Times* for three
years only—there can be no suggestion that they had a hard
and long struggle to get in. The Reform, not surprisingly, had a
cluster of Liberal journalists among its members. William
Howard Russell was a member of the Carlton. Escott, as
has been shown, was a member of the Garrick, as was
F. C. Burnand, editor of *Punch*.[5] It may be objected that these
people were more prosperous and successful than the general
run of the profession, but to this the reply is that the clubs

---

[2] Alan Lee, 106.
[3] Montague Guest papers, BL Add. MS 57938, ff. 67, 69.
[4] Humphrey Ward, *History of the Athenaeum, 1824–1925*, 1926, 117 ff.
[5] T. H. S. Escott, *Club Makers and Club Members*, 1914.

were institutions of the successful whatever their occupations.

A more significant index of journalists' social contacts is found in the history of clubs which had a specifically press membership. By 1890 there was a London Press Club, with an annual income of £3,000, and provincial clubs at Birmingham, Sheffield, Manchester, and Liverpool, with a membership of journalists, and local professional people and 'literary men'.[6] In London, night work in Fleet Street meant that St James's was a relatively inconvenient area. Two clubs, the Whitefriars, which met in Anderton's Hotel, Belle Sauvage, Ludgate Hill, and the Arundel, in Arundel Street off the Strand, had a membership of actors and journalists. The Whitefriars remained a professional club, but the Arundel, in the middle of the century, began to attract high society, looking for entertaining company or perhaps for employment: whereupon there was a secession to a new club, the Savage; 'The bored professionals of studio, stage and press did not then appreciate the opportunities of social advancement that might be opened up by the invading amateurs, and hoped to establish "free and easy" for intellectual toilers only at the Savage Club.'[7] This was in 1855. However the Savage, too, in its turn became fashionable, and in 1881 elected the Prince of Wales to life membership.[8] It would be hard to maintain that journalists suffered from social rejection.

Some, probably a small minority, moved easily among actors, literary people, military experts, travellers, and the aristocracy in the general social vortex. From them they could enlarge and bring up to date their picture of the world. The range of acquaintance enjoyed by Escott, and most probably by others, is impressive. His papers, unusual in being apparently a full unweeded collection of his correspondence during the period of his editorship of the *Fortnightly Review* (1882–5), are filled with very small sheets of very thick, heavily die-stamped paper, bringing invitations to dinner and to Saturday-to-Mondays in country houses. They come from the world of Du Maurier's Mrs Leo Hunter and Mrs Lyon Chacer, and some are from the same people as were pursuing Thomas

[6] Alfred Barker, *The Newspaper World*, 1890, 30.
[7] Escott, 268.
[8] Arthur Griffiths, *Clubs and Clubmen*, 1907, 145.

Hardy when he came to London at about this time.[9] Journalism was socially acceptable: when the seventh Duke of Marlborough succeeded in 1883 to estates which were encumbered with debt, he thought to improve his fortune by starting a newspaper in imitation of the Parisian *Petit Journal* 'to be called *Today* and built up and conducted Yankee style of headings, leaderettes. Bright, short, concise. A flavour of the sporting times *no party politics*—a leaning only to the government of the day.'[10] Escott was invited to be the editor-in-chief. The Duke undoubtedly moved in 'fast' circles; he had been at the centre of the Aylesford divorce case about ten years ago. He would also have had some knowledge of newspaper affairs through his sister-in-law Jennie Jerome. But it is worth noticing that his letter showed no sense of loss of dignity in the scheme, which came to nothing.

G. A. Sala is another, perhaps better, example of the fashionable journalist. Unlike Escott, editor of a weighty review, or a successful war correspondent with the tale of his adventures to tell, Sala had no particular coups or experiences to his name. He was a sociable character and the inexhaustible writer of leading articles in the *Daily Telegraph*, 'the paper with the largest circulation in the world'. He appears again and again in anecdotes and memoirs. In W. P. Frith's celebrated picture of the year, 'Private View of the Royal Academy, 1881', he appears, well placed towards the front of the picture, among such celebrities as Gladstone, Huxley, Browning, and Irving, as the representative of his profession.

Another indicator of the acceptance of the journalist as an important figure in the national hall of fame is the number who were included in the *Dictionary of National Biography*, planned from 1882. Apart from the people mentioned in this chapter, one finds such names as Thomas Ballantyne, once an anti-Corn Law journalist and later founder of the *Statesman*, Dudley Costello, 'foreign correspondent of London journals', James Hannay, editor for four years of the *Edinburgh Evening Courant*, Frederick Hardman, Paris correspondent of *The Times* in 1870-1, and away sick for a good part of that time, and

[9] Robert Gittings, *The Older Hardy*, 1978, ch 6. An example of the literary hostess, entertaining journalists and novelists, is Mrs Mary Jeune.

[10] BL Add MS 58793, letter dated 2 Aug. 1884.

Robert H. Patterson, editor of the *Globe* in 1865 and of the *Glasgow News* in 1872. None of these could be said to be outstanding.

The way in which contacts developed, and could be used, is illustrated in detail in Escott's papers. They can be compared with the equally full record, on the party-political side, of Edward Hamilton, Gladstone's secretary from 1872 to 1885. Hamilton met Escott on 17 March 1883, at a private dinner-party at which Lord Hartington was another guest, and discussed politics with him. Escott then invited Hamilton back ten days later. About a month later Hamilton went to the Cosmopolitan Club, to which he had just been elected, where he met 'a very pleasant gathering', including John Morley, then the editor of the *Pall Mall Gazette*, Frank Harrison Hill, editor of the *Daily News*, Reginald Welby, then assistant financial secretary to the Treasury, and Lord Cowper, who had resigned as Irish Viceroy the year before. On 3 May he was dining at the Devonshire Club and met Escott again, in a party which included Herbert Bismarck. Four days later an 'agreeable little dinner' at the St James's Club included Sir George Trevelyan, and Escott again. On 20 May he dined with Escott and found it 'interesting and agreeable'; other guests included Chamberlain, Irving the actor, Dr Quain the physician, and William Mudford, the editor of the *Standard*.[11] In the Escott papers we find that the young A. J. Balfour met him at Lady Charles Beresford's on 30 April 1885, and arranged to dine with him a little later at the Garrick Club. The papers also record many other visits to the Beresfords. Herbert Gladstone invited him to breakfast with his father 'any Thursday after Easter' in 1883.[12]

Escott has been recognized, both at the time and since, as an associate of Chamberlain, and as the intermediary by whom Chamberlain, a disgruntled member of the 1880 Cabinet, leaked secrets to the *Standard*, to the embarrassment of Gladstone.[13] But this social diary shows how he (and other journalists) could operate independently. These agreeable little dinners gave

---

[11] D. W. R. Bahlman, *The Diary of Sir Edward Hamilton*, 2 vols., Oxford, 1972, II, 410 (17 Mar.), 420 (12 Apr.), 430 (3 May), 433 (7 May), 438 (20 May).
[12] BL Add. MS 58775; 58780.
[13] See Koss, 239–40, 243–4.

opportunities to find out more than the other diners would be willing to divulge. How it could happen is illustrated by an entry in Edmund Yates's diary of 20 April 1885:[14]

E [Escott] . . . said to H [Hartington] 'The Cabinet has sold Herat to the Russians.'

H said 'What rubbish!'

E returned 'I know it.'

Hartington said 'There is not a word of truth in it. You cannot know anything of the sort.'

E said 'I can know it just as well as you can know I wrote that book.'[15]

The Duchess of Manchester said 'That is well said, for you are quite right, Mr. Escott.'

This conversation can be plausibly related to Cabinet meetings held on 14 and 15 April, the week before, at which proposals for a settlement in Afghanistan, involving the withdrawal of forces on both sides from disputed territory, had been discussed.[16] It was the major news story of the moment. Nevertheless, the fact that Yates had thought it worth while to write out the conversation as it had been reported to him verbatim suggests that he thought it something exceptional— though whether he was impressed by the boldness of Escott's tactics, or by the extent of his inside knowledge, it is impossible to tell.

It is difficult to assess the extent of these social networks, which could so easily be put to good news-gathering use. Something probably must be allowed for exaggeration, for the satisfaction which the working journalist may have felt in putting effective pressure on the great nobleman. Some of the examples quoted above, however, are not reported anecdotes, and are based on firm evidence. Probably the number of journalists living in these privileged circles was always low, though slightly later Alfred Milner, J. A. Spender, Henry Lucy, and R. D. Blumenfeld 'went out in Society'. Another

---

[14] BL Add. MS 59871.

[15] 'That book' is *Society in London*, 1885, published under the pseudonym of 'A Foreign Resident'. It reached its ninth edition in 1886.

[16] A. B. Cooke and John Vincent, *The Governing Passion*, Brighton and New York, 1974, 217–20, gives the background to this anecdote.

social gathering, which must also have contributed to the inside information enjoyed by the London press, was described by Wemyss Reid.[17] In the Reform Club there was in about 1873 a 'little coterie', the members of which lunched at the same hour every day at a particular table in the large coffee room. They were known as the 'press-gang'. The group included, as well as Reid, William Black, a sub-editor of the *Daily News*, George Augustus Sala of the *Daily Telegraph*, Sir John Robinson, manager of the *Daily News*, E. D. J. Wilson of *The Times*, J. C. Parkinson (unknown), and James Payn, editor successively of *Chambers's Journal* and after 1883 of the *Cornhill*. It is noticeable that while all were connected with newspaper or periodical publications they did not have the same precise party allegiances. Reid added that thirty years later the group was still in being though the membership had changed. It is one of the institutions which gives meaning to the phrase 'the Fourth Estate'. On the other hand there were important and influential journalists who hardly entered this world. Mudford, by common repute, disliked the pressures which were liable to be exerted at such dinners (although he appeared in Hamilton's list of dinner engagements). W. T. Stead, a more famous figure than any of these, appears not at all. He had, as will be shown, an impressive range of political contacts, but he is not mentioned in these accounts of club life—presumably he was considered to be socially unacceptable in some way.

It is also worth asking how far this infiltration of high society and of the corridors of power was something new. In an illuminating article,[18] Aspinall showed how at the beginning of the nineteenth century journalists, though they might be publicly condemned as hirelings and the scum of the earth, were in fact mingling socially with the political aristocracy. On the whole, with the notable exception of a dinner at which members of Addington's administration welcomed Cobbett back from the United States in 1802, these social contacts were with leading figures in journalism, such as James Perry, the proprietor of the *Morning Chronicle*, Thomas Barnes, the editor of *The Times*, or J. Wilson Croker, a well-known political

---

[17] *Memoirs*, 252–3.
[18] 'Social status of journalists at the beginning of the nineteenth century', *Review of English Studies*, XXI, 1945, 216.

journalist. These people were linked to party politics in a way in which Sala and Burnand, or the meetings of the 'press-gang' were not. A popular early nineteenth-century journalist such as Pierce Egan does not figure in the article. In the mid-century Delane's dining-out, and the deductions he made from slips of the tongue at dinner parties, became legendary; but Delane was hardly a typical newspaperman. It would seem that on balance these contacts had increased substantially in their scale and range and general repute: no one would have described the members of the 'press-gang' as hirelings. The same change of tone may be suggested by an anecdote given by Greville. In 1847 Le Marchant, a minor Whig politician, was visiting Thomas Barnes, the editor of *The Times*, who was already entertaining somebody else.[19] Le Marchant recognized the step and voice of the other visitor, and guessed correctly that it was Lord Durham. He asked what he had come for, and Barnes replied that 'he came on behalf of King Leopold, (who had been much annoyed by some article in the 'Times', to entreat they would put one in of a contrary and *healing* description. As Le M[archant] said, here was the proudest man in England come to solicit the Editor of a newspaper for a Crowned Head!' Thirty or forty years later would it have been reported in that way by a political figure with an equally extensive knowledge of how the political world really worked—for example by Edward Hamilton?

These questions of the ease of social contact are relevant to a small number of London journalists. In the big provincial centres similar problems could hardly have arisen about provincial affairs. By the 1870s and 1880s the proprietors of the leading provincial papers were themselves usually established leaders in their community; this applies to people like the Whitty family of Liverpool, the Leaders of Sheffield, the Baines of Leeds, the Taylors and Garnetts of Manchester, and many others. Nor can one imagine, off-hand, the kind of secrets which would lurk beneath the surface of a provincial town comparable to the government's climb-down over Herat.

Among the fashionable world two or three groups can be

[19] *The Greville Memoirs, 1814–1860*, ed. Lytton Strachey and Roger Fulford, 8 vols., 1938, V, 438–9.

identified who are noticeable for their cultivation of the press. The first of these, perhaps surprisingly, were members of the Royal Family.[20] The Crown Princess of Prussia, in the liberal tradition of the Prince Consort, read British newspapers, particularly the *Pall Mall Gazette* of the 1880s. She gave press interviews.[21] She wrote to her mother, in February 1886 (apropos the formation of the third Gladstone administration), 'Mr. J. Morley I know, and he always struck me as a clever, learned, cultivated man, decidedly quiet and serious and without vanity'.[22] Such a description suggests personal acquaintance over a period of time.

The Prince of Wales and the Duke of Edinburgh mixed with the fashionable journalists. Sala later claimed that he had been dining with the Earl of Fife when the news of the assassination of the Tsar Alexander II arrived:[23] this would have been on 13 March 1881. He was there again in March 1884 when F. C. Burnand, editor of *Punch*, wrote to Escott 'Did you meet Geo. A. S. at Fife's? I was to have been there but got a fair excuse as H. R. H. and Co. bore me'. A year later, in March 1885, there was another invitation to Escott from Fife, to dinner to meet the Prince of Wales.[24] Possibly these were dinners to meet members of the press, and a regular fixture. On another occasion Yates sent the outline of an attack on the Prince of Wales that Escott was to write for *The World*, nasty in tone and intention:

I have positive proof that Tum-Tum did all he could to spoil my dinner, & has been very insolent about it since. So I mean to keep him on the gridiron.

We might start with the German invasion ... And I should go pretty straightly for H. R. H. in it. His fat squat figure, his guttural accent ... In this you can hit all the Bischoffsheim Oppenheim set, and make us generally disagreeable.[25]

On another occasion Escott received a letter from the Prince's secretary assuring him that the Prince did not believe

---

[20] The formal machinery of royal publicity will be discussed later: see next chapter.

[21] Escott MSS, BL Add. MS 58793 from H. M. Stanley, 21 Nov. 1884.

[22] Frederick Ponsonby, ed., *Letters of the Empress Frederick*, 1928, 196.

[23] *Strand Magazine*, July 1892, p. 67.

[24] BL Add. MS, 58776, 58,778.

[25] Escott MSS, BL Add. MS 58796 (n.d.).

him responsible for the recent offensive attacks on him in *The World*.[26]

The most striking example of the contact between Royalty and the press, and the benefits which it could bring, is in the letter-book of the manager of *The Times*, J. C. Macdonald, in July 1883. The Tsar Alexander III was to be crowned in Moscow, and the British press was having difficulty in getting passes for the ceremony. *The Times* having, as he put it, 'never lent countenance to that virulent abuse of Russian Autocracy which British Constitutionalism thinks correct', had obtained passes. But Macdonald's letter went on 'My only wonder is that the Duke of Edinburgh should have attempted to get Sala with his Bardolph face into such a gathering. Even the gold and jewelry could not outshine him, and in his own peculiar style no one has written more bitterly about the Romanoffs.' The Duke of Edinburgh was brother-in-law to the Tsar and it seems that he half succeeded: Sala got into the cathedral, but into a poor seat.[27]

These episodes raise a number of questions. Why did the Prince and the Duke become involved with dinner parties and the like with such people? One suspects that these occasions were, among other things, an expression of the Prince's boredom in a situation where he had no responsibilities. But they also suggest that he was making an attempt to counteract the hostility aroused by the Queen's retirement from public life: his consciousness of this problem was clearly expressed.[28] The need to disarm criticism and to keep the press friendly was, however, greatest, and Yates's letter gives a good example of the kind of threat he was under. Another example of the Prince of Wales's handling of publicity and forestalling of criticism, was the choice, on the visits to Egypt in 1869, and India in 1875, of William Howard Russell (who also acted as *The Times*'s correspondent in 1875) as his 'historian'. In that post he could not utter criticisms (and would not probably wish to): his prestige was such that his would be the definitive account.[29]

[26] Ibid., 58784. The letter was sent by Francis Knollys, and dated 5 Mar. 1884.

[27] *The Times* archives; Macdonald's letter-book, to Charles Lowe, 12 July 1883. Sala gave an account of his presence at the ceremony in an 'Illustrated Interview' in the *Strand Magazine* of 1892.

[28] Sir Philip Magnus, *King Edward the Seventh*, Penguin edn., 1967, 135.

[29] Ibid., 136, 174.

The Prince also took with him an 'artist to the journey', Sidney Hall of the *Graphic*.

The Queen herself was outside such associations. Even if she had been of a very different temperament and reputation, she would, as a woman, have been cut off from such social contacts. Yet even here there are occasional hints—and systematic research might reveal more—that she was co-operating in the machinery of publicity. It does not seem entirely natural that she should decide to publish *Leaves from the Journal of our Life in the Highlands* in 1868. Had she wished to write a memoir of the Prince Consort for private circulation it would have been understandable: such things are often done. But an edition, selling 20,000 copies,[30] of a diary of innocently cheerful holidays in the Highlands, looks more like an apologia, and it seems hardly likely that she would independently have thought of such a thing. In her old age, when she had returned to public life, two contributions may be cited, neither of which would have been possible without her own personal co-operation. The first, 'Queen Victoria's dolls' by Frances H. Low, a fascinating description of her childhood, had been read by the Queen in proof and included her own footnotes. The second, 'The Queen's Hindustani Diary' by Moulvie Rafiüddin Ahmad, included in facsimile two pages with a translation, which she had copied 'expressly for this article'. They appeared in the *Strand Magazine* for July and December 1892, in a widely circulating middle-class magazine: a great coup for George Newnes and a good place in which to insert royal publicity. There was another example on the death of Prince Henry of Battenberg in 1896, when the Home Office apparently refused to allow *Lloyd's Weekly Newspaper* to publish a letter from the Queen on the subject in facsimile, but were overruled through her Private Secretary.[31]

Another set of relationships, probably more directly related to the ambition of the participants, and less purely social, existed between some military and naval figures and their favourite journalistic contacts. Here again the final impression is that the initiative was not taken by the journalists. These officers in the services shared with royalty the disability that

---

[30] Elizabeth Longford, *Victoria R. I.*, 1964, 375.
[31] Simonis, 73.

they could not speak directly to the public in speeches or books; but, while royalty may have had no motive more specific than a desire for favourable publicity, the military, and even more the naval, experts had very definite causes to put forward

The late Victorian navy, in spite of its immense size, or perhaps because of it, saw very little action. Sporadic engagements with Chinese pirates could occur, far away and without warning, and press coverage would have been impossible: a number of these episodes which were the subject of Blue Books were never reported in *The Times*.[32] The bombardment of Alexandria in the summer of 1882 was a rare and exceptional event. On the other hand there were pressures for reform within the Navy very different in character from those in the Army. The bitter arguments in the Army were concerned with organization at the top: in the Navy the reformers were concerned with technical questions, of ironclad ships, gunnery, and torpedoes—fundamentally with persuading the political parties of the need for progressively higher levels of naval expenditure. The important contacts of Lord Charles Beresford and 'Jacky' Fisher therefore tended to be among the editors and naval correspondents of influential London newspapers, J. A. Spender, Arnold White, James Thursfield, and most of all, W. T. Stead, whose 'Truth about the Navy' opened up the general subject of Britain's relative naval strength to the public.[33] Of the two, Beresford was known as someone with a taste for personal publicity, and he had many journalistic contacts, Escott among them. He took care to be reported: at the bombardment of Alexandria in 1882 he was in command of HMS *Condor* and had on board *The Times* correspondent, Moberly Bell, 'in obedience to the orders of the Admiral' (Seymour). A few years later at the Jubilee Naval Review he entertained the Press again, on the Admiralty yacht *Enchantress*. *The Times* correspondent read and reported a private message

---

[32] For example correspondence on an engagement with piratical junks published 13 May 1869 was not reported. Nor was correspondence with Japan, published 31 May 1870. Blue books on brigandage in Spain and Greece, published at intervals in 1870, attracted full reports, suggesting that remoteness was an important consideration in deciding what to report (Parliamentary papers 1868–9 LXIV).

[33] Fisher's contacts can be traced in A. Marder's *Fear God and Dread Nought*, 1952–9, especially II (after 1900). For his earlier contacts with Stead see R. Mackay, *Fisher of Kilverstone*, Oxford, 1973.

which Beresford had transmitted from the Royal yacht, and it was published next day. The Prince of Wales wrote to him 'If you choose to have correspondents on board the Admiralty yacht you must take the chance of their indiscretion.'[34] When the battleship *Victoria* collided with the *Camperdown* during Mediterranean exercises in 1893, with great loss of life and controversy about the reason, Beresford 'happened to be passing the Central News office when the newsboys were shouting out the news, and he at once walked in and talked freely with the editor'.[35] One wonders whether he really 'happened' to be walking near Ludgate Circus at that convenient time.

In the Army, it is clear in retrospect that conditions were almost perfect for the cementing of links with the press. Britain was not engaged in a major European war between the Crimea and 1914: the Colonial campaigns, certainly down to the time of the Boer War, would have been described in the parlance of a later generation as 'side shows'. The commander and his staff found themselves on these campaigns far from civilization in the company of a limited number of war correspondents. The group would disperse at the end of one campaign, to re-form, somewhere else, a few years later. They were not operating under the constraint of pressure from allied governments, or of actual danger to the security of the British homeland—all of which might have provoked some restriction of contact with the press. On the contrary, an ambitious general, in a far-off country, needed to be fully and favourably reported at home: an ambitious correspondent needed to have a story to tell.

Garnet Wolseley stands out from other people by the scale and assiduity of his cultivation of the press. In 1870 the purchase of commissions had been abolished: and the criteria for promotion in the future remained a subject of dispute. At the head of the Army, the Duke of Cambridge remained as Commander-in-Chief till his death in 1895. He was a resister of reform, a cousin of the Queen, and, as the holder of an office which could not hope to operate as adequately as the general staffs of continental countries, he provided a natural target for attack. This was the general situation in which Wolseley and

[34] Geoffrey Bennett, *Charlie B.*, 1968, 75, 142.
[35] Simonis, 170.

his followers, the Ring, were operating. Wolseley's personal ambition for promotion to the highest rank and a peerage was fused with his role as an army reformer, and in a situation where the system of promotion was not clearly established, he aimed at power through the systematic pushing of his favourites—the Ring—and through the cultivation of public fame through the press, both when he was in London and on his campaigns. The object, never realized, of his ambitions was the post of Commander-in-Chief in India. (It was gained, with the support of the Duke of Cambridge, and after many years' service in India, by Roberts in 1885.[36]) Much of Wolseley's lobbying was directed towards this end. In 1879 he wanted to be sent to Afghanistan and enlisted the support of the *Standard* and of Francis Lawley, leader-writer of the *Daily Telegraph*. Lawley told him that he had 'spoken to Levi [sic] Lawson about my case who refused to have anything to do with it, as he said he was still sore about the Billy Russell business[37] and besides the Duke had told him to write down all desire of my going to India.' Nevertheless he retained Lawley's support who urged him to be 'satisfied to stick to the Liberals and the people'.[38]

Sala, who could not by any stretch of the imagination be regarded as a military expert, but who enjoyed a wide following, might also be useful. When Wolseley returned from the defeat of Cetewayo in the Transvaal in 1879 he brought with him some ceremonial sticks, one of which he presented to Sala, who displayed it in his house and proudly showed it to an interviewer from the *Strand Magazine* many years later.[39] Alfred Austin, leader-writer on the *Standard* and no military expert either, also was given 'a shield and several assegais belonging to Cetewayo' which he hung in his house.[40] Sala knew Wolseley well enough to ask favours in return: in 1883, unable to see what was going on in Moscow Cathedral, he

[36] Wolseley's ambitions and career are discussed by Adrian Preston 'Wolseley: the Khartoum relief expedition and the defence of India, 1885–1900' in *Journal of Imperial and Commonwealth History*, May 1978.

[37] See below.

[38] Wolseley MSS, Hove Public Library, to his wife 30 July 1880, and from Lawley, 27 Feb. 1881.

[39] July 1892.

[40] *Autobiography*, 1911, II, 198.

slipped him a note saying 'I must keep telegraphing for dear life. If later on you can let me have half a dozen words of renseignements I should be everlastingly grateful. At present I can only gather that H. I. M. shed tears and that the patriarch Isidore broke down rather in pronouncing the allocution.'[41]

On his campaigns Wolseley had much greater opportunities for influence. He went out of his way to accommodate the war correspondents. When he was travelling out to South Africa in June 1879, he wrote home that he and some others were playing 'a rubber of shilling whist every evening until ten o'clock with Billy Russell', formerly of *The Times* and now working for the *Daily Telegraph*. From then until the end of October, Russell was constantly at Wolseley's table eating his food and sharing his conversation, and presumably reporting the campaign in favourable terms. The association ended when some officers played a practical joke on him and he left in disgust.[42] When Wolseley set off up the Nile in October 1884, on the expedition to Khartoum, 'At the last moment I gave passage to the artist of the Graphic whom I knew in S. Africa and here again in 1882.'[43] Another correspondent, Charles Williams of the Central News, was regarded by Aaron Watson, another journalist, more as Wolseley's associate than as a reporter. He describes him in one of the rooms in a London club loudly reading out a letter from Wolseley to impress the other people there.[44]

Other members of the Ring also wrote for newspapers. Henry Brackenbury is listed as a writer on military subjects for *The Times*; he also offered Escott an article, 'Midsummer in the Soudan', in 1885.[45] Frederick Maurice, who had been described as Wolseley's particular amanuensis and apologist, was the *Daily News* special correspondent in Ashanti.[46] He also wrote for *The Times*. In July 1882, shortly before the campaign of Tel-el-Kebir, and while serving on Wolseley's staff, Maurice offered his services as a correspondent for *The Times* in the

[41] Wolseley MSS, from Sala, 7 June 1883.
[42] Ibid., to his wife, 13 June, 11 and 18 Aug. 29 Sept., and 31 Oct. 1879, when Russell finally left.
[43] Ibid., to his wife, 1 Oct. 1884.
[44] *A Newspaper Man's Memories*, n.d., 79 ff.
[45] Escott MSS, BL Add. MS 58775, 22 June 1885.
[46] Justin McCarthy and Sir John Robinson, *The Daily News Jubilee*, 1896, 115.

forthcoming expedition. They preferred to send a man of their own, but offered him a retainer of £100 to instruct their correspondent in military matters.[47] This was at exactly the same time as Beresford was being offered the post of correspondent of the *New York Herald*, and was being refused permission by Wolseley.[48] Members of his Ring apparently could write for the newspapers, but no other serving officers.

Wolseley's handling of newspaper correspondents was blatant and systematic. It was apparently based on friendship, yet his diary from time to time records his real feelings. Russell was a 'scoundrel and low snob'. His diary of the Khartoum expedition abounds with attacks on the correspondents. They were 'Fellows, the best of whom are weak about their H's, who are mostly cowards and who do not in the least care how they lie as long as they can furnish their employees [sic] daily with a certain amount of sensational rumors reported by them to be facts. Everyone ... knows in his heart what an unscrupulous lying set of vagabonds they are, but no one dare say so.'[49]

These various social contacts were of advantage both to the journalists and to the public figures. For the former it was a liberation from their dependence on particular politicians, and gave them an opportunity to choose whom to ask. For the lobbyists it gave excellent opportunities. It is important, however, to remember how limited was the range of public interests that would find expression in such a milieu. Those who were 'weak about their Hs', teetotallers, clergy of all kinds, and anyone who could not afford to live expensively, were unlikely to be met by Escott or Frank Harrison Hill. Equally importantly, the names that crop up in these circles do not include people with an active concern with trade and industry. This would apply not merely to provincial manufacturers, living many hours from London and unable to leave their businesses—whom one would not expect to find—but also to prominent figures in the City. Escott received letters and invitations from members of the Rothschild family, but they

[47] *The Times* archives, J. Macdonald to Maurice, 20 July 1882.
[48] Bennett, 91.
[49] Adrian Preston, ed., *In Relief of Gordon: Lord Wolseley's Campaign Journal* ... *1884–1885*, 1967, 113-4.

were effectively assimilated into high society. But shipowners, or chairmen of railway companies, do not appear in these letters—since both railways and shipping were the subject of controversial legislation during the period of his editorship of the *Fortnightly Review*, this seems significant.

Another group of people of great political importance who did not mix in such circles were the Irish nationalist MPs, with the exception of Justin McCarthy, a leader-writer for the *Daily News*. Parnell seems to have kept aloof from contacts with the press—even when they might have been useful[50]—and one letter from him, written by a secretary, appears in the Escott papers.[51] The general attitude of the Irish members, which was to emphasize their separateness from the existing parties, would have made such contacts difficult in any case.

The effects of this restricted range of contacts are difficult to guess, and would vary from one individual to another. It is not suggested that the economic concerns of the nation were ignored by the newspapers, either in the news columns or in editorial comments.[52] It is rather that these journalists were constantly exposed to one view of the political world with little to set against it. For a major difference between then and now is that a far smaller segment of political and economic society was then organized to handle the press. Today it is hard to imagine an interest which has not got an organization of some kind, among whose officers there is not an articulate spokesman who can reply to criticism, advocate policies, initiate favourable publicity, or appear on a television interview. People who gather and present the news know that these people are the relevant and essential contacts, irrespective of whether they have social dealings with them or not. Such institutions, had they existed—and existed in the capital—would have counterbalanced these social limitations.

---

[50] See p. 165 below.

[51] BL Add. MS 58789 f. 68: the overwhelming majority of letters were written in senders' own hands.

[52] Compare final section of chapter XI below.

VIII

Access to Information

ACCESS to information depends partly on social and informal contacts, and also, more mundanely, on the routine conventions governing the occasions when reporters are, or are not, admitted. It is obviously unprofitable to try and list all the sorts of occasion with which Victorian newspapermen might be involved. In many the important question would be, not whether they could gain access, but whether the events taking place would be able to attract a report. Journalists' memoirs emphasize that they expected to be treated properly: they must eat with the guests and be given their share of the wine and cigars. The seating plan of one such occasion shows press reporting in action. At the dinner to mark the opening of the new Manchester Town Hall on 13 September 1877, the Mayor and principal dignitaries sat at a top table. Opposite to them all the closest seats were occupied by reporters of the London and Manchester papers, the Press Association and Central News, and, in central positions, artists of the *Illustrated London News* and the *Graphic*.[1] Political dinners were an easy road to publicity for a politician. Other occasions, such as sporting fixtures, gained greatly in importance through regular press reporting and its consequence, the organization of gambling. Entertainment, lectures, annual general meetings of societies, all gained from publicity. There are, however, a number of areas in which the access normally given to the press raises questions of interest.

The first concerns royal occasions. With great public events, weddings, the opening of buildings, Jubilee processions, and the like, there could be no question of denial of access: our interest centres on the extent to which the chief participants would allow themselves to be inconvenienced or would let the press into privileged positions, (into Moscow Cathedral for example). The suspicion already raised that Queen Victoria and her family were actively seeking favourable publicity (in

---

[1] Manchester Central Library, M/68/4/1/242.

spite of all that has been said about the Queen's retirement from public life) is strengthened by a close examination of particular occasions. What happened on them is well recorded, because they were great events in the lives of individual journalists assigned to them, who made the most of what happened in their memoirs.

The wedding of the Prince of Wales in March 1863 was a great state occasion, though its commercial possibilities were not greatly exploited. Sala reported it for the *Daily Telegraph*. He described how 'the authorities showed the greatest consideration and courtesy to the representatives of the press'; about a dozen reporters being in the organ loft in St. George's Chapel, and a carriageful forming part of the Lord Mayor's procession.[2] On occasions abroad, the anxiety of other governments to conciliate the press was apparent. When the Prince and Princess of Wales made a visit to Denmark and Sweden in 1864, Lord Spencer, who had accompanied them, wrote to his friend, Sir Thomas Biddulph, complaining that he had little to say because 'the Newspapers with their Special Correspondents seem to know everything'; at Stockholm they had 'dined one night at the Palace when invited to the Ball'. He thought that 'this adulation of Reporters shows great want of dignity on the part of the Court officials.'[3]

At the wedding of the Queen's second son, the Duke of Edinburgh, to the daughter of the Tsar Alexander II, in Moscow in January 1874, elaborate arrangements seem to have been made for the press. To judge by their reports, they saw the ceremonies themselves, both Anglican and Orthodox, the wedding dinner, and a ball the same evening. Later they were shown a display of wedding presents and were conducted over the couple's new home.[4] By comparison, a recent account of the Coronation of 1953 stated that 'about half-a-dozen writing journalists were admitted to the annexe to Westminster Abbey'—not much change in a hundred years.[5]

On minor occasions the same impression is given, of active

---

[2] *The Life and Adventures of George Augustus Sala, written by Himself,* 1896, 381–6.

[3] Peter Gordon, ed., *The Red Earl: the Papers of the Fifth Earl Spencer 1835–1910,* I, *1835–1885,* 1981, 54.

[4] L. M. Brown, 'Treatment of the news in mid-Victorian newspapers,' *Transactions of the Royal Historical Society,* 5th series, XXVII 35–6.

[5] *The Times,* 20 April 1981.

encouragement of the press. Wemyss Reid has described how, when the Prince of Wales went shooting in Upper Teesdale, he travelled in the special train which was taking the Prince there (and was surprised that local people did not recognize the Prince).[6] On the same occasion, Archbishop Thomson of York invited the press to come and inspect the rooms which he had refurbished for the royal visit. When in October 1881 Reid was asking that one of his reporters from the *Leeds Mercury* should travel on Gladstone's special train, he made use of the precedent set by the Royal Family. A minor journalist, Hartley Aspden, has left a full description of a quite minor royal occasion. In 1881 the Prince visited Welbeck Abbey after the death of the eccentric fifth Duke of Portland: 'The following day the Prince of Wales, with his host, drove through Sherwood Forest. Following close behind were representatives of the press ... At Thoresby ... the party alighted for lunch, the pressmen being entertained in a room adjoining the royal dining room. It was a repast worthy of the spacious days of Robin Hood.'[7]

As well as these special occasions, it seems that regular arrangements existed for informing the press throughout this period. A small, and usually uninteresting, report—for example that Queen Victoria had been for a drive—appeared regularly in the London papers, and there is reference to an official in 1874, the 'court newsman', who provided it: he may have existed long before that time.[8] Kennedy Jones gives an account of reporters travelling to Balmoral in 1854, one having with him a card which said he was from the 'Fashionable Dept. of the *Morning Post*'.[9] We may round off this picture of royal press initiatives with a sour complaint in Hyndman's *Justice* in July 1885, that Queen Victoria had sent a note to the press asking them to contradict the story that her favourite dog had died.[10]

The kind of 'news' generated by these arrangements may seem often to be trivial; and even the great public occasions do

---

[6] Reid, 110–11; Herbert Gladstone MSS, BL Add. MS 46041, Reid to Herbert Gladstone, 1 Oct. 1881.

[7] Hartley Aspden, *Fifty Years a Journalist*, n.d., 18.

[8] Disraeli MSS, box 88, ref B/XX/A/45 (the Conservative *Glasgow News* complained that the *Scotsman* was receiving this bulletin exclusively).

[9] Kennedy Jones, 154.

[10] *Justice*, 4 July 1885.

not attract much interest in the historian. Nevertheless, they mattered very greatly indeed to the newspapers, as one would expect; at the wedding of the Prince of Wales the circulation of *The Times* reached 108,000 compared with an average for the 1860s of about 60–65,000 copies.[11] The regular news of the Queen's movements seems to have been always printed in the London dailies, but given little emphasis. More information perhaps was offered than was really asked for.[12] The question arises how far this provision of royal information was something new: Cobbett commented in 1829 that George IV lived 'in almost total seclusion from the eyes of the people, who were, however, daily informed, by the newspapers, of his dinner parties at his cottage; of his rides about Windsor-Park'.[13] It would seem likely that this kind of reporting went back to 1820, or perhaps to 1812, if no further, to a time when the Regent had been having difficulty with virulent attacks in the newspapers on his character.[14]

In two further large areas of public interest the access of the press was firmly established: in the courts of law and in Parliament.

In the courts, privilege was extended to correct reports of a trial—and had been so since the 1790s. The great political trials in 1820 of Henry Hunt and associates for conspiracy after Peterloo, and of Thistlewood and the Cato Street conspirators, were published without interference, by radical printers in what appear to be verbatim editions. Police court reporting had been the staple ingredient of the mass circulation Sunday papers since their first establishment.

The stages by which proceedings of Parliament became open to the press form a well-known chapter in the history of British liberal institutions. In the eighteenth century the admission of the press to debates had been forbidden under the Standing Orders of the House of Commons. These orders had been

[11] *History of The Times*, II, 358.

[12] Wm. Cobbett, *History of the Regency and Reign of King George the Fourth* 2 vols., 1834, paragraph 492.

[13] A. Aspinall, *Politics and the Press c1780–1850*, 1949, 90, 215.

[14] On 27 Sept. 1883 Hamilton wrote to Gladstone that Queen Victoria 'is suffering from jealousy pure and simple. She takes offence at the big type in which the newspapers head "Mr. Gladstone's movements" and the small type *below* of the Court Circular.' BL Add. MS 44189, f. 249.

regularly ignored, but could be enforced when the Commons were debating controversial questions. From 1802, by a decision of Speaker Abbot, reporters had been regularly admitted to the Gallery. It was decided in the case of *Stockdale v. Hansard* (1839) that the privilege of the House of Commons extended to fair reports published by order of the House. In the case of *Wason v. Walter* (1868), at the beginning of the period under discussion in this book, the privilege was extended to a fair report of parliamentary proceedings published in a newspaper. (The case had been brought against John Walter, the proprietor of *The Times*.)

The right of the public to know what had passed in Parliament had been a strongly-held radical principle since the time of Wilkes, as is illustrated by the effort that Cobbett put into his publication of the *Parliamentary Debates*. The judgement in *Wason v. Walter* came down firmly on the side of the public's right to information:

To us it seems clear that the principles on which the publication of reports of the proceedings of courts of justice have been held to be privileged apply to the reports of parliamentary proceedings. ... If the rule has never been applied to the reports of parliamentary proceedings till now, we must assume that it is only because the occasion has never before arisen. ... Whatever disadvantages attach to a system of unwritten law ... it has at least this advantage, that its elasticity enables those who administer it to adapt it to the varying conditions of society ... Our law of libel has, in many respects, only gradually developed itself to anything like a satisfactory and settled form. The full liberty of public writers to comment on the conduct and motives of public men has only in very recent times been recognised ... yet who can doubt that the public are gainers by the change, and that ... the nation profits by public opinion being thus freely brought to bear on the discharge of public duties? Again, recognition of the right to publish the proceedings of courts of justice has been of modern growth.[15]

The judgement in *Wason v. Walter* was grounded in a doctrine of public interest: it was in the interest of both parliament and the public to have a correct record. In a later passage Chief Justice Cockburn spoke approvingly of the way

[15] Reprinted in D. L. Keir and F. H. Lawson, *Cases in Constitutional Law*, 1948 edn., 112–13.

in which 'Individual members correct their speeches for publication in Hansard or the public journals.'[16] This is a defence of the taking of correct minutes (and a defence which sounds odd to modern ears), rather than a recognition of the news value of debates; but it is nevertheless an expression of the approval of those in authority. The reporting of debates was invested with a constitutional dignity, which spilled over on to the Gallery reporters themselves. There are many accounts of their corporate pride. Wemyss Reid described how, when he first joined the Press Gallery on behalf of the *Leeds Mercury*, he offended his colleagues by having a conversation with one of the members for Leeds, Edward Baines.[17] Henry Lucy and Aaron Watson both wrote in similar terms, and described the increasing respect in which they were held; by the end of the century it was possible to organize a dinner where 'members of Parliament and the chief officials sat down as the guests of those who usually reported or commented on their speeches. It was an amazing innovation.'[18] There was no problem of access: the practical difficulties were concerned with the limited number of seats in the Gallery available for an expanding number of newspapers and their representatives. Tickets were given out by the Sergeant-at-Arms who was slow to adjust his allocation in relation to the rise of new papers and the decay of others.[19]

In fact, there was an element of shadow-boxing in all this; it will be shown in a later chapter that the space and emphasis given to Parliamentary debates declined from about 1870 to the end of the century, and that these coveted seats were often empty in practice. Even in 1869 Lucy, slipping in without authority, found that the seats at the back were all empty.[20] At that time the London papers, apparently, were anxious to keep provincial papers out. In practice, newspapers liked to possess a ticket to the Gallery so that they could attend debates of particular interest to them without further trouble.[21]

Access to individual members of Parliament, to question them or hold conversation with them, was a different matter.

[16] Ibid., 114.
[17] Op. cit., 123–4.
[18] Watson, 219.
[19] See below.
[20] H. W. Lucy, *Peeps at Parliament*, 2nd edn. 1904, 1–4.
[21] C. Seymour-Ure, *The Press, Politics and the Public*, 1968, 245–6.

As will be shown in a later chapter, interest was shifting in the newspapers away from the content of parliamentary business to the events of the day at Westminster and their interpretation—a shift accelerated by the dramas associated with the Irish Question. Access to this kind of inside story could come from a variety of sources: in the first place from the sort of informal contacts described in the last chapter. Or it could come through an institution such as the so-called 'vestry' which met in the National Liberal Club in the 'smallest smoking room, which is now monopolised by an amiable clique consisting entirely of journalists and politicians. Nothing happens, of note, that we don't hear of and discuss there . . .'[22] It seems also to have been fairly normal for the Member of Parliament for a provincial town to use his good offices in introductions, or the provision of information, on behalf of the local newspaper. H. J. Wilson, MP for Holmfirth, offered in 1890 to provide the *Sheffield Independent* with information 'or any other service'. This was an offer to a paper he did not much approve of, and which he was in the process of criticizing vigorously.[23] Where an MP was closely linked to a newspaper, as, for example, Joseph Cowen, the proprietor of the *Newcastle Daily Chronicle*, or Joseph Chamberlain, who relied in his constituency heavily on the support of the *Birmingham Daily Post*, the amount of advice and support might well be very much greater. Certainly Cowen's correspondence with the London office of his paper shows detailed advice on political matters. Such contacts, however, would be restricted, and probably restricted to contacts within the same political party. They increased the chances that any one editor would become a mouthpiece of a particular group, unable to sift and evaluate information for himself. Access to the Lobby was therefore something different in kind from the beginning. Entry into the Members' Lobby by journalists was first restricted in 1871, though the restriction soon lapsed. In May 1880, Mitchell Henry, an Irish member, 'thought the manner in which Hon. Members were jostled about in the Lobby was also a ground of complaint. There was a constant influx of strangers, besides gentlemen reporting for the newspapers, thus preventing anything like confidential communica-

[22] Charles Payne to R. E. Leader, 23 June 1886. Leader MSS.
[23] H. J. Wilson to Leader, 17 June 1890, Leader MSS.

tion between Members.'[24] Entry was restricted again in 1884, after a bomb exploded in Westminster Hall, and in 1885 the modern Lobby system was initiated, entry being restricted to journalists on a Lobby List prepared by the Sergeant-at-Arms. The system developed the same weaknesses as had developed in the Gallery, since the allocation of tickets lagged behind the realities of the situation: it was hard for a new, up-and-coming paper to gain admission.[25]

How valuable the system was as a source of news is perhaps open to question. The Members' Lobby before 1900 was not surrounded by the secrecy which has been normal in modern times (this in itself suggests that it was not seen by contemporaries as a vital piece of political machinery). There are several descriptions of the life of lobby correspondents which leave a general impression that they found their work interesting but not important: (this contrasts with the memoirs of the foreign correspondents who tended to write as if the fate of empires depended on their efforts). These reminiscences tend to emphasize the lobby correspondent's menial status relative to the Member of Parliament. John Boon, a journalist working as lobby correspondent for the Central News in the later 1880s, and later for Exchange Telegraph, described how reporters and leader-writers attended, 'the latter being admitted once or twice a week for an hour or two'. They were 'supposed to stand in rows and have paragraphs of very little value posted into them as if they were pillar boxes'. He added, which sounds like a true memory, that Members of Parliament were supposed to speak to the journalists, who should not themselves initiate conversation. He mentioned Labouchere as a politician who made active use of the system.[26] Aaron Watson worked as a lobby correspondent, both in the early 1880s and for a time after 1902 as London correspondent of the *Yorkshire Daily Observer*. He said that he hated work in the Lobby, and implied that particular skills or particular status were needed to make effective use of the privilege.[27] One of his friends was 'expert at "swapping stories", and when members of Parliament are

[24] *Hansard*, 27 May 1880, vol. 252, col. 534.
[25] Jeremy Tunstall, *The Westminster Lobby Correspondents*, 1970, ch. 1.
[26] John Boon, *Victorians, Edwardians, and Georgians*, 2 vols., 1927, 71.
[27] Ch. 22. The *Yorkshire Daily Observer* had formerly been known as the *Bradford Observer*.

strolling about the Lobby they expect to be told something funny, in return for any scrap of political information they may impart. Pitt, . . . who represented *The Times* in those days, could swap stories as well as anyone; . . . [but] in his case members did not require to be bribed by an anecdote; they ran to him with what they knew.' Watson also noticed the use to which the system could be put by particular members: 'It is not always . . . that the Lobbyist has to seek information. It often comes to him unasked . . . Lord Charles [Beresford] was, indeed, a notorious offender, with an insatiable appetite for publicity.'[28] It seems that, in general, the Lobby was a handy meeting place for those people whose contacts already existed, and was not much more than that. Joseph Cowen's papers give a practical example of the system in operation. In March 1888 he needed copies of the Local Government Bill in advance of publication: MPs would get it on the previous day. He wrote to his London correspondent 'If you look about the lobby on Monday night you may be able to obtain a copy from the bill office. Any friendly MP will get you one.'[29] There is no mention in any of the reminiscences of the systematic dissemination of information by press conferences and briefings which are described as part of the work of the modern Lobby correspondent.[30]

In interpreting these reminiscences some account must be taken of the distortion liable to occur in any account which is anxious to show the growth in power of an institution, or the growth in status of the writer.

The information available in government departments, and the arrangements for informing the press, were increasingly important. A number of different questions which are ultimately related to general constitutional changes are involved. In the early nineteenth century there had been no formal barrier on civil servants writing in the press; for example Sir Charles Trevelyan had written in 1843 to the *Morning Chronicle* on tariff policy, at that time a controversial question, though he was criticized for doing so.[31] The sharp division between

[28] p. 206.
[29] Cowen MSS D 386.
[30] Tunstall, 43 ff.
[31] Peel papers, BL Add. MS 40449 ff 84–5, Sir James Graham to Peel 14 Oct. 1843.

politicians and non-political permanent civil servants had not yet come into being, and the favouring of papers friendly to the government was generally accepted.

The full implementation of the Northcote–Trevelyan reforms after 1870—and more particularly their implementation by the zealots Robert Lowe and R. R. Lingen—initiated a change. By a Treasury Minute of 3 June 1873, civil servants were forbidden to communicate official information to the press on pain of dismissal. The prohibition was reaffirmed in 1875 under the Conservative government,[32] the occasion being the formation of a company to publish the *Civilian and Civil Service Review*, which was to be directed towards criticism of the current civil service reforms.[33] The imposition of the ban was circulated to departments, who disclaimed responsibility for the projected publication. The reply from Thomas Erskine May, then Clerk to the House of Commons, gives an interesting picture of the Press Gallery from the other side:

There are few offices to which early information is so often entrusted, as those of the House of Commons. The lobbies and galleries are crowded by representatives of the press, in search of intelligence; yet no instance has occurred in which any officer of the House has been accused, or even suspected, of communicating information irregularly to the newspapers.[34]

The prohibition on unauthorized disclosure was respected, certainly in form, as is shown by a number of letters about articles in the *Fortnightly Review*, where signed articles were usual. Sir Charles Fremantle of the Mint, asked to write about the coinage, replied, 'We permanent officials must not enter into the arena of controversy when the matter in question is one which concerns our own Department'. He went on to recommend Robert Giffen, 'Though he is in the Board of Trade, he might with propriety sign an article about coinage, which has nothing to do with his Office.' Another civil servant, F. G. Walford, fearing that the author might be recognized as

[32] PRO T1 7439/B.
[33] T1 7385 B. Lingen's memorandum on the subject deserves quotation. Editorship of a newspaper 'necessarily (or almost necessarily) implies the unauthorized use of official information which is the worst fault a Civil Soldier can commit. It is on the same footing as cowardice in a soldier. It is unprofessional.' Ibid. A publication called the *Civil Servant Review* eventually came into existence.
[34] T 9470/73.

an official, wished to sign with his initials only. Even Wolseley, with all his links with the press, could write, concerning an article on the Channel Tunnel; 'I am very sorry I could not in my present position in the War Office allow my name to appear in any way as the author of, or sponsor for, any article.'[35] The only exceptions seem to be the occasional employment of serving officers as war correspondents.[36]

This prohibition would not prevent informal contacts, for example at dinner parties or in the London Clubs, indeed it might well encourage them. It also made it clear that sooner or later some kind of formal and official arrangements would become necessary, such as are now provided by information officers, or the press officers of government departments. These became general after the First World War.[37] But even if the role of government was far smaller in the 1870s and 1880s than it has been in the present century, there were occasions on which there would be need for clarification of technical legislation, or reassurance of the public, or the provision of up-to-date news on a crisis abroad. This was the period in which there were complaints about 'grandmotherly legislation', 'constructionism', and socialism, all of them stemming from increased state intervention.

News from government departments, published with the approval of the Permanent Head, was very different from unauthorized leaks. The way to circulate such news was the subject of intermittent discussion within departments. As with tickets to the Press Gallery, or the Lobby List, problems were created by the constantly increasing numbers of newspapers, all tending to demand equality of treatment. Departments, in a time of rigid economy, were unwilling to add increasing numbers of provincial papers to their circulation lists. In practice the department chiefly concerned was the Foreign Office, which was the one which most often had news to impart. In 1863 it had been ordered that copies of Blue Books should be distributed to the eleven main London morning papers.[38] In 1870 the *Manchester Guardian*, the *Sheffield Indepen-*

---

[35] Escott papers, BL Add. MS 58779, from Sir Charles Fremantle, 9 May 1884; 58795, from F. G. Walford 26 July 1883; 58796 from Garnet Wolseley 12 Jan. 1883.
[36] See last chapter.
[37] M. Ogilvy-Webb, *The Government Explains*, 1965, ch. 2.
[38] FO 83/814.

dent, and the *Glasgow Herald* were included. In 1872 the Central News was added, and there followed a stream of similar demands, always agreed to, and including an increasing number from the trade press, in search of consular reports.[39] It is noticeable that, as with Press Gallery tickets, newspapers were not willing to entrust the collection of news to the agencies: they wanted direct access as well. In 1876-7, with the growing Eastern crisis, there were interdepartmental attempts to harmonize their practice. The Colonial Office wished to assimilate its rules to those of the Foreign Office: the two departments should consult about each application. The Admiralty had a simple system, almost designed to enrage the press: 'information of a brief nature' was sent to the morning and evening papers, and to the *Scotsman* and the *Glasgow Herald* outside London; 'information of a lengthy nature' was sent to *The Times*, with a request that slips be given to other papers on a list.[40] There is in all these arrangements a sense of unreality: no feeling that, if the information being circulated was important, then it was desirable to assist its publication, nor the sense—shown by Wolseley or Beresford—that for better or worse the newspaper press existed and needed to be provided with material. In January 1887 it was proposed to end free distribution of Blue Books because it was thought to be invidious. Lord Salisbury's comment was hard-headed: 'I doubt. I think you are bringing a hornet's nest around your ears and may save £50 annually.'[41]

What was the content of the material being distributed? Some of it consisted of official announcements of the kind now put out by the Central Office of Information: for example in 1875 applicants for passports were to be told to mark the

---

[39] Ibid. It is interesting to notice that the applicants assumed that papers friendly to the government would be given preferential treatment. In July 1876 W. E. Forster wrote that 'It is true that the Observer is a liberal newspaper but it is the only morning paper in Bradford and would be generally admitted to be one of the oldest and most respectable journals in the North of England.' On 18 August 1886 S. Rowe Bennett of the *Western Morning News* wrote to Lord Iddesleigh, then Foreign Secretary 'I ask for this favour not only as a Unionist ... but as a Devonshire man who has always sought to do justice to your Lordship's high character.' (FO 83/1328). In practice, a note by Hertslet (librarian of the Foreign Office) stated, political opinions were not taken into account (ibid.).

[40] FO 83/814.

[41] FO 83/1328.

envelopes accordingly; and the public was told that Swedish banks would no longer cash Bank of England notes because of the number of forgeries in circulation. Sometimes the Foreign Office was circulating news which the agencies were unlikely to get because it came from remote places: thus on 5 March 1874 they reported that the Chinese New Year had passed off quietly in Peking: in May 1881 there were details of an eclipse of the sun reported from Cairo. But there were also examples of news that might have an important bearing on major events: on 18 July 1876 the Foreign Office circulated a telegram from Sir Henry Elliot stating that a 'Turkish functionary of high position' was being sent to investigate and punish the Bulgarian atrocities.[42] This was in the early stages of the Atrocities agitation, when the government was attempting to play down the accounts of massacres. Another example (there are very few of them recorded), was a statement on the Afghan boundary question of 17 August 1886. This notice, also dealing with an important question, was reported to have been 'sent by the private secretaries' rather than by the officials.[43] The general impression given by these departmental records is that the information being given was regular and non-controversial. The establishment of the *Board of Trade Journal* in 1886 provided a vehicle for information on foreign tariff regulations and consular news, which had been formerly sent out by the Foreign Office.

Journalists agree in their memoirs that they got a chilly reception in government offices. Boon of the Central News described them being looked upon as 'pariahs'.[44] Kennedy Jones, talking of the 1890s, used similar language, but believed that when Joseph Chamberlain became Colonial Secretary in 1895 he initiated change: 'There was no other Government Department at that time where a journalist was so certain of obtaining accurate and authentic information from a responsible official ... and the newspaper man left Downing Street with the pleasant but unusual feeling that his visit had been welcome.' Then, at the time of Fashoda, there was the need to explain the crisis to the public; thanks to Chamberlain, 'For the

[42] FO 83/814.
[43] FO 83/1328.
[44] p. 24.

first time Fleet Street was invited to the Foreign Office, the Daily Mail representative was received by the Permanent Under-Secretary within half an hour of the Cabinet breaking up and given definite information.'[45] Boon also singled out Chamberlain for his handling of the press: 'no man responded more quickly to a sensible question and his general attitude was appreciated'.[46]

Yet examination of the news columns of the dailies shows that information was being given long before the end of the century. It was bound to be so. The preferred way of making Government announcements was by a statement in Parliament, but there were many times and occasions when Parliament was not sitting. In time of war announcements came from the War Office or the Admiralty. The latest news of a crisis came from the Foreign Office. Not to give news would have given an incentive to the newspapers to look for it elsewhere. A close reading of the Afghan frontier dispute of 1885 illustrates briefing of the newspapers in action. In the spring of 1885 the Russians were advancing into Afghanistan: Britain was anxious to demonstrate that their advance would be resisted. The British also had a party of their own, led by Sir Peter Lumsden, in Afghanistan on a frontier demarcation expedition, or ostensibly so. During the period March to May British newspapers carried a series of articles, all originally stemming from the Press Association, though different papers presented the facts with variations. On 26 and 27 March long articles appeared on war preparations in Britain (a proclamation calling up reserves was issued on 27th). These articles gave detailed news, specifying which ships were being prepared in which ports, stating that 'the Press Association understands'- that only 20,000 out of a possible 70,000 reservists were being called up, giving lists of names, and much more.[47] In April there were moves towards an agreement: in early May, when the Russian reply was still awaited, there appeared more accounts of naval preparations: 'the Press Association understands that orders have been sent to all the admirals'. On

[45] Kennedy Jones, 94–6.
[46] Boon, 53.
[47] This is based on the files of the *Glasgow Herald*, *Manchester Guardian*, *Yorkshire Post*, *Times*, *Standard*, *Daily News*, and *Daily Telegraph*. All, except *The Times* quoted the material.

5 May, when Russian agreement to accept arbitration had been received, the Admiralty 'understands that contracts already entered into will be carried out'.[48] As well as this, the unfolding crisis was punctuated with announcements cast in the form 'The Press Association says "We are in a position to state . . . " '. So, far from being treated as pariahs, the reporters of the Press Association were being used as the expounders of government policy. None of the reports received contradictions or disclaimers. The Vienna correspondent of the *Standard* reported on 28 March, 'Even the Queen's Message calling out the Reserves, and the newspaper reports of war preparations in India and England, are taken as a mere demonstration with the object of preventing war.'

It is likely that the Press Association was chosen, in preference to individual papers, as it automatically ensured a wide distribution of the news, particularly in provincial papers where the Liberals believed they had their main support. It is hard to tell how often it was briefed in this way. There is a parallel at the end of the century, when it is stated that the Under-Secretary at the Foreign Office saw Reuters agent regularly, and thus official news was widely disseminated.[49]

The distribution of war news and the handling of war correspondents presented their own problems. The uncensored printing in England of military information from the Crimea, from the correspondents and from soldiers' letters home, was not forgotten twenty years later. In 1876–8 discussion revived, with the fear that war with Russia was about to break out again, and the problem became a real one after 1879 on the North-West Frontier and in Egypt. The problem was surveyed by the Intelligence Department of the Quarter-Master-General's Department, who included two of Wolseley's close associates, Maurice and Hozier. Another of the group, Lt. James Ross, produced a set of proposals for the future. The presence of newspaper correspondents

is an evil of modern warfare which cannot be avoided. The public will not consent to be shut out from all news of the theatre of war; nor is it wise that they should be. But, on the other hand, the presence of

---

[48] *Glasgow Herald*, 1 and 5 May.

[49] Zara Steiner, *The Foreign Office and Foreign Policy*, Cambridge, 1969, 36; and chapter X below.

the agents of newspapers, whose sole desire is to gain as much authentic information as they can, and who publish it to the whole world without considering the consequences, is most detrimental to the well-being of the army . . . Now it is a fact, that in England, there is the most energetic press in the world, and that none can pay so highly for an able staff of correspondents, or for correct news which comes without delay.

Therefore, he argued, they should be made to realize that it was in their own interests to co-operate in accepting some control. They should be licensed, wear uniform, and be subject to military law. Serving officers would have the best understanding of military questions, but would be unable to criticize the actions of superior officers: retired officers would be an acceptable compromise. Their movements should be restricted and they should be kept away from the front line. The Turks (presumably in the recent war) had kept them all together so that 'they can be got at at once and, if necessary, marched off in a body. The Turks were too undecided to carry this out.' In return for these substantial limitations on freedom they should receive help and explanation from the military, who should forward their messages, after censorship, through field telegraphs. He added the interesting item of information that the censor in the recent Turkish war had been a trusted person who 'was a secret agent of Reuter'.[50]

These proposals bear a close resemblance to the technique of handling the war correspondents that Wolseley was to develop.[51] It also explains why *The Times* was offered assistance from serving officers on more than one occasion. Wolseley skilfully kept the correspondents happy while strictly limiting their scope. Roberts, in the Afghan campaign of 1879, was less successful in dealing with them. In 1879 questions were asked in the Commons whether it was in accordance with Army regulations that staff officers should hold appointments as newspaper correspondents, and a few days later, whether the secretary of state had seen that the *Standard*'s reporter had been sent away by Roberts and one of his own aides-de-camp appointed in his place. Roberts was in the wrong and had been written to. Whether the questioner, G. Anderson, a member

[50] WO 33/32.
[51] See previous chapter.

for Glasgow, was spokesman for an outraged press, or a participant in the feud between Roberts and Wolseley, is not known.[52]

The general issues raised by these episodes are familiar from the time of the Crimea and have changed little down to the present day. War correspondence presents particular problems, in the danger of giving information to the enemy, and in the greatly enhanced public demand for news. It also presents difficulties to the reporter in grasping what is happening and assessing it. Whereas access to the Parliamentary debates, or Town Council meetings, meant that the reporter produced a record of a body of transactions, the nature and extent of which was agreed by all parties, there was no such agreed body of war information, other than the official communiqués.

A final question concerns the conventions governing interviews. It is claimed that W. T. Stead invented the interview: and that this was one of the novelties which combined to make up the 'new journalism'.

The idea is older than that, and involves a number of separate notions: the journalist has personal contact with the great man, discusses some matter of public moment, and makes the fact of the interiew plain in his published report. A private hint or briefing or leak could hardly be described as an interview. Even so, the 'interview' can cover very different kinds of transaction: situations where the famous person makes his opinion known or where he receives the journalist at home and talks in general terms of his life and interests, or again occasions when a prominent person is beset by the 'media' and has to speak to get away. In none of these, except perhaps the 'at home' kind, was W. T. Stead the innovator. The *Oxford Dictionary* gives the earliest reference to the word interview, in the press sense, as taking place in 1867. Some very striking interviews were carried out then. Beatty-Kingston of the *Daily Telegraph* wrote that he interviewed both Pope Pius IX and Victor Emmanuel at that time.[53] As will be described in another chapter, Bismarck gave an interview to Alfred Austin

---

[52] *Hansard*, vol. 244, cols 1318 and 1436, 20 and 21 Mar. 1879.
[53] W. Beatty-Kingston, *Men, Cities, and Events*, [1895], 102, 186 (he also interviewed Leo XIII in 1888).

in 1870.[54] During the Franco-Prussian War William Howard Russell claims to have interviewed the Crown Prince of Prussia on a number of occasions.[55]

George Augustus Sala records a number of interviews at a slightly earlier date. In 1865 he was sent to cover the progress of Napoleon III through Algeria for the *Daily Telegraph*. He claimed to have had an interview with the Emperor: 'and at seven o'clock one morning I had an audience with Napoleon III himself. His Majesty was fresh from the bath . . . he was most condescending, and gave me permission to follow the Imperial Cortège.' In the Austrian campaign in Italy in 1866 Sala claimed that he had had a long interview with Garibaldi: 'He received me in the friendliest manner . . . there was no need for a letter of introduction because the *Daily Telegraph* was so friendly.'[56] The last sentence of this quotation provides the clue to the success of both Sala and Beatty-Kingston: the *Daily Telegraph* was the fastest growing paper in England, and these public figures would have found it useful to have favourable publicity there: if Garibaldi was interviewed, then Victor Emmanuel and the Pope needed a vehicle for their points of view. It is also worth quoting a letter from G. C. Glyn to Gladstone in 1867: 'There is a curious and I believe *genuine* account of an interview with Bismarck in today's Telegraph. I saw the original letter from which it is extracted.'[57] This letter is a good pointer to the status of the newspaper interview at this time: Glyn could not quite believe it, which suggests that it was a recent innovation.

It is doubtful if the public statement of opinion would have been regarded as acceptable by politicians at an earlier time. Brougham and Palmerston were active in the management of the press. Peel commented on proofs of articles in the *Quarterly Review* on occasion, offered to him by Croker, who was a party propagandist rather than a journalist.[58] But the disparity in status between the Minister of the Crown and the journalist was wide enough to make questioning probably an impertinence: an example of a working journalist dealing with a

---

[54] See chaptr X.
[55] W. H. Russell, *My Diary During the Last Great War*, 1874, 211.
[56] *Life and Adventures*, 416, 442.
[57] Gladstone MSS, BL Add. MS 44347, f. 43 dated 28 Sept. 1867.
[58] Norman Gash, *Sir Robert Peel*, 1972, 97, 283.

politician in the early nineteenth century was given to Thomas Frost by William Bean, founder of the Liverpool *Albion*:

Canning ... was so extremely fastidious about the rounding of his periods, notwithstanding his eloquence, that he was always anxious to have the reporter's notes submitted to him for revision. His alterations were so numerous as to be equally annoying to the reporter and the printer; but Bean had a greater annoyance ... in the insulting behaviour of the wife of Colonel Bolton, whose guest Canning was whenever he visited Liverpool. Mrs Bolton had a great contempt for 'newspaper men', and evinced it ... by invariably desiring the servant to bring a chair from the kitchen for his use while he was engaged with the statesman. Bean is said to have felt the insult very deeply ... but it does not appear that he ever resented it, and the story illustrates very forcibly the distance which separates the present time [1886] from fifty years ago ...[59]

Where Stead, fifty years later, was an innovator was in the systematic use he made of the interview. The *Pall Mall Gazette* employed as 'Chief Interviewer' a woman named Hulda Friederichs, to conduct the interviews, which were lengthy and general. Interviews of this kind seem to have become popular at the lighter end of the periodical press. Yates of *The World* ran a series called 'Celebrities at Home' in the late 1880s. Soon after its inception in 1891 George Newnes's *Strand Magazine* began a series of illustrated interviews, lighter in character but similar to those introduced by Stead in the *Pall Mall Gazette*. These interviews described the home and life-style of such people as Sala himself, Edward Lloyd, the Baroness Burdett-Coutts, and famous artists such as Sir Frederick Leighton.

It is clear that interviewing of this kind represented no great advance in the power of the press. The great personages who were interviewed were those people who were willing to have some personal publicity. Where interviews with political figures at times of crisis were concerned, such as that of Alfred Austin with Bismarck, it seems likely that they also took place when the great personage was anxious to make his views known. The journalist was being received in audience. In most cases the journalist represented a newspaper which was working in some friendly relationship with the political person or faction involved. Stead's most spectacular interview, with the

[59] Frost, 121–2.

Tsar in 1888, was of this kind.[60] When Beatty-Kingston interviewed Victor Emmanuel in October 1867, he was told by the King's minister, Rattazzi, that 'He will talk frankly enough because he knows that the journal you represent is a sincere well-wisher to Italy and an earnest advocate of Italian unity.'[61] Antonio Gallenga, the Italian patriot who spent the second half of his life working for *The Times*, took a jaundiced view of interviews as he looked back from the mid-1880s: he had not been

sufficiently *flunkyish* for an 'Interviewer'. It was but seldom I came into contact with Monarchy or statesmen and it was generally at their own request; it was seldom that they had anything of importance to say to me, and still more seldom that I durst report what they had said without their leave, or that I felt that they said what they thought when they allowed or bade me report their sayings.[62]

Things may have been changing in the thirty years after 1870. Stead, though he did not invent the interview, developed efficient techniques for extracting information from less willing informants. He would work up a subject, write something on it, and then ask his target for comment. He introduced himself to Gladstone in this way. But his stalking of an unwilling subject is best illustrated in his dealing with Carnarvon. Carnarvon had first attracted his attention by being the anti-Turkish member of Disraeli's cabinet. On 2 July 1884 Stead returned to him, asking for comments on pamphlets on the House of Lords' attitude to the Redistribution question. Carnarvon was too busy to write anything for the *Pall Mall Gazette*. On 31 July Stead returned to the attack with more pamphlets. Carnarvon was still too busy. On 18 September Stead wrote again, 'My Lord, At last I hope we have a subject on which we shall not disagree' and went on to ask a question about coaling stations for the navy. This time Carnarvon gave way and wrote on 20th 'the question is too serious for me not to reply'. By return of post Stead asked for 'a sight of your Colonial Defence Committee's Recommendations? I have hitherto not been allowed to see it,' and asked on 24th for a signed article. Carnarvon replied that he could 'not wholly refuse but as chairman of a

---

[60] J. Saxon Mills, *Sir Edward Cook*, 101.
[61] Beatty-Kingston, 102.
[62] Antonio Gallenga, *Episodes of my Second Life*, 2 vols., 1884, II, 364.

highly confidential committee' could not enter into detail.[63] Throughout the correspondence Carnarvon protests that he is being asked for confidential information and proceeds to give it. This aggressive skill in wearing down a suitable informant was something new in journalism, but at that time it was probably also unique.

If we return to the reporting of the Afghan frontier dispute in the spring of 1885 we find a number of occasions where interviews were being used in a routine way. Thus on 5 March the *Daily Telegraph* printed a Press Association interview with a 'high military official' who asserted that the Russians would respond to a show of firmness, and explained to readers how a large army could be moved quickly to the North-West Provinces. On 16 March M. Lessar, a Russian diplomat, gave an interview, explaining his country's peaceful intentions, and the *Pall Mall Gazette* commented

When M. Lessar arrived in this country he declined to be interviewed. Experience however has enlightened him as to the uses of the interview. On Monday all the papers but *The Times* published a report of his interview with the Press Association, and today *The Times* publishes a translation of his interview with the London correspondent of the *Cologne Gazette*.[64]

Then on 13 May a Mr Stephen, on Sir Peter Lumsden's staff, returned to Britain: the Press Association sent a reporter who interviewed him at Dover.[65] The Lessar interview attracted attention, but none of these occasions involved a great celebrity, and they do not seem, to a modern eye, much different from those interviews which appear daily on news bulletins.

A different slant on the development of the interview can be found in the recorded attitudes of politicians. The general impression is that they saw it as something new-fangled and possibly dangerous. In 1874 Edmund Yates was refused an interview by Disraeli, who disliked the system, when he asked

---

[63] BL Add. MS 60777 (not foliated). They continued to correspond frequently through 1884 and 1885 on a good variety of political subjects. As Irish Lord Lieutenant in Salisbury's Caretaker Government, Carnarvon was a most valuable contact.

[64] *Pall Mall Gazette*, 20 Mar. 1885. The *Glasgow Herald* printed the interview *verbatim*.

[65] Reported in the *Glasgow Herald*.

on behalf of James Gordon Bennett of the *New York Herald*.[66]
Chamberlain, a much younger politician, reacted in the same
way in 1886: '[Henry] Lucy wanted Chamberlain to give his
views in an "interview" on the situation, this he does not seem
prepared to do.'[67] It is noticeable that Labouchere, the writer,
still used inverted commas. In 1880 Tim Healy wrote of
Parnell

I am doing an 'interview' supposed to have taken place between
Parnell and Redpath for the *Tribune*, New York ... Parnell is an
extraordinary man. He would not even give me five minutes for a real
interview, but simply told me to write it, and then only made a slight
suggestion after he read it, as if I and not he would be the man who
would be responsible for what appears.[68]

A fuller picture of the development of the interview can be
derived from the Gladstone papers, thanks to his long fully-
recorded political career, and the overwhelming contemporary
public interest in him. In October 1881 J. A. Godley
reported[69] that

'the London correspondent of the N. Y. Herald has telegraphed a
long rigmarole to Mr. Gladstone asking for an "interview" respecting
Ireland ...
   'Mr. G. has written the letter which I append ... Is it too high a
compliment to a paper of this kind that Mr Gladstone should write to
it himself? The letter could be turned into one from a Private
Secretary beginning "I am directed by Mr. Gladstone ..."'.

In Gladstone's correspondence with W. T. Stead there are
repeated requests for interviews and statements of opinion,
particularly in the later 1880s. In March 1887, with characteristic effrontery, Stead wrote 'I am going to Rome this Easter to
see the head of the Catholic Church ... and it has occurred to
me that it would be useful considering the questions which his
Holiness is likely to ask me for me to have some conversation
with you.'[70] Gladstone sent a chilly reply but saw him. In
September 1889 Gladstone made a complaint which suggests
that he retained a radically different idea of what an interview

[66] Disraeli MSS, box 88, Yates to Corry, 24 Dec. 1874.
[67] Herbert Gladstone MSS BL Add. MS 46016 f. 100, 16 July 1886.
[68] T. M. Healy, *Letters and Leaders of my Day*, 1928, I, 97.
[69] Gladstone MSS, BL Add. MS 44222 f. 197, (to Herbert Gladstone).
[70] Ibid., 44303, f. 367.

should be: 'I had believed it to be in England a well understood rule and practice that an interview accorded to an Editor of a newspaper is meant simply to supply him with material which he may use *if* he thinks fit for his own guidance.'[71] That is, it should be non-attributable. He went on to complain that he had been misrepresented.

The cumulative impression left by these examples is confused. Newspapers were printing interviews—to be precise, inquiries made, person to person, of named individuals, about specific questions—as if this were an established practice. Politicians appeared to distrust or misunderstand the system. From their point of view it is easy to see why. Unlike the foreign public figures who gave interviews, they had no difficulty in getting publicity in Britain when they wanted it. A speech in Parliament, prepared in advance, would be fully reported in *Hansard* and *The Times* at the very least. A speech outside, to a meeting, would get similar treatment in the papers. An interview in private was subject to editing, misunderstanding, or distortion—a real risk when the interviewer was someone of Stead's headstrong temperament.

The question of interviews is bound up with another—how much harassment or pressure were the newspapers likely to exert? The evidence is far too scattered and subjective to allow any definite reply to be made. Complaints were expressed from time to time, especially in the early 1870s. A 'swarm of special correspondents and reporters' converged on Sandringham at the time of the Prince of Wales's illness;[72] Queen Victoria was being dogged by the press in the Highlands[73]—deservedly so in view of her best-selling book; there was a sense of outrage when a Liverpool journalist attempted to interview Gladstone in Hawarden Church.[74] In a totally different quarter:

The only portions, fortunately, of the English press which up to the present evince any disposition to imitate the American 'interviewing' nuisance are the sporting journals ... It is a fine thing, no doubt, to win the Derby or the St. Leger ... but these triumphs are dearly bought at the cost of all the torture involved in being perpetually

---

[71] Ibid., f. 409. Another case of misrepresentation is complained of at f. 364.
[72] *Printer's Register*, Jan. 1872, quoting the *Freeman*.
[73] Ibid., Nov. 1873.
[74] Ibid., Oct. 1873, quoting the *Hour*.

hunted by sporting editors and occasionally libelled into the bargain.[75]

The detail of Gladstone's later career leaves a rather different impression. This is in spite of the Hawarden Kite, undoubtedly an occasion when journalists succeeded in extracting information from his son which he himself was unwilling to make public. But on that occasion the leak came from Herbert Gladstone, MP for Leeds, to Wemyss Reid, editor of the *Leeds Mercury*, and one of his main supporters. It is more appropriate as an example of the effectiveness of political and social contacts than of the intrusiveness of reporters.[76] From the mid-1880s onwards Gladstone's health, and the possibility of his retirement, were matters of great public interest: journalists watched his movements, they went to church to hear how he read the lesson, they interviewed his oculist, but they did not disturb his privacy at home.[77] Earlier in his career, the whole long story of his nightly expeditions of 'rescue' would have been impossible had the press been more aggressive—not merely on account of the threat of scandal, but because the whole enterprise demanded privacy and confidentiality.

Contemporaries agreed that intrusiveness and interviewing were American vices. T. M. Healy, not sufficiently appreciating that Irish affairs might be more newsworthy in the United States than in Britain, was surprised when American journalists invaded his hotel when he went there in 1881.[78] When in September 1886 Justin McCarthy went to the United States with Mr and Mrs Campbell Praed, they too were astonished at the difference. Since McCarthy was going shortly after the failure of the first Home Rule Bill, to raise funds on behalf of the Irish Nationalists, they should have expected extreme public interest, but they found American reporters unmanageable:

One very important journal was already in possession of the sitting room ... In the course of a few minutes that one journal had gathered to itself half a dozen other journals; and when that seven had departed there came other and still other sevens. Mr McCarthy's

[75] Ibid., Jan. 1870, quoting *Macmillan's Magazine*.
[76] See Koss, 276–9.
[77] *Daily Chronicle*, 15 Jan. 1894, *Standard* 4 and 5 Jan. 1885 and 28 Feb. 1894.
[78] Op. cit., I, 142.

voice grew faint, but the interviewers lingered on ... apparently determined that while there was any 'copy' to be got the hero of the occasion should not eat nor sleep until he had provided it ...[79]

One does not find the British press described in such terms.

To a certain extent direct access to eyewitnesses and participants mattered less then than it does today, when it is standard journalistic practice to round off a report of an event with a quoted comment from someone directly involved, as if to demonstrate the truth of the report. Reports of accidents, disputes, or lawsuits, generally include direct comment from interested parties. This kind of reporting involves a multitude of minor interviews which are made much easier by the existence of the telephone: they have no exact counterpart in nineteenth-century newspaper reporting.

The general conditions of the time favoured the work of the journalists to an extent which is perhaps surprising. A limited number of political journalists moved easily among those who conducted the nation's business and were accepted into 'Society'. They were a small proportion of the whole profession, but what they had to say was widely read and copied. In the later nineteenth-century world of conspicuous expenditure and unashamed display of wealth or inherited privilege, newspaper publicity was no bad thing; hence the ease with which would be obtained the accounts of celebrities at home, and the lists of wedding presents, guests at balls, and descriptions of the clothes on fashionable occasions. The conventions of easy access for the press were reinforced from an entirely different direction by the dominance of liberal ideas of freedom of information. By the 1860s there could be no practical question about the reporting of Town Council meetings, trials, or parliamentary debates. The important uncertainties lay in relations with the executive government. The problems of handling war news were not really tested between the Crimea and 1914, but were a potential source of friction. The attitude of the civil service is hard to disentangle. The unofficial distribution of official information was prohibited and there is no evidence of regular arrangements for the supply of what was

[79] J. McCarthy, *Our Book of Memories: Letters of Justin McCarthy to Mrs Campbell Praed*, 1912, 4.

necessary; a situation which enhanced the value of private contacts. Social contacts could be supplemented by interviews, and these were increasingly used, though apparently with restraint and decorum, in the last thirty years of the century.

IX

Political News

POLITICAL speculation was at the centre of the London newspapers' interests: it was rare to find a day on which at least one of the leading articles was not concerned with the heart of the body politic. Such articles would be concerned not with analysis of events which had taken place, and which had been observed from outside, but with the immediate future—with political motives and relationships, the effects that speeches or actions were likely to have, the political and diplomatic choices ahead, and of course with advice. There was, as there still is, a strong emphasis on inside knowledge, or the appearance of it.

The present chapter is concerned with the extent and sources of such political knowledge. So far we have seen the work of the lobby correspondents, and the official record of *Hansard*. Information on some subjects came from government departments, but hardly inside information. Unless there was some urgent reason to the contrary, it was likely to be minimal, and given grudgingly. And there was the gossip of dinner parties and evenings in the clubs. The element still to be discussed is the systematic briefing of journalists by politicians. The facts of such contacts are familiar: any archive of a nineteenth-century statesman which has survived to a substantial extent is likely to contain correspondence with political journalists, not necessarily with the most notable editors, but with one or two minor figures, who were personally known and trusted.

Gladstone, with his long and fully documented career, is a natural starting-point. He showed a developing skill in his public relations. One of the best examples of him at work was given by an American journalist, E. L. Godkin, the editor of the *New York Evening Post*. He visited England in the summer of 1889 and was invited to dinner by James Bryce:

Suddenly 'Mr. and Mrs Gladstone' were announced, and there, sure enough he was, and my eyes fastened on him as they never fastened on any man since I was twenty. The first words he said on shaking

hands with Bryce were 'Is Mr. Godkin here?' And then he began apologising to me for not having sooner taken any notice of my card ... I sat by him at dinner and had a most delightful talk.

A few days later he was invited to the Gladstone's house, 'and had nearly two hours' very interesting talk with him'. They talked about church matters, and then went on

about the Liberal Unionists whom he denounced with curious fire, eyes glowing, hand uplifted, his face close to mine; we talked of Ireland and the Irish members whose conduct considering everything he thought very good ... It was most interesting and I think would alone have repaid me for coming to England.[1]

At the age of eighty he would not miss the opportunity of giving an interview to an American journalist who might enjoy an Irish-American readership.

Gladstone's dealings with the popular press began in the 1860s, as has been made clear by the publication of volume VI of his diaries, which covers the period down to the end of 1868.[2] At this time the *Daily Telegraph* was becoming the penny paper with the largest circulation in the London area, and its politics were radical in inclination. The diaries show the development of his day-to-day relationship with Thornton Hunt, an editorial writer on the paper. Hunt, the son of Leigh Hunt, had previously worked for the *Morning Chronicle* which had been bought by the Peelites in 1849: it may have been through this connection that he came to know Gladstone. He was a somewhat disreputable character who had broken up the marriage of G. H. Lewes, and not, one might suppose, a person particularly congenial to Gladstone. Professional reasons, however, brought the two into frequent contact: the diary records nearly one hundred occasions on which Gladstone either wrote to Hunt or saw him between March 1864 and December 1868. These meetings were not evenly spaced over the whole period; they were concentrated in times when Parliament was sitting. At such times Gladstone might be seeing Hunt once or twice a week.

From Gladstone's point of view, the advantages of this relationship are obvious. He gained personal publicity and

[1] R. Ogden, ed., *The Life and Letters of E. L. Godkin*, 1907, 153.
[2] Ed. H. C. G. Matthew, Oxford, 1978. See his introduction, to vol. V, xliv–vi.

support in the daily paper with the nearest thing to a mass circulation at that time. He could also, which was particularly important down to October 1865, while Palmerston was still alive, put his own slant on the interpretation of political events: for example he could stress the need to economize on defence spending. In all these actions Gladstone was using again the systems of publicity which had been so well exploited by Palmerston, and using them to shift Liberal ideas in a Gladstonian direction. An example where this was clearly being done is found in June 1865. On 9 June Gladstone saw Hunt. On the 12th the *Daily Telegraph* published a leading article summarizing the events of the session and discussing the question (not under that title) 'Where do the Liberals go from here?' The article argued that they must first stick to a sound financial policy, secondly support the unification of Italy, thirdly extend the franchise, and fourthly have a policy for Ireland. It needs a minimal acquaintance with Gladstonian ideas to see where that particular list of Liberal objectives had originated.

Gladstone was enjoying a very strong position. His guidance was being followed to a very substantial extent: if one compares the dates of his meetings with Hunt it is possible, not always but on most occasions, to see his influence in the paper a day or two later. It may well be that the files of the *Daily Telegraph* contain his own writings: on two occasions, each after a meeting with Hunt, the paper carried articles on the national finances which, in their spare and cogent presentation, read far more like the work of Gladstone than of the paper's own staff.[3] Left to itself the *Daily Telegraph* of the 1860s was flippant in tone. He may not have gained so much in personal publicity: any speech by a major political figure was fully reported in the 1860s, and indeed until the end of the century. When Gladstone went in the autumn of 1864 to open a public park in Bolton, the Tory *Standard* devoted marginally more words to the occasion than the *Daily Telegraph*.[4] If publicity in Lancashire was the objective, Gladstone would have received it automatically: the papers of the district would have been equally full in their reports.

The *Daily Telegraph* certainly gained great and immediate

---

[3] *Daily Telegraph*, 24 May and 23 Nov. 1865.
[4] See p. 248 below.

practical advantages. They gained explanations of what the government was doing, and occasionally exclusive advance information. A clear-cut example occurred in February 1865. On Saturday the 4th, three days before the opening of the Session, Gladstone saw Hunt. On the following Monday the *Daily Telegraph* published a leading article which gave a preview of the Queen's Speech to be delivered the following day. Out of the seven proposed items of legislation that it listed, five duly appeared next day: the only ones that did not were proposals for a Royal Commission on the railways, and for new museums to spring from the matrix of the British Museum. The Royal Commission on the Railways was Gladstone's own project, and he failed to get it accepted by the rest of the Cabinet at a meeting on the Monday afternoon.[5] Comparison of the two lists proves that it was Gladstone who had told the *Daily Telegraph* what was happening. Advance information about the Speech was exclusive information of the greatest value, the kind of success on which Delane's reputation had been built in previous decades. Many of the subjects dealt with were far less spectacular. For example, on Friday 10 March 1865 Gladstone saw Hunt. Three days later two items appeared; one a report of the failure of a private bank, the other an article explaining that this bank failure gave relevance to Gladstone's Bill for the regulation of country banks. It continued by explaining how *The Times* and the *Economist* had misrepresented the Bill. The *Daily Telegraph* was well informed, and Gladstone could clarify and justify his actions. In much of this no question of political ideology arose.

The history of Gladstone's relations with the *Daily Telegraph* after the 1860s is obscure. Thornton Hunt died in 1873, but there is no record, in the Gladstone Papers, of their having corresponded after 1870.[6] Gladstone's position had changed: as Prime Minister and leader of the Liberal Party he could call on his assistants to guide and influence the press: many of his later dealings (though not all) were carried out by his secretaries or by the party Whips. He continued to regard the *Daily Telegraph* and its effective proprietor, Edward Levy, as friends of his administration. George Carr Glyn, the Liberal Whip,

[5] *Diaries*, VI, 320, 332.
[6] Nor does he appear in the *Diaries*. Matthew, VII, 1982, xciv of introduction.

began to have some suspicion of the *Telegraph* in 1868, in writing to Gladstone: 'The Telegraph I really cannot make out at all but I think it will not dare to break with you.' In fact the relationship survived the fall of Gladstone's first administration for a short time. In January 1875 Glyn wrote again, 'I am content to stand upon Levy's article in *today's* Telegraph which seems to put the position so well. He writes boldly and is, as he has ever been, loyal and true.' The relationship did not survive much longer. On 4 December 1875, a few days after the announcement of the purchase of the Suez Canal shares, Glyn wrote again of the Tory administration; 'They have got the London papers clearly with them—poor Levy bought by *early* information!'[7]

The old association was not repaired. In 1876–8 Gladstone joined and led the popular movement against the Turks: the *Daily Telegraph* favoured the Turks against the Russians. Personal disagreements between Gladstone and Edward Levy-Lawson, as he had become in 1875, led in 1878 to a libel suit. This estrangement between the popular penny paper and the People's William was well known: various explanations were offered. It has been said that the Levy-Lawsons were anti-Russian because of Russia's anti-semitic policies, or alternatively because they had invested in Turkish bonds.[8] These explanations may both be true, but the estrangement needs to be seen in a more general context. In this context the intrinsic difficulties of the management of newspapers by politicians are illustrated.

The situation must be seen from the newspaper's side. Out of office, Gladstone, or any other politician, could no longer provide inside information about the Queen's Speech, or about diplomatic moves. The more closely a paper was attached to one party, the more unlikely it was that it would establish confidential relations with the opposing side. It seems likely, in fact, that the *Daily Telegraph* had never been solely the mouthpiece of Gladstone, valuable as his contributions had been. A letter from Edward Levy to Disraeli's confidential secretary,

[7] Gladstone MSS, BL Add.MS 44347 f. 114 (14 Apr.); 44349 f. 56 (15 Jan.) and f. 74.

[8] The dispute is outlined in a letter from Labouchere to Herbert Gladstone BL Add. MS 46015 f. 1, 19 Mar. 1881. The accusation that the Levy-Lawsons were influenced by their investment in Turkish bonds was made endlessly in *Truth* in 1877–8.

Montague Corry, apparently dating from late 1868, begins 'My dear Corry' and runs as follows, 'I have tried to track you down for two days without success. I suppose your whole mind has been given to the corruption of our future electors.'[9] This suggests that they were on easy and informal terms while Hunt was cultivating Gladstone. The correspondence of Lord Carnarvon, Conservative Colonial Secretary from 1874 to 1878, shows that by the summer of 1875 he was conducting a regular and informal correspondence with Edwin Arnold, a *Daily Telegraph* leader-writer.[10]

Secondly, the *Daily Telegraph*'s involvement with the Near East went back well before the Bulgarian Atrocities and the Ottoman financial crash of 1876. Two leader-writers, one of them Edwin Arnold and the other Edward Dicey, were both ardently pro-Turkish and had been appointed as early as 1861.[11] These appointments might have been related to the family's investment in Turkish bonds, but they could equally well have been a matter of accident. It may also be that the *Daily Telegraph* was thinking of its market. The vehemently pro-Turkish attitude of Londoners has often been commented on,[12] and newspapers were conscious of it. In June 1877 Edwin Arnold wrote to Carnarvon asking him for 'fifteen minutes' talk' to offer him 'some ideas derived from the knowledge of public opinion which my work and duty give me'.[13] Macdonald, the manager of *The Times*, wrote in similar terms to Mackenzie Wallace, then in St. Petersburg, 'All the inconveniences of a strongly neutral position are most severely felt by us who have besides to cater for Readers, the great majority of which are fiercely Turkish in their sympathies.'[14] Apart from the crisis of the Eastern Question the political climate was changing: both the Westminster and Middlesex constituencies became Conservative strongholds in the 1870s. The *Daily Telegraph* was swimming with the current. The change is suggested by an ingratiating letter of congratulation sent by Edward Levy-Lawson to W. H. Smith when he became First

---

[9] Disraeli MSS, box 88.
[10] BL Add. MS 60778.
[11] *D.NB.*
[12] E.g. in R. T. Shannon, *Gladstone and the Bulgarian Agitation*, 1963, 155.
[13] Carnarvon MSS, loc. cit.
[14] *The Times* archives.

Lord of the Admiralty in 1877, 'Do you remember coming down here one night to tell me that you were going to stand for Westminster; and in the Conservative interest? I fought you then: but I have helped you much since. How right you were! And how right I have always been about you.'[15] (In the 1865 General Election the *Daily Telegraph* had supported J. S. Mill.) It seems probable that the paper moved towards the centre of the political spectrum, though it did not formally abandon the Liberal label until 1886. It was the natural ally of the Whig-Imperialists within the Liberal Cabinet of 1880, and there is some slight evidence that it received advice from Hartington or from his active secretary, Reginald Brett.[16] In any case it is important to notice that the change of politics was accomplished without loss of circulation; rather there was a marked increase.[17]

Gladstone, increasingly conscious that his main support lay in the north, attempted to widen his contacts by giving encouragement to W. T. Stead, editor of the *Northern Echo*. Stead opened the correspondence, in accordance with his usual technique, by sending Gladstone copies of his paper describing the anti-Turkish agitation in 1876, and inviting comments. Gladstone in reply began to try and influence the editorial line being taken—'Were I in the place of Editor of your paper I should take the following for my general clew ...' He received the reply 'I thank you for your "clew". I shall bear it in mind ...' and Stead's letter went on to say that his own line of attack on Conservative foreign policy had been precisely the same. The correspondence continued, Gladstone constantly trying to direct Stead's energies in the proper direction, 'It is ... right and needful to point distinctly & steadily to the Prime Minister as the root of all this mischief and scandal', and Stead asserting his own opinions. By February 1878 Gladstone's views appeared too moderate, and Stead wrote back stating his own 'very decided dissent'.[18] It is a fine display of editorial independence; the David, in his late twenties editor of a halfpenny paper circulating in the Durham coalfield, defying the Goliath at the pinnacle of his popularity among Liberals. The *Northern*

---

[15] Hambleden MSS, PS/5/38 A, letter dated 7 Aug. 1877.
[16] See p. 197 below.
[17] See chapter II.
[18] Gladstone MSS, BL Add. MS 44303, ff. 230–86.

Echo could not possibly have filled the place of the *Daily Telegraph*, but proved unavailable as well.

The main weight of Liberal propaganda was directed to the *Daily News* in both Gladstone's first and second administrations, and we are fortunate in having two valuable examples of the kind of instruction it received. The *Daily News* had been reorganized in 1868, when the price was reduced to a penny, and it had become the official party organ. Its editor from 1869 to 1886 was Frank Harrison Hill. He received guidance throughout the period after 1870 from Granville, Foreign Secretary from 1870 to 1874 and from 1880 to 1885, whose style of advice is best illustrated by quotations. On 17 March 1872 he wrote: 'I trust in your discretion, not to let it appear that you know or have had any hint of the answer which we shall give to Parliament tomorrow.

'But it will be to the effect that the answer [of the United States] is civil, but declines to adopt our views.'

On 18 April, 'It is probable that the American answer left yesterday.' A week later, on the 26th, 'The Americans are on the totter ... With your pen of a ready writer you could paint a glowing picture of the respectful and cordial feeling any honorable settlement would be received with here.' There followed many more letters on the subsequent tortuous stages of the *Alabama* arbitration.

After the defeat of the Liberals in February 1874 there is a gap in the correspondence, apart from a few miscellaneous topics, until April 1880, when the Liberals returned to power. On 24 April Granville wrote assuring Hill that he would be kept informed about Ministerial appointments. On 9 July 1882 Hill received information of some importance: 'The Egyptians are continuing their armaments—Sir B. Seymour will announce tomorrow morning that unless there be a temporary surrender of the forts for the purpose of disarmament, he will open fire in 24 hours.' Alexandria would be bombarded in two days' time, as in fact it was. (The question whether or not to allow Admiral Seymour to issue this ultimatum had been under discussion for some days, so this news would not have been a total surprise.)[19]

---

[19] The events leading to the bombardment are given in detail in R. Robinson and J. Gallagher, *Africa and the Victorians*, 1961, 110 ff. Granville's letters are all taken from Granville MSS, PRO 30/29/426.

The letters continue on a number of subjects, and include a number on Afghanistan. On 5 March 1885: 'It might be inconvenient for the Daily News to confirm or to contradict the Observer's note about the Telegrams to St. Petersburg.

But pray say that you understand that communications are being continued between the English and Russian Governments.'

A few days later, on the 11th: 'Lumsden has not to my knowledge yet done any of the things mentioned in the Times.'

On 3 May, at the time when it will be remembered that the reserves were being called up,[20] Granville sent an important message:

I see no objection to your stating, though not as a communiqué, that it is believed that M. de Staal presented the answer of the Russian Government, which is of a conciliatory character, on Saturday. That it has been considered by the Cabinet and that any answer will be given (tomorrow) Monday.

That it may safely be concluded from Lord Granville's guarded remarks at the end of his speech to the Academy that he is confident peace will be secured: unless in the case of some unexpected events.

Further, equally substantial, briefing was given to the *Daily News* by Edward Hamilton, Gladstone's secretary after 1880. The two sets of letters, dealing with different subjects, are sufficiently alike in their general range of activities and information to suggest the normal established way of dealing with the press. Thus, on 10 February 1883, Hamilton wrote 'Thanks for so kindly acting on my note of yesterday. The article seems faithfully to carry out the cue which I was instructed by the Cabinet to give yesterday.'[21] Then on 11 May 1884, among much advice on how to handle the Gordon question, Hamilton sent a draft defence of government action:

'It is rumoured that some of those who waver in their confidence in the Government intend to abstain from voting, in order to mark their sense of the misconduct of the Government, not only in the Soudan, but also in Egypt proper ... Can anything be more foolhardy, or less calculated to serve the interest, not only of the Government, but also of the country and of Gordon himself?'

[20] See p. 157 above.
[21] This, and Hamilton's other letters, are taken from Hamilton MSS, BL Add. MS 48619.

On 11 February 1885, after the fall of Khartoum, he wrote, 'I have no doubt you will comment favourably on these announcements. The accession of Lord Rosebery may I think be considered a strength to the Government; and you will probably agree that it is an act of patriotism on his part to be willing to join the Government at this particular moment.' This was followed by a closely similar leading article the following morning. On 18 April Hill was asked to hint very delicately that a withdrawal from the Sudan might be desirable, in order to prepare the way for the Government's doing precisely that.

As with Granville's letters, the guidance was detailed and precise. There was also a third channel of advice, and there may well have been others. Lord Richard Grosvenor, the Liberal Whip, had regular meetings with Henry Lucy, the lobby correspondent of the *Daily News*, though we do not know what kind of information was given.[22]

The correspondence is full enough to make assessment of the politicians' objectives possible. The handling of the *Alabama* dispute and, more doubtfully, the Afghan question, show that they were thinking of their foreign audience. The Americans might be coaxed into accepting terms satisfactory to the British government. This hope may have been partly based on the news-sharing arrangement between the *Daily News* and the *New York Tribune*: something written in the one was likely to reach readers of the other. Similarly with the Russians in Afghanistan: just as it seems that the press was being used (it is not known exactly by whom) to demonstrate British preparedness and determination, so Granville may have wished to cool the situation once the Russian reply had been received.

More often these pieces of guidance were directed to the backbench MP, as for example Hamilton's attempt to prepare the way for a retreat from the Sudan in 1885. It was natural therefore that the Whips and the Prime Minister's secretary should be the people primarily involved in managing the *Daily News*. The need to find a quick, effective, and unobtrusive way of putting pressure on MPs is the dominant motive behind these letters. By contrast, there is no example where Hamilton and Granville appear to be attempting a direct appeal to the public in the manner of a modern party-political broadcast.

[22] Ibid., f. 114, 2 May 1885.

The propaganda objectives of a minister in power and a provincial activist, such as W. T. Stead, were very different. The latter were concerned with vigour and consistency, the former with defending current necessities. Thus their techniques differed also. The latter could build on a powerful leading article or the report of a public meeting; the former needed to publish a hint in the right place at the right time, possibly in a leading article, but, as often, in the series of short miscellaneous paragraphs which appeared in the London papers immediately below the leading article. The reader opened his paper at the centre page, where he found a summary of the main political news, followed by the leading articles, and followed in turn by these paragraphs. They might include, among such items as the comings and goings of Royalty, or news of the opening of new plays, some carefully and unobtrusively presented political news. There is no exact counterpart to these paragraphs in modern papers. Among them would also be found what Granville termed communiqués;[23] paragraphs in the form 'We understand that' or 'We are authorized to state', where the connection with the government was explicit. Both Granville and Hamilton display a constant and close attention to these distinctions: they not only offered information, but were anxious to control how it should be presented. The distinction between what could or could not be attributed to the politician was generally made.

These paragraphs, denials of false rumours and so on, could be inserted at the last minute. Leading articles were written after dinner, and small items could be inserted relating to the events of one evening, for publication the following morning. For example, one of Hamilton's letters reads, 'Your note of yesterday only came into my hands after midnight on my return home, and I have no one at that hour whom I can despatch with a note.'[24] Dilke's manuscript memoirs contain an anecdote about how 'on the night of the 13th [May, 1882] between 1 & 2 o'clock in the morning' he had gone to the *Daily News* office to get them to write a leading article attacking any plan of renewed Irish coercion.[25] Such stories, involving late-

---

[23] The word, later much used by Northcliffe, came in from France, meaning an official announcement, and is first recorded in 1852.

[24] Hamilton MSS, BL Add. MS 48619 f. 114.

[25] Dilke MSS, BL Add. MS 43934 f. 172.

night cabs to Fleet Street and confidential discussions, explains why the main political influence, and the exclusive news that went with it, were bound to remain concentrated in the London press at the expense of the provincials.[26]

How well did Hill follow his instructions? If the files of the paper are compared with these letters it seems that they were usually followed. But it is impossible for a modern reader, insensitive to the precise nuances involved, particularly in the diplomatic situations, really to judge how well he responded. Granville and Hamilton both expressed themselves well satisfied. Hamilton, when leaving his job for a post in the Treasury in June 1885, wrote of his 'sense of the great value which the Govt. has derived from the unswerving support which you have given to them', and Granville about the *Alabama* claims, had written about the 'constantly judicious and successful manner' in which Hill had supported him.[27] Nevertheless he was bitterly criticized and finally dismissed in January 1886. About him Chamberlain had written: 'Can anything be more stupidly ineffective than Hill's management? ... You know that it is no use putting him up to things. He never takes a hint ...'[28] According to Labouchere, one of the proprietors, and shortly before his dismissal, 'He is a bad Editor and the Liberal party suffers owing to his inability to present political matters in a popular manner, whilst two thirds of the Cabinet have complained to me of him.'[29] It seems that it was impossible to satisfy all sections of a party so divided, both on general social and political objectives and on the tactics for particular situations: it was difficult to be the organ of a party which itself was a widely based coalition.

The needs of the *Daily News*, the reciprocal benefits that they expected, emerge clearly. Hill complained from time to time, not of the political influence that was being exerted over his editorial judgement, but that some other newspaper, especially the *Standard*, might be getting an item of news before he did. Perhaps the most striking feature of both correspondences is not the value of the inside news that was being passed

[26] But cf. below.
[27] HamiltonMSS f. 134; Granville MSS, PRO 30/29/426, letter of 28 June 1872.
[28] Dilke MSS, BL Add. MS 43885 f. 288, Chamberlain to Dilke, 9 Dec. 1882.
[29] Herbert Gladstone MSS, BL Add. MS 46015, f. 28, Labouchere to Herbert Gladstone, 13 June 1885.

on, but the explicit pledge given, more than once, that Hill would be given priority. 'As far as Downing Street is concerned I say most positively that we never give hints to anyone save yourself', wrote Hamilton; or 'You may be sure you will always get the earliest information possible about Ministerial appointments.' Or, making the back-scratching nature of the relationship plain, '[Mr Gladstone] is only sorry that you should be under any impression that you are not shewn an adequate amount of the favour to which the useful support of the Daily News so amply entitles you.'[30]

A final element, other than the needs of the politicians and the editor, can be seen, though dimly, in the picture; that is, the desire to provide the public with a reliable record. From time to time, Hamilton, and more especially Granville, took the initiative in contradicting false rumours, and keeping Hill posted with the general state of affairs. For example, in September 1880, there was 'no truth in the report of the Cabinet on Monday in today's Daily News . . . an announcement in your paper is regarded as more or less authoritative'.[31]

Were affairs conducted in a similar way on the Conservative side? There had been continuous attempts since the 1830s to organize a network of Conservative newspapers over the country, though these efforts were primarily directed towards mobilizing support at elections. Here however we are concerned with the business of explaining government actions to an influential and widely-circulating newspaper. Processes similar to those of the Liberals were at work, though specific detail is lacking. Disraeli's handling of the *Daily Telegraph* has already been suggested.

It is probable that *The Times* also was to some extent associated with the Conservatives. The *History of The Times* describes how the paper was in difficulties after the death of Palmerston in 1865, and how it came round to the general support of Disraeli.[32] There is a description of how Disraeli gave advance copies of his speeches to *The Times* alone.[33] After 1880 *The Times* employed Algernon Bourke (known under his nickname 'Button') to advise the editor, Chenery. Bourke was

---

[30] Hamilton MSS, f. 114.
[31] Ibid., f. 43.
[32] Vol. II, *The Tradition Established, 1841–1884*, 1939, 393 ff.
[33] T. H. E. Escott, *Platform, Press, Politics and Play*, Bristol, n.d., 335; Koss.

the Conservative spokesman on foreign affairs in the House of Commons; the archives of *The Times* show that he was paid a salary in 1880, but say nothing about subsequent years.[34] Furthermore it has been shown that the paper published the Pigot forgeries in 1889 on the advice of W. H. Smith, then the Leader of the House.[35] These facts taken together suggest some kind of linkage between the party and *The Times* newspaper.

The newspaper which looked most like the Conservative equivalent of the *Daily News* was however, the *Standard*. The *Standard* was an old-established Conservative paper; in 1870 it had been under the direct political editorship of the Conservative Whips. After Mudford had become editor at the end of 1874 great emphasis had been placed upon his independence of political pressure. In practice, however, the *Standard* needed news and established a relationship at least with Lord Salisbury: there may have been others. The link, which was a generally known one, was through Alfred Austin. Austin had been a writer for the *Standard* since the 1860s. He appears to have come into contact with Lord Salisbury through the organization of a Conservative periodical, the *National Review*, in October 1882. A process of briefing began. On 15 June 1884 when the House of Lords was obstructing the passage of the franchise reform bill, Salisbury began to offer editorial advice: 'May I take the opportunity of saying that I hope you will do what you can to prevent a certain influential organ of opinion from throwing cold water on the action of the Peers', perhaps a reference to the 'great unreasonableness of The Times' referred to in a later letter. A week later, on Sunday 22 June, this first approach was followed by a long and fully worked-out letter from Salisbury's nephew A. J. Balfour, who was working as his political secretary: 'In accordance with the suggestion you made to me on Friday I send you the outline of the advice which the leaders desire shall be followed by the House of Lords. If you could press this advice in the manner you know of you would I am sure be doing a Service to the party',[36] followed by the draft of a leading article.

---

[34] W. S. Blunt, *Secret History of the English Occupation of Egypt*, 2nd edn. 1907, 217.
[35] F. S. L. Lyons, 'Parnellism and Crime' in *Transactions of the Royal Historical Society*, 5th ser, XXIV, 1974, 123–40.
[36] Alfred Austin MSS, Bristol University Library.

The letters received by Austin, some printed in his autobiography and some in manuscript in the Bristol University Library, are few and make it impossible to assess the frequency of such briefing. There is a long and informative letter on the general state of European affairs of 10 September 1886, followed by a leading article in the paper along similar lines on 16 September, one from Balfour on 30 July 1895 on the election of the Speaker, and one from Salisbury on 17 August 1896 on the question of Port Arthur. This is enough to show that the process of briefing continued, and it seems likely that the letters are sole survivors of a much larger volume of information, which may have been handed over verbally in interviews.

The *Standard*'s needs and interests were similar to those of the *Daily News*. They wanted information on the probable course of events—'Gladstone *will* resign' on 12 July 1886; and after his resignation, and the formation of Salisbury's Government, another letter on 14 August; 'Referring to an article in the Standard today—do not expect any statements of policy or controversial matters in the Queen's speech. We treat the short session merely as one for winding up the business and passing the estimates.' And they expected most-favoured treatment; when the *Standard* did not find out the date of the opening of parliament as soon as *The Times*, Salisbury was profuse in his apologies.[37]

How I came never to think of it—how it happened that you never asked—how you missed hearing people talking of it here . . . is hard to explain. I can only say it was a piece of bad luck. The thing had been decided the Monday before—and was no secret. Till I got your letter I was not aware that The Times had had exclusive information. I think the remedy is to be found in a greater freedom of communication with private secretaries.

The briefing of official newspapers by leading members of the Government was only a part of the situation.[38] Many politicians had their outlets. W. E. Forster, at odds with Chamberlain's Radicals, was associated with Wemyss Reid,

[37] Ibid., Salisbury to Austin, 29 Nov. 1886.
[38] Harcourt also supplied Hill with information: see Peter Fraser, *Lord Esher, a Political Biography*, 1973 35.

who wrote his life.[39] Dilke, whose family had long owned or managed newspapers, was, to judge by his unpublished memoir, obsessed with them.[40] Carnarvon and Chamberlain, both of whom steered an individual course, maintained correspondence with a variety of journalists. Carnarvon's papers show him trying to maintain a position as a trimmer. He had extensive and often purely social relations with Delane and Henry Reeve of *The Times*, Meredith Townsend of the *Spectator*, W. T. Stead, Frederick Greenwood, the Conservative editor first of the *Pall Mall Gazette* and later of the *St. James's Gazette*, and Edwin Arnold of the *Daily Telegraph*.[41] He crossed party boundaries unhesitatingly. It is probable that the most powerful influence would be exerted over papers at the extreme of the political spectrum, or over minor papers not in a position to play rivals off against each other, or to sift out the information offered while rejecting the advice on how to use it. The influence of Lord Randolph Churchill over the *Morning Post* was of this kind, with its well-defined and limited readership among the gentry who might be expected to be in general sympathy with the stance of the informant.

For the *Daily News* or the *Standard* there was the same problem as there was for the *Daily Telegraph* after 1874; how does a paper regarded as authoritative, which derives its information from privileged access to official information, fare when its party is out of office? There is no evidence to show whether the *Daily News* had any private sources among the Conservatives: it seems hardly likely, and particularly unlikely in the embittered political atmosphere after the Home Rule split. The *Standard* learned secrets from the Liberals after 1880 through Chamberlain, who was disaffected by his lack of status in the new administration, and passed information to Escott, his associate, who was also a leader-writer on the *Standard*. But it must remain doubtful how useful this source actually was, and how long it continued. There were three occasions on which the *Standard* achieved conspicuous success: the first on 11 November 1880 when it published a leading article showing

---

[39] 2 vols., 1888.
[40] Dilke MSS, BL Add. MSS 43932–40.
[41] Carnarvon MSS, BL Add. MSS 60776–8.

inside knowledge of the previous day's Cabinet on Ireland, the second on 6 April 1881 when they gave advance information on the terms of the 1881 Land Bill and the third on 17 January 1882 when they again showed inside knowledge of Cabinet discussion on Ireland. All three leaks aroused shocked reactions from Gladstone and Granville. In Escott's and Chamberlain's papers responsibility for the first leak is implicitly acknowledged, and the *Standard* crops up from time to time between 1880 and 1882.[42] There is no reference to the *Standard* after that time, and a letter from Morley to Chamberlain, written two days after the third leak, said that he had met Mudford, editor of the *Standard*, at Escott's. He had been 'very pleasant but certainly no longer the editor of Chamberlain's Journal'.[43] It seems possible that the source dried up. Whatever happened it is clear that a source such as this, going through an intermediary, and based on the accidental circumstance that Chamberlain was critical of the Government's Irish policy, could not be compared with the steady flow of advice which came to a paper whose party was in office. The efforts put by the *Daily News* into their investigation of the Bulgarian atrocities, and by the *Standard* into displaying an inside knowledge of the Gladstone Cabinet's proceedings, may have been stimulated by the need to show the public that they were still actively in business. It could be argued, with some plausibility, that one factor leading to a weakening of the old dependence on individual politicians was the swing of the pendulum in elections between 1868 and 1886. In Palmerston's day, by contrast, there were very few months, between 1846 and his death in 1865, when he was not in office in some capacity.

How difficult was it to provide an adequate news service without accepting domination by politicians? Granville, writing to Gladstone of the difficulty of handling the press, noticed that 'what they want is constant information and briefs'.[44] In 1886 Labouchere in his role as proprietor of the *Daily News*, and complaining of Lucy as editor, said 'What we want is a

[42] A. Ramm, ed., *The Political Correspondence of Mr. Gladstone and Lord Granville, 1876–1886*, Oxford, 1962, I, 231, 253, 332. BL Add. MS 58777, Chamberlain to Escott 20 Nov. 1880. There are 49 letters in the Chamberlain papers and 60 in the Escott collection, giving a fairly full picture of their dealings with each other.

[43] Chamberlain MSS, Birmingham University Library, JC5/54/438.

[44] Ramm, 213.

man who, when he wishes to write about foreign politics goes to
Rosebery and when he wishes to write about Irish matters goes
to Morley.'[45] Morley himself, on being appointed editor of the
Pall Mall Gazette in 1880, wrote to Dilke 'I am not yet grown a
sufficiently cool hand to be a good editor. It would be worth
silver and gold and jewels if I could have ten minutes with you
about three times a week.' Dilke agreed to do this, and
Chamberlain gave information on domestic affairs. Dilke
added that Morley 'used this so well that no complaint ever
arose with regard to it, although there was great complaint
with regard to Chamberlain giving information to another
man—Escott of the *Standard* and the *World*'.[46] It is noteworthy
that Morley, with his great ability, and with impeccable
standards of intellectual propriety, should have felt the need
for constant guidance: if he needed it, how much the more
would others?

W. T. Stead's conduct of the *Pall Mall Gazette*, after Morley
left it, provides another, very different test. Stead's own views
were developed in an article on the 'Future of Journalism' in
the *Contemporary Review* in 1886. He set his sights high:

There ought to exist such relations of confidence as to render it
possible for the editor to be put in possession of the views of any
personage whose opinion he desires to know.[47] This of course is a
work of time, and even after many years the most successful editor
must be content to know many of the most important personages at
second-hand. But it is better to be intimate with the confidant of a
Minister than to be merely on friendly terms with the Minister
himself. There are some Ministers who never tell anything when their
journalistic acquaintances seek information. Others profess to tell
everything, and mislead the enquirer in every direction. Those
Ministers are very rare who make a confidant of an editor, and still
rarer are those who do not make a thorough-going support the
condition of such confidences.

The terms of course are absolutely impossible. No consideration
whatever, in the shape of exclusive and official information, can
compensate for the loss of the right of individuality, of independence,
and of criticism.[48]

---

[45] Labouchere to Herbert Gladstone 17 Feb. BL Add. MS 46016 f. 10.
[46] Dilke MSS, BL Add. MS 43934 f. 216–7.
[47] Defined a little later in the article as 'everyone from the Queen down'.
[48] *Contemporary Review*, 1886, 666.

The journalist should seek information from all, and be dominated by none. In defence of this stand may be cited Stead's 'decided dissent' from Gladstone in 1878, when he was editing the *Northern Echo*. But it is a doubtful description of the way in which he was running the *Pall Mall Gazette* a few years later. The *Pall Mall Gazette* was notorious for the support which it gave to certain causes. Of these, one was the Russian Government. This dated back to Stead's anti-Turkish crusade in the mid-1870s and to his meeting with Madame Novikov. It is easy to find examples of Russian influence in the files of the paper.[49]

Another of Stead's guiding lights, later in his career, was Cecil Rhodes. They met in 1889, at the end of Stead's spell at the *Pall Mall Gazette*. On a personal level, Rhodes found Stead in one of his recurrent financial crises, and paid his debts. Stead was an enthusiastic follower until, to his great credit, he became an outspoken critic of British policy in South Africa at the time of the Boer War.[50]

The 'Maiden Tribute' revelations in support of the Criminal Law Amendment Bill of 1885, which are probably the best known of Stead's campaigns, cannot be linked to an external influence, unless perhaps he was given encouragement by the Salvation Army. Stead certainly continued to be close to the Booths after 1885. (It is suggested that later, in 1890, they lent him the money with which he bought out George Newnes' share of the *Review of Reviews*.)[51]

An important and long-running campaign, where it is easier to assess the extent of the influence exerted over Stead, was concerned with the state of the national defences. By definition it was a field in which expert knowledge and access to confidential information were of the greatest importance. The *Pall Mall Gazette*, which came out at tea-time and was much read in the London Clubs, was an admirable vehicle for the ventilation of these questions. In August 1884 H. O. Arnold-Forster, secretary of the Imperial Federation League, and

---

[49] See p. 236 below.

[50] John Flint, *Cecil Rhodes*, 1976, 115–16; J. W. Robertson Scott, *The Life and Death of a Newspaper*, 1952, 175 ff.

[51] J. O. Baylen, 'W. T. Stead as publisher and editor of the *Review of Reviews*', *Victorian Periodicals Newsletter*, Bloomington, Ind., 1978–80, 70–84. There is a wealth of detail about Stead's contacts in this article which is based on Stead's papers.

advocate of naval rearmament, went to see Stead on the subject of defence. He introduced Jacky Fisher, and possibly other naval officers, to him. The articles on the 'Truth about the Navy' began to come out in September, in a long series which ran to the end of the year. (Examination of the file of the *Pall Mall Gazette* shows that in the first half of the year it had paid little or no attention to the navy as a news topic.) These articles ventilated a series of naval grievances which mostly derived from the fact that the British navy, with its immense number of ships, was not provided with the newest and best-armed ships. The newest ships in the French Mediterranean fleet were superior to anything projected in Britain. The French fleet, if it acted in conjunction with the Russian fleet in the Mediterranean, would be far more than a match for the British. These arguments, appearing in the second half of 1884, were followed in December by proposals by Lord Northbrook, First Lord of the Admiralty for increased naval construction.[52] It is an example of the efficiency of a lobby rather than of the power of the press.

Army reformers also found their way to the *Pall Mall Gazette* office. Their influence, however, is more to be seen in the paper's general views on foreign and imperial affairs. In 1880 Stead had been introduced by General Gordon to Reginald Brett, who since 1878 had been secretary to Hartington. Hartington was Secretary for India between 1880 and December 1882, when he became Secretary for War for the remainder of the Liberal administration. Both offices gave plenty of scope to anyone preoccupied with the questions of strategy, and Brett acted as adviser and informant to Stead[53] (and possibly to others, but other contacts are not documented). Wolseley and Gordon had known one another since they first met in the Crimea, and Brett, in contact with both men, gave Stead advice from 1884 to 1886 on the handling of the Egyptian question. These letters, which have survived, allow us to assess Stead's capacity for independent judgement.

Stead has been given credit for initiating the plan of sending Gordon to Khartoum: the *Concise DNB*, epitomizing his career,

[52] Stead's dealings with Arnold-Forster and Fisher are described in R. Mackay, *Fisher of Kilverstone*, Oxford, 1973, 179–82.
[53] The connections are explored by Peter Fraser and R. Mackay.

states that he was 'directly responsible for the dispatch of Gordon', and this, together with the subsequent Relief Expedition, are often quoted as prime examples of the power of the press. The facts are that Stead interviewed him on 8 January 1884 when he landed at Southampton from Belgium, and wrote a leading article next day arguing that he be sent out 'to assume absolute control of the territory'.[54] Before that however, on 1 January, *The Times* had published a letter from Sir Samuel Baker, who had travelled in the Equatorial Nile region, also recommending that Gordon be sent. Dilke explained the course of events more plausibly. He quoted a letter from Granville to himself: 'The papers seem to think that Gordon is a new discovery by the Government under pressure of the press. It happens that I consulted Malet on the subject months ago.' Dilke added, 'it was Wolseley, Gordon's friend, who suggested that he should be sent'.[55] Who suggested to Stead that he go and interview Gordon is not known, but not difficult to guess. The Gordon expedition came out of the initiatives within the government, and at most was endorsed by the press.

Gordon arrived in Alexandria on 16 February 1884. That same day Brett wrote to Stead 'agreeing with every word in this day's paper' and continuing

We ought to send out to *Egypt proper* at once, a reinforcement sufficient to enable a flying column to move immediately to any point on the Nile ... they ought to be sent at once to Alexandria.

Nobody wants them to attempt to avenge Baker or reconquer the Soudan; but they should stand, sword in hand, ready to strike if anything happens to Gordon.[56]

The agitation for a relief expedition had already begun, and again it was not being initiated by the press. Brett also gave advice on the conduct of the campaign against the Mahdi. On 23 February:

With regard to Tokar, I think it is well-nigh settled that a consider-

---

[54] Quoted by Lord Elton, *General Gordon*, 1954, 327.

[55] Dilke MSS, unpublished memoir, BL Add. MS 43938, 23–4. Sir Edward Malet had been British Consul-General in Egypt 1879–83.

[56] *Journals and Letters of Reginald Viscount Esher*, ed. M. V. B. Brett and O. S. B. Brett, 4 vols., 1934–8, I, 89. Baker Pasha (Valentine Baker) in command of an Egyptian force, had been defeated on 4 Feb. in the eastern Sudan.

able force is to remain at Souakin to prevent the rebels threatening the place . . . Some of the troops will return to Alexandria and shortly a force will be despatched to Assouan . . . This force must start while the Nile remains navigable. Some of Wood's army would doubtless accompany it.

This is not definitely settled, but there is very little doubt that it will shortly be sanctioned by H.M.G.[57]

Two days later:

There are two points of immediate importance

1) Strengthen the British garrison at Cairo and Alexandria—from England. If force is required at Assouan send *Wood's* army . . .

2) . . . defend Souakin from the place itself as a base, unless there are military reasons to the contrary. Forbid advance to Teb.

These messages need some explanation. Wood's army was the Egyptian army under its British general. Tokar, Suakin, and El Teb are places in Eastern Sudan on or near the Red Sea: the rebellion had spread to them. They were much closer to Khartoum than was Cairo, but the only access was by a route across the desert. In 1884 controversy was vigorous between those who favoured relieving Gordon through Suakin, and those, notably Wolseley, who argued that the force should advance up the Nile from Cairo. In sending these letters Brett was treading in a very controversial area. He was also handing over sensitive information about troop movements which were about to take place. It might be thought that this is another example of the briefing of a friendly paper, of the kind that Hamilton was also carrying out, but in fact the second letter coincided with the sending of orders by Hartington to advance on El Teb, where an Arab force was defeated on 29 Febru-ary.[58] As Dilke put it, Brett was using Stead 'to bring pressure upon the Government on all occasions when he did not personally agree with what they were doing'.[59] It is an illustration of what could happen when the system of handing out exclusive information went wrong.

What use did Stead make of the information he received? This question is most easily answered by a specific example. Brett continued through 1884 and 1885, until he was dismissed

[57] Ibid., I, 91.
[58] Adrian Preston, *In Relief of Gordon* etc., 1967, xxvii.
[59] Dilke MSS, unpublished memoir, BL Add. MS 43933, f. 190.

by Hartington in the spring of 1886, to send advice on a variety
of subjects. One letter, dated 25 November 1884, began by
recommending that 'Egypt had better be dropped *altogether* till
after next Monday, & final shots fired to the Admiralty and
War Office'. It then gave a list of 'principal points', which
among a number of others included '3. The responsibility of
the W O and Lord H almost as great as the responsibility of
Lord N[orthbrook]; 4. No attempts to shuffle responsibility on
to each other', and finally '6. Personal appeal to Lord H,
possible P.M., all the greater responsibility. Fitness and courage for the post judged by the result of this struggle with the
Tsy and electioneering agents.'[60]

The arguments in this letter, a blow in the campaign for
increased naval construction, appeared in a leading article
entitled 'A test of backbone' on page one of the *Pall Mall
Gazette* on 1 December. Brett's points were dealt with as
follows:

[3] The efficiency of the navy depends almost as much upon Lord
Hartington as upon Lord Northbrook,

[4] ... nor must there be any attempt on the part of either to shuffle
off responsibility on the other.

[6] Everyone recognizes in him the future chief of the Liberal party.
As the future Prime Minister of England it is doubly incumbent
... [on him to see that the country was not imperilled] ... Nor is
that the only consideration ... This accession to supreme office
... will largely depend on the estimate which the nation forms of
his capacity for power. ... It is impossible to believe that the
Marquess of Hartington speaking with the authority of his
department and in the cause of Imperial Security can be baffled
by the Treasury, even if its resistance is reinforced by wirepullers
potent at contested elections ...

This close correspondence could be paralleled by many other
letters in the collection. Brett's interventions are noteworthy:
the first reaction must be astonishment that he could carry
them on for so long; the connection was well known to
contemporaries. It suggests that the general standard of confidentiality was not high; there is an ironic contrast between
Lingen's opinion that the handing out of official information

---

[60] Printed in Fraser, 52.

was as 'unprofessional' as cowardice in the army,[61] and the casual way in which private secretaries could operate. Stead's treatment of his information also deserves comment. His article in the *Contemporary Review* bore no relation to his practice: he was good at establishing contacts, but exercised little control over their contributions. He deserves some sympathy however. The *Pall Mall Gazette* was a daily journal of comment, and its small staff were working under pressure. If it was to maintain its position as fashionable, informed, and influential it was liable to fall prey to advisers who could offer sketches of articles with which Stead was in general agreement. It can be argued that the causes which have been discussed were all ones that Stead himself enthusiastically embraced, and that therefore no question of the loss of independence actually arose. Nevertheless the agents—the glamorous Madame Novikov (and Stead was easily attracted to women), the terrifying Fisher, the bossy and clever Brett, and the immensely rich Rhodes—were a formidable band against whom to maintain an independent line. A final point is that the name of the proprietor, Yates Thompson, figures not at all in any of the correspondence. So, far from determining the policy of the paper, he was ignored.

The *Pall Mall Gazette* is an extreme example of external influences at work, and the metropolitan press, more accessible and more likely to be read by politicians, was more subject to such approaches than were provincial papers. An article, or an idea, or a little publicity for an individual, if it appeared in a London paper, also stood a chance of being repeated in the provinces. By contrast, a provincial report might well be ignored by the London papers. Joseph Chamberlain's correspondence betrays a constant concern that London heard nothing of his schemes in Birmingham, until the Improvement Bill for the building of Corporation Street came before Parliament in 1876.[62]

This does not necessarily mean that the provincial editors were excluded from inner political circles: as people with

---

[61] See previous chapter. On standards of confidentiality see Cooke and Vincent, 187–8.

[62] For example, to J. T. Bunce, 3 May 1876, 'The London Papers are really beginning to take a friendly interest in Birmingham. Their silence never did us any harm. I hope their patronage will be equally innocuous.' Chamberlain MSS, JC 5/8/13.

expert knowledge of public opinion outside London they were valuable contacts. Some—Wemyss Reid of the *Leeds Mercury*, Charles Cooper of the *Scotsman*, E. R. Russell of the Liverpool *Daily Post*, and J. T. Bunce of the *Birmingham Daily Post*, were close confidants of politicians.[63] Cooper's autobiography contains a number of references, as close contacts, to W. P. Adam, the Liberal Whip, and to H. C. E. Childers, Chancellor of the Exchequer between 1882 and 1885, and MP for South Edinburgh in 1886. He spoke of his links with easy assurance:

Never have I published or allowed to be published statements as to facts or intentions made known to me by statesmen or other men, without their consent ... hundreds of times have I seen in other newspapers statements as to Ministerial intentions or individual movements about which I have often known weeks before.[64]

Chamberlain's papers provide some insight into the way in which things worked. In the 1870s and 1880s his position was rather similar to Gladstone's at the time of his association with Hunt—a new challenger to the existing leadership, except that until 1876 he lacked parliamentary experience, and was a provincial. He was very conscious of the need to project himself and his programme. The main vehicle for his radical ideas was the *Fortnightly Review* under the editorships of both Morley and Escott, particularly in the diary of events called the 'Chronique' which was compiled under his guidance by both men. But he was also trying to establish a range of provincial newspaper supporters. In Liverpool, Russell began to receive advice and outlines of his views from 1882, when Chamberlain had made a successful speech there. In the summer of 1885, in the weeks leading to Chamberlain's Unauthorised Programme, he received a good deal.[65] Chamberlain's closest contact was with Bunce of the *Birmingham Daily Post*, and his letters to him include a number of a familiar kind—long, carefully drafted expositions, particularly of international affairs, which could have been used as leading articles. The attempt to compare them with the files of the newspaper fails to reveal the kind of

[63] Correspondence between Russell and Gladstone (fairly formal) and Morley is contained in BL Add. MS 62993. The information from Morley mostly dates from after the Home Rule split.

[64] Charles A. Cooper, *An Editor's Retrospect*, 1896, 403.

[65] Chamberlain MSS, JC 5/62.

correspondence which has been seen between Brett's letters and the *Pall Mall Gazette*; Bunce digested the advice he was sent, and then used his own judgement. The *Birmingham Daily Post* remained a general supporter of Chamberlain after the secession of the Liberal Unionists, but was independent. In September 1885, before the split, this independence led to a quarrel. Chamberlain wrote:

I have delayed writing for some days, but I cannot refrain from saying now how much I have been pained by your recent articles on my London speech and Free schools . . .
I cannot bear the thought that just at the moment that what has scornfully been called the Birmingham policy is receiving almost universal support, the journal which has been its most able and consistent exponent should seem to be falling into the lines of the Leeds Mercury or the Western Morning News.

This produced a reply arguing that the Liberals should not destroy the voluntary schools and continuing

Believing this, I could not, from the very nature of my position, keep silence. By abstaining from expressing my opinion I should fail to discharge my duty towards the journal I am permitted to direct, and I should, I think, do injury to Liberalism by shrinking from the frankness and independence which are essential to influential and honourable journalism.[66]

Chamberlain backed down. This letter is a valuable document to those who argue for the superiority of provincial over London journalism. There appears, on this very limited evidence, to be a difference in standards of independence between the main London and the main provincial papers. One explanation has already been offered, that London papers and their leader-writers were simply closer to hand, and in circulation among those that mattered. Another lies in a difference of environment. A leading provincial paper—like the *Birmingham Daily Post*—had a secure status in its own region. It could easily fill its columns with advertisements; it had an unchallenged position in its locality as the most authoritative source of regional news. In many cases—again like the *Birmingham Daily Post*—it had established a reputation as a leader of local political campaigns. It could afford to snub a Cabinet Minister.

[66] Ibid., JC 5/8/79, 80.

A third explanation lies in the differing news objectives of the London and provincial papers. According to Cooper, editor of the *Scotsman*, defending the provinces strongly, the provincial papers at the end of the century gave more parliamentary news, about the same amount of foreign news, and far more general news.[67] Put another way it might rather be said that the London press gave far more attention to political speculation, particularly on the British conduct of foreign affairs. Possibly this was a survival from the period when *The Times* and Palmerston dominated the scene: possibly in the capital of a great commercial and political empire such interests were bound to predominate. Cabinet meetings were often announced in the papers in advance, and there was a habit of marking the occasion with leading articles on the next day discussing what had been transacted. For example, the Cabinet met on 2 January 1885, and the next day *The Times*, the *Standard*, and the *Daily News* all published leading articles discussing what had happened. It is possible that Cabinet meetings were regarded as pieces of governmental machinery which would one day be publicly reported as the proceedings of parliament had come to be, but it is certain that they received plenty of notice in the papers. The papers did not, as they would today, analyse major questions and then speculate as to the way in which the Cabinet would handle them; they would make a straight guess about what particular business had been transacted. Sometimes they wrote with inside knowledge, sometimes they may have bluffed their way to the truth, since the topics discussed usually fell within a narrow range of probabilities. Sometimes they guessed entirely wrong. So long as it was a matter of prestige for a paper to look as if it had inside knowledge, the Cabinet minister had a valuable lever.

We can see the system at work if we compare the day-to-day account of the years 1885–6 given by Cooke and Vincent with the accounts given in the newspapers.[68] At critical times one can find clues to the identity of a particular newspaper's contacts. Thus, in the spring of 1885 the Cabinet was waiting to receive the French reply to proposals for the regulation of

[67] Op. cit., 70.
[68] Op. cit., 173 ff.

the Egyptian Debt. These proposals were received and made
public in mid-January and included a suggestion for an
international body to investigate the working of the debt
administration—the 'Enquête'. The Cabinet met on 20 and 21
January and were bitterly divided between those led by
Gladstone, willing to accept the French proposals, and those
led by Hartington, who found international enquiry humiliat-
ing. Leading articles in the *Daily News* and *Daily Telegraph* on
21st both took the latter view. The next day both papers
returned to the subject: the *Daily News* (which we know had
been inspired by Hamilton) now reassuring its readers that
nothing approaching international control was in prospect,
and the *Daily Telegraph* explaining the causes of the dispute
within the Cabinet.

We find the divisions within the Cabinet echoed in the press
again in April and May of the same year. By that time, with
the crisis in Afghanistan, and after the fall of Khartoum, the
immediate question for decision was whether Wolseley's expedition should return home, or make an attempt to reconquer
the Sudan in the autumn. Three Cabinets were held on 13, 14,
and 15 April. The first two of these were concerned with
Afghanistan, and the last, on the 15th, with Upper Egypt.
Comment appeared on the 16th. The *Standard*, believing
rumours that the Afghan situation had taken a more pacific
turn, thought wrongly that the Cabinet of the 15th had been
concerned with Afghanistan. The *Daily Telegraph* argued for a
middle course in Egypt; there must be no withdrawal unless an
effective defence against the Mahdi was provided. On 18 April
Hamilton wrote asking the *Daily News* to prepare the way for a
change of policy, and on the 20th the paper argued that the
situation in Egypt was now so much improved that troops
could be withdrawn. On the 20th the *Daily Telegraph* also
believed that a decision to withdraw had been taken, and
approved it: it was a safeguard that Berber, on the Nile, could
be reached by the new railway being built from Suakin on the
Red Sea. Within the Cabinet, Hartington had made the
completion of this railway the condition of his acceptance of
withdrawal.[69] The coincidences both in January and April
between the views of Hartington and the *Daily Telegraph* are

[69] Ibid., 220.

noticeable. So is the lack of relevant comment from the *Standard*.

We can make a further study of the London press's grasp on events in the last eighteen months of Gladstone's fourth ministry. Stansky's *Ambitions and Strategies* gives a day-to-day account of Cabinet actions and decisions which can be compared with what was being printed in the London papers.[70]

In September 1892 the future of Uganda was in dispute. The East Africa Company wished to withdraw from the area which was proving unprofitable. The Church Missionary Society was anxious lest withdrawal be followed by the revival of the slave trade. Imperialists emphasized that if Britain left the area, others, in particular the Germans, would move in and a market which should ultimately become profitable would be lost for ever. These disagreements were also felt within the Cabinet, Rosebery being for retention, Gladstone and Harcourt being for withdrawal.

On 19 September 1892 Rosebery circulated a moderate memorandum to the Cabinet in favour of retention. The question was discussed in correspondence between ministers: there was no reference to this in the press. On 23 September Rosebery received a deputation from the CMS. This was the occasion for reference to the question in an article in the *Morning Post* on the same day from a correspondent, and again another article and a leader on 24 September, both making the case for retention, as did the *Scotsman*. Apart from that there was little press discussion on the subject. On 27 September it was generally announced that the Cabinet had been summoned for the 29th. The newspapers' habit of confidently announcing Cabinet agenda to the public had not changed since the 1880s: the *Standard* held that 'No doubt ... the essential character of the scheme for Home Rule is still to be determined.' The next day, the 28th, the *Morning Post* speculated that the Cabinet would be concerned with Home Rule, and the *Scotsman* also thought it would be on Home Rule, or perhaps on the Permissive Bill.[71] On the 29th, the day of the

[70] Oxford 1964. The following paragraphs are based on a reading of the *Standard*, the *Daily Chronicle*, the *Morning Post*, the *Daily News*, the *Daily Telegraph*, and the *Scotsman*.

[71] The Permissive Bill, allowing for local veto on the sale of intoxicating liquors, had been included as part of the Liberal party's Newcastle Programme in 1891.

Cabinet meeting, the *Daily Chronicle* believed, like the *Scotsman*, that a general discussion of the programme of the session was to take place. But the *Daily Telegraph* guessed, or had been told directly, that 'Uganda is believed to supply a chief reason for the meeting of the Cabinet today'; a leading article added that Rosebery 'would not scuttle though some of the Liberals might', and added that the *Daily Telegraph* would like a commissioner under the control of the Foreign Office to be sent to Uganda. This was Rosebery's own idea also. This detailed and accurate leading article showing knowledge of the discussion in the Cabinet is in strong contrast to the guesses of other papers, and suggests private information.

The next day (30 September) it was reported generally that the Cabinet would meet again: and the *Daily News* argued the case for evacuation of Uganda authoritatively: 'After the speeches of Mr. Gladstone and Sir William Harcourt and other Liberals . . . we cannot doubt that Government will take good care . . . not to . . . involve the nation in the Company's acts.' The second short meeting decided on a compromise—to support the East Africa Company in Uganda till March 1893. This decision was communicated to the East Africa Company in a letter of the same day, and this letter was generally published and discussed by the newspapers.

In this affair the London papers, in spite of their political editors and lobby correspondents, showed no knowledge of the importance of the question of Uganda within the Liberal Cabinet, and guessed wrongly what was afoot, except for two informed articles, one supporting Rosebery in the *Daily Telegraph*, answered from an anti-Imperialist side in the *Daily News* next day. Newspapers may have had better inner knowledge than that, but they certainly did not show it.

The sequence of events leading to Gladstone's retirement in 1894 offers another opportunity to test the newspapers' understanding of events. The Liberal Cabinet was dealing with two problems in the winter of 1893-4. One was the opposition of the House of Lords which had rejected the second Home Rule Bill and was mutilating the Employers' Liability and Local Government Bills. The other general problem concerned the Naval Estimates for 1894. Public agitation for increased naval construction had been heard on and off since W. T. Stead's

'Truth about the Navy' campaign. It had always been widely discussed and reported in the London papers, and the agitation revived again in December 1893. Both problems were therefore common knowledge: what was not known was the state of opinion of the Cabinet or the extent to which decisions had been reached.

On 14 December 1893 the Cabinet met and discussed the naval question, following a public meeting which had been held two days before. The Cabinet showed a division between the First Lord of the Admiralty, Lord Spencer, on one hand, and the Chancellor of the Exchequer, Sir William Harcourt, and even more Gladstone himself, on the other hand, both of whom resisted increased government spending. The *Standard* and the *Daily Chronicle* both correctly predicted that the Cabinet would discuss the naval question: the *Daily Chronicle* quoted an incorrect report from the Central News that the Cabinet would agree to the increased expenditure. The *Daily News* had printed a leading article on the 12th and an article on the 15th, both attempting to allay public anxiety: the Navy needed to be strengthened and government plans were in hand.

On the 19th there was a debate in the House of Commons on the question: on the same day the *Daily Chronicle* published an article by 'Our Special Representative' stating that Mr Gladstone's speech would be 'short, direct—and unanswerable' and proceeded to forecast, correctly, the line that he would take. Discussion of the debate on 20 December in the *Standard* and the *Daily Telegraph* included no reference to Cabinet disagreement.

The question continued: after Christmas the *Daily News* printed articles on 6 and 8 January 1894 from their correspondent at Plymouth on the measures to strengthen the Navy being currently taken by the Admiralty. The *Standard* correctly stated that Harcourt was converted to increased naval spending. On 9 January the *Daily News* continued to describe the government's existing programme: and a similar article was published by the *Daily Telegraph*. A Cabinet was held on the same day at which Harcourt agreed to accept the estimates put forward by the Admiralty, but Gladstone continued to oppose them and threatened resignation. On 10 January the *Daily Chronicle*, the *Daily News*, and the *Standard* made no comment.

The *Daily Telegraph*, however, reported that an agreement had been reached. It discovered and corrected its mistake in articles on the 11th and 12th which ended with a report that Gladstone and Harcourt were now arrayed against Spencer, the First Lord. The *Daily Telegraph* argued strongly both then, and later, for increased naval spending. In these reports the *Daily Telegraph* had got half the story, but not the significant half, which was that Gladstone was not leading a party within the Cabinet but was an isolated figure determined to force agreement on his colleagues.

The deadlock in the Cabinet was eased when Gladstone left on 13 January for four weeks' holiday in Biarritz. The subject faded from the press until on 31 January the *Pall Mall Gazette* published 'an outrageous canard' that Gladstone had resigned, which elicited a telegram of denial from Biarritz.

Gladstone returned on 10 February. *The Times*, welcoming him back, hoped that he would control his followers and decide whether or not to dissolve parliament and fight an election on the issue of the House of Lords.[72] Among other points being made was that the Employers' Liability Bill had been badly mangled in the House of Lords. The Cabinet was held on 12 February: comment the following day focused on rumours of dissolution, which were then denied; 'The Central News has received Ministerial . . . authority to state . . . that the Cabinet was unanimously agreed . . . and there is absolutely not the shadow of a crisis.' Comment in a leading article in the *Daily Telegraph* shows the machinery at work: 'If it were possible . . . to boil down the incoherent phrases in which Sir Algernon West through no fault of his own . . . embodied the Prime Minister's ideas we should get as a result simply this "Nothing is changed—only my eyes are a bit weaker".' What the newspapers did not know in all this discussion of the affairs of the House of Lords was that Gladstone had put forward a plan of dissolution from Biarritz, and that it had been already rejected by the rest of the Cabinet.[73]

For the next few days the situation within the Cabinet remained at loggerheads. Among the newspapers there was

[72] *The Times*, 12 Feb. 1894.
[73] A. G. Gardiner, *The Life of Sir William Harcourt*, 2 vols., 1923, II, 256. West, a former secretary, was with Gladstone in Biarritz.

plenty of comment and little information. The exception was the London Letter of the *Scotsman* on 19 February—'There are rumours that the Admiralty programme has after all, not been settled, . . . and that, after all, the crisis at the Admiralty is still to deal with. I do not know whether this statement is accurate, but it comes to me with much better authority than the mere gossip of the lobby.' The writer of this London Letter returned to the same point on 22 February saying that rumours of a serious division within the Cabinet had not died down and that the Admiralty programme might be one of the bones of contention. (This seems like leaked information: Charles Cooper, the editor of the *Scotsman*, had good political contacts and the London Letter could have been his own work.)

At the Cabinet of 23 February Gladstone talked of ending his co-operation with the rest of the Cabinet and the same day made his first approach to the Queen, asking through her secretary, Ponsonby, if he could write to her in confidence.[74] The general tone of press comment was that the question of the House of Lords was still predominant. After the weekend, on Monday 26th, a leading article in the *Daily Telegraph* held that 'We are comparatively speaking in smooth waters.' Gladstone, they thought, was extremely well, apart from his eyes: 'There is no prospect at present of committing the duty of leadership to other hands'.

On the following day, the 27th, rumours of his resignation were current and were fully discussed in the *Standard*, the *Daily Chronicle*, the *Pall Mall Gazette*, and *The Times*. These were followed on the 28th by a statement from the Press Association denying any intention of resignation—'His position is still accurately reflected by Algernon West's telegram from Biarritz'.[75] The same evening Gladstone was seen going to see the Queen, and even on the following day, when Mr Gladstone did in fact resign, the *Daily News* and the *Daily Chronicle* were still publishing disclaimers.

This dry narrative of events shows how difficult it was for the newspapers to find out what was going on, unless information was being leaked to them. They were trying to find out what was going on within a small circle, and the Cabinet of 1892–4

[74] Stansky, 75.
[75] *Daily Telegraph*, 28 Feb. 1894.

has had the reputation of keeping its secrets exceptionally well, unlike that of 1880–1885. Whether on Uganda or on the possibility of a fight with the House of Lords the papers guessed wrong. The development of political editors and lobby correspondents had not made them any better able to find out without inside information voluntarily given. The sort of information which they could find out was the relative popularity of Rosebery and Harcourt, among back-benchers, as successors to Gladstone. In dealing with that sort of question, the lobby correspondents' system worked adequately. In this intrinsically difficult area of Cabinet decision and discussion it seems doubtful whether they were any more successful than Delane had been in the middle years of the century.

In general the newspapers remained co-operative and deferential in their relations with political leaders. In the autumn of 1892 and the winter of 1893–4 they published a number of disclaimers and explanations which appear to be inspired— denials that Gladstone was resigning, denials that there was a crisis, or accounts showing that all was activity and development in the dockyards. These appeared in the Liberal *Daily Chronicle* and *Daily News*. There seems to be no significant change since the 1870s.

The fact that newspapers were receiving these communications was certainly well known throughout the period. In February 1874 when the Conservative news agency, the Central Press, began publishing the *Sun*, the *Printer's Register*, a trade paper circulating not among politicians but among printers, commented: 'No paper has been more quoted of late because of the "communications" it receives from Conservative friends in high positions.' Politicians were adept at guessing where inspired paragraphs had come from. Morley wrote to Chamberlain in November 1873, when neither was yet in the corridors of power, 'Did you see a strong article in the Telegraph on Monday or Tuesday? That looks as if the government was going to turn.'[76] Later, Salisbury's association with Austin was well known. In the Gladstone–Granville correspondence the attributing of opinions to politicians from

[76] Chamberlain MSS, JC 5/54/29.

newspaper articles, or of articles to the influence of individuals, occurs again and again.[77]

Nevertheless, the forms of secrecy were preserved with some care: letters from Balfour or Hamilton were marked 'Private and confidential'. It was often emphasized that the political hints being given must be on a non-attributable basis: Gladstone, for example, writing to Stead, said 'I drop these remarks, on which it may be better not to quote me as my name is rather often before the public.'[78] Hamilton, asking Hill to prepare the way for a withdrawal from the Sudan, added, 'Any such article would have to be written with special care; and, as I have said, it must bear no traces of anything like inspiration; otherwise it would fail in its object.'[79]

Sometimes there might be sound tactical reasons for secrecy; Gladstone might, in both of these examples, have been planning to appeal to the judgement of public opinion in advocating policy. But the urge for secrecy seems to have gone deeper than that. Austin, for example, never makes it clear in his autobiography that he was a paid intermediary between Lord Salisbury and his newspaper. He presents the relationship, rather, as one of two persons deeply concerned with foreign affairs. Wheeling and dealing in newspaper offices appeared as a disreputable course of action. The conflict between the need and taste for publicity and the desire for secrecy is seen at its clearest in Gladstone and his closest associates. He saw Hunt nearly a hundred times between 1864 and 1868, yet in those same years there are only thirteen letters from Hunt preserved among Gladstone's papers. It seems that most of such correspondence must have been weeded out; the long series of meetings would not have been possible without some kinds of arrangement being made by letter.

The Gladstone–Granville correspondence also shows a consistent distaste for contact with the press. For example on 29 February 1872 Gladstone wrote 'I got a query from L[evy] after seeing you this afternoon . . . He is a sharp fellow but I do not expect to see him sensibly ahead of his contemporaries tomorrow, though he beats some of them and especially Delane

---

[77] Ramm, I, 64, 66 (Dec. 1877 and Jan. 1878).
[78] Gladstone MSS, BL Add. MS 44303, 30 Sept. 1876.
[79] Hamilton MSS, BL Add. 48619, f. 108.

in continually hanging about the Houses of Parliament & among us at least picking the brains of the likeliest people.' One would not recognize here the Levy who was being described about this time as 'ever loyal and true'.[80] About six months after the formation of Gladstone's second administration, Granville lamented that he could not handle the press. Gladstone replied 'If you are a bad manager I certainly am worse ... No doubt under the late government there was a continuous action—my very imperfect practice has been to express a readiness to ask and I find they do not ask.'[81] This takes no account of the letters going out from 10 Downing Street signed by Hamilton.

The reasons for this defensive, hole-and-corner atmosphere lie partly in the nature of the business being done: British governments in the last twenty years have shown a similar sensitivity. They are also related to the particular circumstances of the time. The 1860s to the 1880s was a period of reform, of seeking out and removing improper influences—whether they were corruption in the boroughs or favouritism in the Civil Service. In place of these influences there should be, it was thought, the body of the electorate, willing the common good as it cast its vote, and informed by a fearless press which found out and proclaimed the truth. The gap between this fantasy and the way in which things could actually be made to work from day to day provides the background to the government's handling of the press at this time.

On one side was the London press, constantly asking for information, and skilful in finding likely alternative informants. Hill, for example, asking for sight of a parliamentary paper in advance added, 'I fear that the interest of some other newspapers with certain foreign Embassies may put them at an advantage as compared with us, and by implication the Liberal government'.[82] On the other side were the needs of the government, which must be allowed some discretion in what it publishes and what it conceals. It has to prepare the public for changes in policy, the reasons for which it may have to gloss over. The midnight hints to editors were often sent in the hope

---

[80] See p. 174 above. The phrase dates from Jan. 1875.
[81] Ramm, 213–4.
[82] Hamilton MSS, BL Add. MS 48619, letter of 3 August 1884.

that suitable editorials might influence the vote in critical debates. In general the ways in which information could be disseminated were more limited than a critic, viewing the situation from outside, might expect. The amount of parliamentary questioning grew very fast during this period,[83] but it is not clear how much use there was of the prearranged question to enable a minister to make a statement. Political speeches could give an excellent opportunity to make some point, but the occasion might not arise at the right time. A letter of Gladstone's on the subject of the Queen's unpopularity, which at first sight seems merely comic, shows how awkward a tool the political speech could be:

About that republican business, I have sometimes thought whether, though I should not like to make a political splash of it, I could have a sort of talk to neighbours at Hawarden in the village schoolroom which might be reported. I should like to please the Queen in the matter, if I could do it without injuring her.[84]

The need for organized arrangements for government information is clear to a late twentieth-century eye. It was seen occasionally, but not at all generally, then. To a modern observer it would seem that the best way of keeping the press friendly would be to keep it informed, and that it would be better to inform all editors than one political crony. The first signs of this view of things appear at this time though in a small and patchy way.

From the mid-1880s we can begin to see a significant number of occasions when the people with news to give offered it to the Press Association or to newspaper correspondents in general. In Wolseley's dealings with correspondents general acclaim and not party advantage was the objective, and his favours were distributed to correspondents at large. This can be shown in a particular episode on the way to Khartoum. On 1 January 1885 a messenger slipped into his camp at Korti with a piece of paper saying 'Khartoum all right. 14.12.84. C. G. Gordon'. It was the size of a postage stamp, to be swallowed in case of

---

[83] A count of the number of questions asked in a week of ordinary business in the House of Commons yields the following result: May 11–15 1874 a total of 44 questions; May 12–16 1884, 111; May 21–25 1894, (a week later on account of Whitsun), 130 (*Hansard*).

[84] Ramm, op. cit., Camden 3 series v. lxxxi, 291, 22 Dec. 1871.

capture. Next day the *Standard*'s correspondent reported at some length that he had been privileged to see this dramatic document. So did the correspondents of the *Daily News* and the *Daily Telegraph*: they had all been favoured equally.[85] A similar tendency lies behind an angry letter from Macdonald, manager of *The Times*, to Moberly Bell, their correspondent in Cairo: He was

not surprised and not sorry that Baring[86] has at last kicked at the persecution to which he must have been subjected by 'The Specials'. But that he should make the News Agencies alone the recipients of his confidences may in the long run prove an unwise proceeding both for himself and the govt. he serves. Obviously it releases us from any sense of favour ... and justifies us in treating the whole Egyptian question in a more independent and scrutinizing spirit than ever.

He added that agencies could not have the influence possessed by *The Times*.[87]

There are signs that at home the Liberals were beginning to adopt a policy of even-handedness. One comes in a letter from Spencer, at the time Irish Lord Lieutenant of Ireland, to his relation Horace Seymour, who was one of Gladstone's secretaries, and employed as an intermediary with the press from time to time: 'Could you, as you see the Central News people, check them in their repeated intelligence about the movements of informers and witnesses?'[88] If the Central News was regularly briefed, someone presumably 'saw' the Press Association also.

Gladstone also began to adopt a similar policy. The history of the Press Association describes how a certain reporter, Walter Hepburn, was preferred by him: he travelled in the special train, and Gladstone would not speak until he was settled in his place.[89] This story is corroborated by a letter from Herbert Gladstone to Lord Richard Grosvenor, the Liberal Whip, dealing with the final arrangement for Gladstone's journey to Edinburgh in November 1885,

---

[85] For Wolseley and the press see chapter VII.

[86] Baring was Consul-General in Egypt.

[87] *The Times* archives; letter dated 19 Nov. 1884.

[88] Peter Gordon, *The Red Earl: the Papers of the Fifth Earl Spencer, 1835–1910*, I, 1981, 250, letter dated 3 Aug. 1883.

[89] George Scott, *Reporter Anonymous: the Story of the Press Association*, 1968, 77.

At Lord Rosebery's request I have arranged for a compartment next
our saloon to be reserved for Reporters, and I would see that one of
them is admitted into our carriage to take down anything that is said.
Would the Press Association like to supply the man or who? He would
have to give his copy to other reporters so that each speech might be
published locally promptly.[90]

It is easy to see how Gladstone, during an election campaign,
preferred to speak to the Press Association, who would distribute his words to the northern towns where he knew his
strength lay.

We also have an account by John Boon of Gladstone's
announcement of the formation of his third ministry in February 1886. 'The Press were invited to attend ... When I say
"the Press" I mean the representatives of the news agencies
and two or three of the great London papers.'[91] They received
the list of the new Cabinet. This occasion, if it is the first such
press conference, represents a minor landmark in constitutional history.

It also seems that the habit of sending minor news items to
the Press Association was increasing. A few samples illustrate
this point. On 3 May 1892, in the last months of Salisbury's
administration, the Press Association was officially informed
that the Board of Trade had received many objections to canal
dues proposed by the companies; on 5 May they were authorized to deny a rumour that Sir J. Fergusson was to become
chairman of the Board of Inland Revenue; on the 11th Ulster
unionists denied through the Press Association that Ulster was
arming against Home Rule. In 1894, under Gladstone's last
administration, the Press Association on 4 May reported that
West End dressmakers and milliners were organizing strong
opposition to Asquith's proposed regulation of the industry,
and denied a rumour that the Speaker was about to retire. On
9 May they understood that the Cabinet of 8 May was held to
clear up outstanding business before the recess. On 12 June
they were officially informed by the Foreign Office that the
Sultan of Morocco had died, and were asked to clear up a
misunderstanding about Anglo-French discussions about the

[90] Gladstone MSS, BL Add. MS 44317, f. 94.
[91] John Boon, *Victorians, Edwardians, and Georgians*, 2 vols., 1927, I, 61.

Congo.[92] These news items may seem humdrum and uninteresting, but twenty years earlier even such minor events were counters in a political game: for instance in September 1868 the editor of *John Bull* thought it worth while to ask Disraeli for exclusive news of the identity of the new Bishop of Peterborough.[93] By the 1890s such a request would surely have seemed odd.[94]

A process of regularizing and organizing the distribution of official news was going on imperceptibly, but even so the extent of change seemed slight. Simonis, writing in 1917, emphasized the difference between Britain and the United States: 'The American politician courts the newspapers. Even the President meets the journalists in conference regularly twice a week, and allows himself to be cross-examined freely, with the result that his views are clearly expressed in the newspapers ... Can you imagine Downing Street doing such a thing?'[95]

[92] These items are taken from the *Glasgow Herald*, which was more meticulous than some papers in stating the source of its news.

[93] Disraeli MSS, box 88.

[94] Nevertheless Koss quotes an example of the traditional way of handling the press from the First World War when the *Daily News* lobby correspondent was excluded from ministerial briefings because of the paper's attacks on Lloyd George (II, *The Twentieth Century*, 1984, 243).

[95] H. Simonis, *Street of Ink*, 1917, 321.

X

Foreign News

THE collection and assessment of foreign news presented far greater difficulties, and the London papers, following in the tradition laid down by *The Times* in the middle of the century, put great stress on their ability to cover the general course of diplomatic activity and the general state of British overseas interests wherever and whatever that might be.

Foreign correspondents seem to have been a species which evolved separately from the kinds of journalist who have appeared in previous chapters. British journalists changed their jobs frequently, and entered the profession from school:[1] an able man might rise from being a provincial reporter to the editorship of a great daily. The foreign correspondent was likely to remain in the same place for many years, if not for life. He was more likely to switch the paper he worked for than to switch the place where he worked: George Saunders in Berlin, initially working for the *Pall Mall Gazette* and working up, via the *Morning Post*, to *The Times*, and William Lavino, in Vienna, first for the *Daily Telegraph* and then for *The Times*, are examples. They needed specialized skills and influential contacts; such people were not easy to find, and not willingly dispensed with. They came with their contacts already made and were usually older than their counterparts at home: Blowitz was forty-five when he joined *The Times* and Donald Mackenzie Wallace thirty-seven. It must be emphasized that the number of well-recorded lives of foreign correspondents is very small, particularly outside the staff of *The Times*. They were a very mixed collection. Sometimes they were merchants resident abroad, like Edwin Pears of the *Daily News* in Constantinople, or Moberly Bell of *The Times* in Alexandria.[2] Sometimes the choice seems eccentric: Mrs Lynn Linton in Paris is an example.[3] Another is Pierce Connolly, the anti-

---

[1] See chapter IV.

[2] *DNB*.

[3] See p. 77 above.

Catholic propagandist, who was the *Daily Telegraph*'s correspondent in Florence for a time in the 1850s. He had studied for
the priesthood in Rome, and thus knew the language.[4] By the
end of the century such people were less likely to be found:
more were professional journalists, or, like Valentine Chirol,
recruits from the diplomatic service. What they could all offer
was the ability to cope with a particular locality. At a time
when it was unusual for educated middle-class Londoners to
have travelled far afield, the foreign correspondent had an
expertise which his superior at home could not share. It would
not be very easy for the office in London to assess what
influences were being exerted over him.

Alternatively, as will appear later in this chapter, the foreign
correspondent was a foreign national. The course of nineteenth-century nationalism threw up *émigrés* from a number of
countries—Poles, Italians, Hungarians, and others—who had
a command of languages and who could be expected to be
articulate and politically informed. Among them one may
include Karl Marx, a correspondent of the *New York Tribune*
after 1849.[5] The employment of such people was common in
the 1850s and 1860s: later, as they retired from active work,
their place was taken by British nationals. The fact that
foreigners were employed on a general scale demonstrates the
lack of competent Britons. The former could prove difficult to
handle: one example is the Hungarian Ferdinand Eber, *The
Times* correspondent in Vienna to 1885. In November 1883,
when he was near to retirement, he received a comprehensive
rebuke from Macdonald; there were

... repeated complaints from Chenery about the suppression of all
interesting News in your correspondence ... Chenery's notion is that
as a patriotic Hungarian you ignore Croat, Bosnian and in general all
South Slavic aspirations ... and that the other Papers are full of
incidents and movements of political opinion which are passed over
in perfect silence by us. He tells me that at the Foreign Office great
surprise is expressed that we appear to know so little of what is going
on ...[6]

In choosing correspondents at the end of the century, *The*

---

[4] My thanks are due to Dr Denis Paz for this information.
[5] Isaiah Berlin, *Karl Marx*, Oxford, 1939, 184.
[6] *The Times* archives, letter dated 13 Nov. 1883.

Times regarded good contacts within the diplomatic service as an important qualification. This feeling was shown clearly in a letter to Wallace as correspondent in Constantinople: 'The other day Mr Walter had a letter from Lord Dufferin written in the most complimentary terms about you, and had your position here needed backing up of any sort, nothing could be more effective than the manner in which his Excellency expressed himself.'[7]

The tone of this letter suggests, not only the value of a good source of information, but also the importance of correspondents who echoed the ideas of the British government. With the same general objective *The Times* eagerly exploited the good relations of Donald Mackenzie Wallace with Lord Dufferin. Dufferin was sent by the British Government to Egypt in November 1882 to advise on the reconstruction of the Egyptian administration. He took his friend Wallace with him; and Moberly Bell, *The Times* correspondent in Cairo, was told that Wallace was there on holiday, though he was in fact there as special correspondent, to keep the paper posted with confidential information about Dufferin's proposals.[8] (A similar association of politician and journalist has been described for the years leading up to the Boer War, between the South African High Commissioner, Alfred Milner, and Edmund Garrett, then editor of the *Cape Times*.)[9] The same deferential attitude was shown in another letter, this time to *The Times* correspondent in Madrid:

When Mr. Arthur Walter was at Madrid in the Autumn our Ambassador appears to have left upon him the impression that you were adverse to his policy and too disposed to favour that of the Spanish government in its relations with our own. I cannot say that your correspondence has lent the slightest colour to this impression and I would not have referred to it, except to put you on your guard and to point out to you the importance of cultivating good [later amended to 'fairly good'] relations with the official representative of England in Spain.[10]

[7] Ibid., letter, also from Macdonald, dated 29 Mar. 1882. Lord Dufferin was at that time ambassador in Constantinople.

[8] *The Times* archives, letters from Macdonald dated 3 Nov. 1882, 19 Jan. and 8 Mar. 1883.

[9] A. N. Porter, 'Sir Alfred Milner and the Press, 1897–1899' in *Historical Journal*, XVI, 2 (1973), 323–39.

[10] Letter dated 7 Mar. 1883.

It is interesting to compare this with a letter from North-cliffe thirty years later, after his takeover of *The Times*:

This involves the question whether or not Maxwell should go to India. We do not want any bowing down to Officials there. I have a natural horror of that sort of Journalism and suffer a great deal from it at Printing-house-square, where I am trying to break it down.

My views on this matter are those of Delane: that a Newspaper is meant to publish news, and not to please highly placed people.[11]

These tendencies, to make use of foreigners, but to prefer correspondents with the outlook of the diplomatic service, were not peculiar to *The Times*. It arose in part from the conditions in which they worked. The resident foreign correspondent in a foreign capital had not been educated within the same political culture as the people he was reporting on. He was less able to judge what was normal, who was likely to know what, which newspapers were officially inspired and by whom, and how far the conventions of what was legitimate differed from those he had known at home. He was inevitably working in greater isolation than he would have been in Fleet Street. He was likely to gravitate towards the society of other expatriates. The number of foreign correspondents in any place was small: a photograph of a farewell presentation to Blowitz in Paris in 1902 by the foreign press corps shows about thirty-six people.[12]

Otherwise the most obvious place for advice and support was the British Embassy. The successful correspondent needed some of the qualities of the courtier; Alfred Austin described how the correspondent of the *Standard* in Rome, Thomas Adolphus Trollope (the eldest brother of the novelist), 'had free access to the British Embassy ... every day while I stayed, I either played lawn tennis at the Embassy or rode with Sir Augustus [Paget, the Ambassador] his wife, and daughter, in the Campagna'. When Austin was sent on a fact-finding expedition in 1880–1, he was invited to dinner at the Embassy in Constantinople and by the Minister in Bucharest. All along he relied on British official sources for information.[13]

---

[11] Northcliffe MSS, BL Add. MS 62198, Northcliffe to Marlowe 10 February 1911.

[12] Frank Giles, *A Prince of Journalists*, 1962, reproduces the photograph, 192.

[13] *Autobiography*, II, 135, 149. His host in Constantinople was G. J. Goschen, on a special mission to the Sultan.

George Saunders, who became *The Times* Berlin correspondent in 1896, showed the same tendencies. His letters home are full of descriptions of the miseries of life in Berlin and of his links with the Embassy, where he could find congenial companions who would go curling on the ice with him. In January 1896 he wrote home, 'They have been greatly pleased at the Embassy with my first fortnight's work. ... One can't have everything. I can't go about *dining* as The Times correspondent. I have to *work* first of all.'[14]

The other side of the picture is represented by the criticisms made by Wilfrid Scawen Blunt in his *Secret History of the English Occupation of Egypt*. He criticized the

> sort of manipulation of the organs of public news in the interests of our diplomacy [which] exists in nearly all the capitals where our agents reside and is a potent instrument for misleading the home public. The influence is not as a rule exercised by any direct payment, but by favour given in regard to secret and valuable information, and also largely by social amenities. In Egypt it has always within my knowledge been supreme, except at moments of extreme crisis when the body of special Press correspondents at Cairo or Alexandria has been too numerous to be kept under official control. In ordinary times our officials have had complete authority both as to what news should be sent to London, and what news, received from London, should be published in Egypt.[15]

If a newspaper wished its foreign correspondents to reflect the views of British diplomatists abroad, as *The Times* apparently did, well and good: it might be better than that they should be the mouthpieces of someone else. But for all these reasons the problems raised by an item of foreign news would be greater than those raised by a domestic item. So would the difficulties of assessment in the office.

A foreign correspondent might well run into other difficulties. In some countries, notably Russia, there was an effective censorship on outgoing telegrams. There was the difficulty of having to discover whether he was collecting true information or was unconsciously helping another government to 'fly a kite'. Austin complained of this:

---

[14] Saunders MSS, Churchill College, Cambridge, GS 1/106, letter dated 23 Jan.
[15] 2nd edn. 1907, 176.

... the position of a newspaper correspondent in a foreign capital especially at critical international moments, is in the nature of things not easy and sometimes far from pleasant. His object is, of course, to make as much use of Ministers and Ambassadors there as possible: and their object is to do the same by him.

It is open to them to give him true information, or information scarcely true, so that he may disseminate, and thereby produce the effect they desire. Personal and political regard for truth are two distinct things in their minds.[16]

He particularly blamed Bismarck for misleading journalists. It could be replied that misleading half-truths might come, just as easily, from British politicians to British journalists. Nevertheless, it was probably easier to detect in politics at home, and it might be offered less frequently. Whereas party intrigue in domestic politics might be settled face to face within clubs, and at the dinner table, international negotiations might employ articles and counter-articles in the press.

The great bulk of the foreign news came not from independent investigation, but from sources in the capital city—or the city where the resident correspondent was stationed. For example, a proposal to cover a number of provincial elections in the French general election in 1877 was criticized by Macdonald, the manager of *The Times*, as interesting but difficult on the grounds that the correspondent would not be able to select a representative sample of elections for study.[17] The resident correspondent read the press of the country concerned, saw politicians, and the core of his reports was derived from material of this kind. George Saunders described his day in 1896 as follows: he spent the morning reading nine or ten of the morning papers and visited political people, he then spent the afternoon off, and returned to the office at 5.00 where he read German newspapers from 5.00 to 7.00 p.m. From then to about 10.00 or 10.30 p.m. he would prepare his despatch to London: it had to be 'on the wire' by 11 o'clock. He had an assistant in Berlin, but he would not have had the opportunity to travel round and find things out for himself.[18] There was, similarly, a staff of two in Paris and Vienna.

In *The Times* and the *Standard* the bulk of the correspondence

[16] *Autobiography*, II, 115.
[17] *The Times* archives, Sept. 1877.
[18] Saunders MSS, GS 1/106, 23 Jan. 1896.

from European capitals would be concerned with international affairs and national politics. But as one descended to the lighter papers such as the *Daily Telegraph*, or some of the evening papers, the proportion of reporting on these serious subjects would diminish, and its place be taken by international social gossip. This is particularly true of the news from Paris and Florence, two cities with which the Victorian tourist was familiar. Many papers filled their columns with news of fashions, of local events, of gossip about prominent personalities, and about what was being currently talked about in those places. Readers were not given similar news of the cafés and sidewalks of Berlin, Vienna, and Constantinople. The news from these places was strictly diplomatic. Thus, even in places in Western Europe where there was freedom and safety of movement, the foreign correspondent confined himself in general to international affairs and miscellaneous comment: he did not investigate things for himself very much.

The war correspondent, covering a war to which Great Britain was not a party, had other problems. The idea of an accredited war correspondent, who travelled with the army and reported to his paper, was generally accepted by governments from the time of the Crimea. There was not, however, agreement on what he could expect to be told, or where he could go. In particular, the French government was consistently unwilling to give war correspondents much scope. Unlike the resident correspondent, the war correspondent would need to move about in areas where normal traffic was restricted: he would need papers which would establish his status and protect him, and he would greatly benefit from access to the telegraph system. All these things made him particularly dependent on the goodwill of the country whose armies he was attached to.

Unlike the foreign correspondent, the war correspondent moved from country to country and army to army, and would have had no opportunity to develop special relations with particular politicians. The war correspondents were a small group of specialists, with special qualities—courage and enterprise, an understanding of military matters, and, not least important, the ability to ride a horse. They had often a tendency towards self-dramatization. The regular band who

reappeared in one campaign after another—Archibald Forbes, G. A. Henty, Bennet Burleigh, 'Billy' Russell—were not drawn from any particular walk of life.

The phrase 'special correspondent' had no very precise meaning, nor had the phrases 'occasional correspondent' and 'special commissioner'. These titles were used at different times by different papers or journalists to describe someone who was working on a particular assignment: some examples are Sala's tour of the United States after the Civil War, or Archibald Forbes's investigations in 1874 of a famine in Bengal, (or, most interestingly, a long series, by an unidentified author, of the state of individual constituencies in the General Election of 1880).[19] Such investigations would normally be presented in a series of letters in successive issues of the paper. Whatever problems the special correspondent might encounter would be specific to each particular assignment.

In these conditions it is not surprising that newspapers should have entered into special relationships with various foreign powers and interests. The foreign interest wanted British publicity; the British paper needed access to information. The bare fact that this was so was widely known in the middle of the nineteenth century, and Edward Stanley recorded a conversation with the Prince Consort in 1861 when he said, of the Conservatives, 'The country is governed by newspapers, and you have not a newspaper.' The Prince then went on to say that 'the whole English press, except the *Times*, was influenced by foreign governments: (which is true of some journals: the *Chronicle* being in French hands, the *Daily News* acting as the agent of Sardinia): the Queen broke in, saying the *Times* was as corrupt as the rest.'[20] To this list could be added the *Standard*, said to be working in the service of Napoleon III, and the *Morning Post*, in some relationship with the Turks. The links did not necessarily mean that money was passing; merely that there was a recognizable association: they existed in the middle of the century and did not all survive. What they meant in practice is best considered in relation to a number of specific

[19] Sala's tour and the election studies (by 'One of the Crowd') appeared in the *Daily Telegraph*; Forbes's investigations in the *Daily News*.

[20] J. Vincent, ed., *Disraeli, Derby and the Conservative Party. Journals and Memoirs of Edward Henry, Lord Stanley, 1849–1869*, Hassocks, 1978, 165.

cases. These examples are taken from a variety of times, places, and situations: and are mostly concerned with fairly short episodes. It is a difficult area in which to find definite evidence, and these are examples where it is possible to draw on reasonably solid information, rather than examples of great intrinsic historic importance.

1. The Daily News and the Sardinian Government

Prince Albert believed that the *Daily News* acted as the agent of Sardinia, and there is some evidence to support his belief. It is possible that the connection came through Charles Wentworth Dilke (the grandfather of the late-Victorian politician), who was a friend of Keats and a lover of Italy, and who sent his son to finish his education in Florence in the house of the British Consul. Dilke acted as manager of the *Daily News* between 1846 and 1849.[21] In any case the character of the *Daily News* as a Liberal–Radical organ, and the presence of Italian refugees in London, made the association a natural one. At some time in the 1840s he made the acquaintance of Antonio Gallenga, a political refugee who, according to his own autobiography, was 'struggling to make his country known in England'.[22] In 1854 Gallenga, though resident in England and in fact nominally Professor of Italian at University College, London, was elected a deputy in the Sardinian parliament for the district of Cavour at the instigation of the politician Cavour. At the same time, the correspondent of the *Daily News* in Turin was Ruffini, a politician and friend to Gallenga. Gallenga then replaced him as correspondent. The former was probably Giovanni Ruffini, a writer and politician, (the author, among other things, of the libretto of *Don Pasquale*), who had been in Britain since 1833, and a deputy in the Sardinian parliament after 1848. He had then become ambassador in Paris in 1849. Thus the new and struggling *Daily News* had as its Turin correspondents not British residents, nor yet professional journalists, but two Italian politicians in succession, each of whom can be seen to have had close links with the Sardinian government. Gallenga made himself unpopular in Turin and returned to

---

[21] *DNB.*
[22] Antonio Gallenga, *Episodes of my Second life*, 2 vols., 1884, II, 107.

London in 1857 to write, on and off, for the *Daily News*.[23]

On 29 April 1859 Austria invaded, or was provoked into invading, Piedmont: on 3 May the French declared war on Austria in their support. The London papers were anxious to despatch correspondents to this, the first European war since the Crimea. Gallenga, having paid a quick visit to Turin, called at the *Daily News* office to offer his services, but found that he was too late, another Italian, Carlo Arrivabene, having started that day by the seven o'clock mail. Gallenga then went on to *The Times* office. There he was accepted as correspondent, but he was told by Mowbray Morris, the manager, that he had learned from Turin that no '"press-gang" will be allowed at the front', to which Gallenga replied, 'Let that be no hindrance. That rule will only apply to civilians and aliens. But I can don a uniform and go as a combatant. Cavour is my friend; I was till lately a deputy. Surely exception will be made in favour of me—an old patriot' to which Mowbray Morris replied 'That is what we thought'.[24]

It did not work out like this. The ban on correspondents at the front had been initiated by Napoleon III. Gallenga did not get near to the action in Lombardy. He went on to Florence and attached himself to the army of the Prince Napoleon. He wrote to *The Times* from there, but nothing was happening in that area. Examination of the press reports of the campaign and of the battle of Magenta show that the London papers merely received copies of official communiqués from their correspondents in Turin. Significantly, these included the *Standard* and the *Morning Post*, both of which were strongly suspected of being linked with the French. There was, however, one exception; at the last minute Napoleon III decided to allow Hungarian correspondents to move forward with his armies: and the correspondent of *The Times*, Eber, benefited by the concession.[25]

To all this the *Daily News* was a conspicuous exception. Arrivabene, like Gallenga, was an Italian exile in London, and had deputized as Professor of Italian while Gallenga was sitting in the Sardinian parliament. He too was known to

[23] Ibid., 279.
[24] Ibid., 291–3.
[25] Ibid., 303.

Cavour, and possibly had been entrusted with a specific mission to England. In a letter, which seems on internal evidence to have been written immediately before the campaign, Cavour had written to him

I have received the two articles of the *Daily News* you have kindly sent me, and I have no doubt they have produced a good effect, and that they must have convinced our adversaries of the patience shown by Piedmont.

Now that, in spite of everything, this war is approaching, I must beg you to do all that is in your power to persuade our friends in England of the necessity of hostilities: so that, if we cannot secure the material support of the great English nation, we should *at any price avoid its enmity*.[26]

Arrivabene, unlike the other correspondents, saw the field of battle at Magenta. 'In possession of the magic *permis* which Count Cavour had kindly obtained for me ... I had authority to follow either of the two allied armies, and to go to and from the headquarters of the one to those of the other, to pick up news for the benefit of English readers.'[27] The advantage enjoyed by the *Daily News* is visible in the press reports of the battle of Magenta. The battle was fought on Saturday 4 June: on Monday the 6th the *Daily News* reported a decisive victory; *The Times* was not sure and remained unsure till 9 June. As far as the *Daily News* was concerned, an isolated advantage like this might not do much for the circulation, though had the war continued, as was generally expected, a consistent superiority in information would have been an advantage (and even on a single occasion a special edition, on a subject of great popular interest, could sell in immense numbers). It would be hard to make any estimate of the benefit to the Sardinians. It so happened that the reports of the battle of Magenta arrived on the same day as the celebrated meeting in Willis's rooms at which the various sections of the Liberals agreed to unite and try to bring down the Derby administration, which, it was feared, might intervene in the war on the Austrian side. In the ensuing debate, in which Derby was defeated, the crisis in foreign affairs was the main subject of discussion. Possibly the *Daily News* had an influence on Liberal members. It was

[26] Charles Arrivabene, *Italy under Victor Emmanuel*, 2 vols., 1862, I, 12.
[27] Ibid., 118.

certainly a good example of well-timed press support, and an example of the advantage which could be enjoyed by a favoured newspaper. A movement like the campaign for Italian unification was the sort of thing which stood to gain a great deal from favourable press comment and the general benevolence of uninvolved nations, since the case rested, not on points of legality, but on general acceptance of an emotional or moral idea.

The subsequent sudden armistice, after the victories of Magenta and Solferino, provides an opportunity of assessing the kind of support being given to Napoleon III by the *Standard* and the *Morning Post*. The armistice was a bolt from the blue. On 8 July the papers were discussing the next stage in the campaign. On the 9th the armistice was reported: both immediately turned to praise of Napoleon III's military genius, in extravagant terms. The *Standard* thought him a '*veritable soldat de Dieu*'; the *Morning Post* said 'The greatness of the Monarch has overcome the just pride and ambition of the soldier.' Their defence of the French change of direction was immediate and automatic. The *Morning Post*'s knowledge of the change was received exceptionally, and perhaps unnaturally, early: the armistice was announced in the French *Moniteur Officiel* in Paris in a notice timed at 9.45 p.m. The *Morning Post* printed this announcement together with a leading article of its own composition in the following morning's edition.

The subsequent adventures of British correspondents in the Italian war are not so well recorded: a number, including Arrivabene, were in Sicily with Garibaldi in 1860. In 1866 a most unlikely group of correspondents, H. M. Hyndman (*Pall Mall Gazette*), G. A. Sala (*Daily Telegraph*), George Meredith, the novelist (*Morning Post*), G. A. Henty, the novelist (*Standard*) and Bullock-Hall and Spicer (both from the *Daily News*) went out. We find them, somewhere in the Tyrol, with Garibaldi's army, in a scene which belongs to the world of operetta: 'Where we stood the [Italian] rank and file were obviously wavering. This was too much for Bullock-Hall. He rushed forward, caught a horse belonging to one of the officers who had fallen, mounted it and, revolver in hand, led a charge himself.' It was pointed out to him that the enemy would be justified in shooting him out of hand, because as a non-

combatant he was taking part in the action.[28] The ban on correspondents at the front had been imposed by Napoleon III: once he had retired from the Italian campaign the ban clearly no longer applied.

2. *The Times and the American Civil War*

In the Civil War the papers attempted to have correspondents at the headquarters of both armies. Most papers had a regular correspondent in New York as well. The war attracted very great public interest, and very large-scale reporting. The British press as a whole supported the South, as British public opinion did. Nevertheless, this provides an occasion where we can see the processes of favouritism and penalties being administered to the newspapers by the contending parties. Since the war was over before the completion of the Atlantic cable readers in England received, in effect, a series of essays well after the events described. Of the London papers, the *Daily News* and *Morning Star* supported the North, and the former was accused of being in the pay of the Washington authorities. The charge was indignantly denied by their correspondent E. L. Godkin, who had been domiciled in the United States since 1857: he had no favours, 'not even a pass'.[29] On the other hand a letter from him in January 1862 from Paris, to C. L. Brace in New York, reads 'The Southerners have beaten us hollow in the management of public opinion on this side of the water':[30] the reference to 'us' suggests, not an objective British observer, but a partisan of the North. The main champion of the South was, as an earlier chapter has shown, the *Standard*, together with its sister paper the *Morning Herald*, both of which received information and perhaps money from the Confederates.[31]

Much more is known about the operations of *The Times*. Like the *Standard*, it supported the Confederates. It had a correspondent with them, F. C. Lawley, from the autumn of 1862. He sent about a hundred despatches home (through the French Consulate in Richmond, Virginia), which were sufficiently full and valuable to have been reprinted in recent years.

[28] H. M. Hyndman, *The Record of an Adventurous Life*, 1911, 35–6.
[29] R. Ogden, *Life and Letters of E. L. Godkin*, 1907, 217.
[30] Ibid., 202.
[31] See chapter III.

He sent back eye-witness accounts of the later battles of the war, seeing Gettysburg in the company of the Confederate High Command.[32] *The Times*'s readers were well served. Things were much less satisfactory on the Northern side. *The Times* had a correspondent, Charles Mackay, resident in New York from 1862 to 1865. It sent William Howard Russell as correspondent with the Federal army, and he arrived in March 1861, before the outbreak of hostilities. (This is a good example of Delane's foresight.) Russell, whose sympathies lay with the South, sent home what was described as an 'outspoken' article criticizing the Federal Army's tactics and efficiency at the Battle of Bull run on 21 July. The article was bitterly resented in the United States, and he was refused permission to accompany the Federal armies in their march south to Richmond in the spring of 1862. With nothing to do, he returned home in April, and was replaced eventually by Gallenga who described himself as an 'out and out' supporter of Secession. Gallenga arrived in New York and, by his own account, called on Charles Mackay: he found him 'almost exclusively surrounded by New York *"Copperheads"* (as Northern men sympathising with the South were called).' He then went on to Washington, where both the British and the Italian ambassadors supported his application for a pass to the Federal Headquarters, but unsuccessfully: he was told that 'No man from Printing House Square shall ever come within sight of the Stars and Stripes banner on the battlefield'. Gallenga, too, had to return to Britain two months later, and then went to Denmark to report on the Schleswig–Holstein question.[33] The relations with the Confederates were as easy as the relations with the Federalists were difficult. As well as Lawley's despatches *The Times* received information from Hotze's information service, and on occasion was given exclusive information.

3. The Standard, The Times, and the Franco-Prussian War

In the Franco-Prussian War Napoleon III again imposed a ban on correspondents at the front, and indeed the French treatment of them became well known. According to Mason

---

[32] W. S. Hoole, *Lawley covers the Confederacy*, Tuscaloosa, 1964, 15. Hoole states—as an example of pre-telegraphic reporting—that these despatches average 3,600 words each.

[33] Gallenga, II, 342–6.

Jackson of the *Illustrated London News*, 'About a dozen newspaper correspondents were there, [in Metz] and they became a
united body through persecution. There was always about a
fourth of their number in prison.'[34] Examination of the press
reports of the war shows that the ban was effective, news from
the French side consisting usually of communiqués from the
French headquarters rather than the personal impressions of
the correspondents. The Emperor's determination to maintain
the ban was probably strengthened as the series of military
disasters unrolled.

The Prussians were less restrictive. *The Times* sent William
Howard Russell, who was accredited to the headquarters of the
Crown Prince, and Captain Hozier, at that time a serving
officer, who was with the headquarters of the King of Prussia.
(The British War Office had initially forbidden him to go: it
would be interesting to know how they changed their minds.)
Also with the Crown Prince were William Beatty-Kingston for
the *Daily Telegraph*, Archibald Forbes for the *Daily News*, and
others. Beatty-Kingston describes how ten or eleven British and
United States correspondents (and one German) spent Christmas Day 1870 together with Prussians at their Headquarters at
Versailles: he adds that while they could visit Prussian positions, it was very difficult for them to get to 'the absolute front'
at any time.[35] But it is noticeable that the Prussians, like the
Federalists, made things difficult for their enemies. Henty, an
experienced reporter, who had been on a number of campaigns
for the *Standard* since the time of the Crimea, was not given a
pass, and the elaborate measures taken to find an acceptable
replacement have been fully recorded by his successor, Alfred
Austin.

Austin had written from time to time for the *Standard*: unlike
that paper's his own views were strongly anti-French. When
the French declared war on 19 July 1870, according to his own
account 'I rapidly wrote, compelled by indignation, The
Challenge Answered [a poem furiously attacking the French],
and sent it to one of the daily papers—I do not remember

---

[34] Mason Jackson, *The Pictorial Press, its Origin and Progress*, 1885, 333. On 20 Aug.
1870 the *Illustrated London News* published a picture of two English correspondents, tall
and imperturbable, being led away by the Metz police to the execrations of an
immense crowd. One of them was their own man, W. Simpson.

[35] *Men, Cities, and Events* [1895] 65.

which of them I sent it to, of course with no ulterior purpose, but I shall tell, directly, how serviceable it turned out to be.' He was then approached by the editor of the *Standard* to persuade him to try and get permission to join the King of Prussia, their own correspondent having 'met with a curt refusal'.[36] The editor added that Austin would have to rely on his own personal contacts to get permission. Acting on these instructions Austin obtained introductions to the two Bunsen brothers in Berlin, one of whom, George, was known to Bismarck. He 'at once communicated with Count Bismarck, standing personal guarantee for my trustworthy conviction that France had put itself in the wrong by the Declaration of War, and that, if admitted to the King's Head-Quarters, I should write with unfettered independence, and in no degree hampered by the editorial opinions of the *Standard*.'[37] Political partisanship was an essential qualification.

This application was accepted at the third time of asking, Bismarck having presumably noticed the advantage of having such a correspondent in the field. It is hard to see Austin as other than an agent on the German side; for example he mentions that Bismarck's secretary Baron von Keudell cashed his cheques for him. Certainly Austin saw Bismarck on a number of occasions: on 5 September (on which occasion The Challenge Answered was mentioned), 6, and 12 September. Napoleon III had abdicated on 4 September after the defeat of Sedan. By 12 September, with the decisiveness of the Prussian victory, political circles abroad were beginning to discuss possible peace conditions, and to express the view that the French should not be too harshly treated. These interviews were held on the initiative of Bismarck, not of Austin. That on 12 September was in fact a detailed statement, almost a press-release, of the tougher peace terms that Bismarck wished to see. On 13 September these appeared in an issue of the *Standard*, in which the interview was reported at length on one page, with a hostile leading article about it on the opposite page. The episode is a good example of the way in which the government used a paper's urgent need for news for its own purposes.

The Paris Commune and its suppression provide a further

[36] *Autobiography*, II, 21 ff.
[37] Ibid.

example of political leaning on foreign correspondents, in a different context. *The Times* had been clearly pro-German during the war: Russell's enthusiasm for the Prussian armies stands out from his despatches. In London Gallenga, who now worked as a leader-writer, was able to revenge himself on Napolen III's betrayal of 1859 with the approval of Delane: 'When Paris surrendered, and Moltke and I had triumphed over prostrate France, my dear Delane drew a long breath, and wrote to me a kind letter of congratulation.' Delane in turn was complimentary about Gallenga's work.[38]

In Paris, *The Times* office in normal times acted as a collecting point for other European news; it was by far its most important foreign post. In 1870 *The Times* Paris correspondent was the newly-appointed Frederick Hardman. According to Dasent, Hardman went with the French government to Tours in the early autumn of 1870, and in subsequent years spent much of his time in Rome on sick leave, returning to Paris just before his death in 1874. It seems possible that he returned briefly to Paris at the end of the Commune in May 1871: another authority describes how Hardman was horrified at the way in which the Commune was suppressed, and sent back critical accounts to London.[39] It is true that Hardman was replaced till his death by an acting correspondent, Laurence Oliphant, and that Blowitz acted as Oliphant's assistant: Blowitz had been taken on, it is said, on the recommendation of Thiers.[40] The hint that there had been some kind of political pressure to moderate criticism in *The Times*, and that this was connected with the arrival of Blowitz, gets support from what was actually printed in the paper.

Paris was recaptured on 22 and 23 May, 1871. On 26 May *The Times* printed despatches dated 23 and 25 May. In these the tone was strongly sympathetic to the defeated Communards. The first described the pathetic parties of prisoners being taken to Versailles, and wondered if their record was any worse than that of the government at Versailles. The second considered that the city was not much better off than it had been under the Commune because of the over-bearing behav-

---

[38] Gallenga, II, 357; A. I. Dasent, *John Thadeus Delane*, 2 vols., 1908, II, 271.
[39] P. Henderson, *Life of Laurence Oliphant*, 1956, 178.
[40] Frank Giles, *A Prince of Journalists*, 1962, 66–7.

iour of the troops of the party of order. The correspondent had seen a party of some three hundred persons going to execution. On 27 May *The Times* printed a telegram dated the 26th, which was very different in tone. The telegram minimized the amount of damage that had been done to the city (the Tuileries had been burnt on the 25th). The telegram said how the female prisoners that the writer had seen were 'very furious-looking', and that he had been with an English friend round the Paris boulevards. They were, he said, 'crowded with troops of the Line and with civilians fraternising with them'. On 29 May there were printed two postal despatches both dated the 26th. One described further executions of women in the style of correspondent *A*, the other was a further despatch from correspondent *B* saying that 'instant execution is only ordered in the more extreme cases' and that the prisoners were 'hang dog and villainous in expression'. Two quite contrary accounts were being printed side by side in *The Times* office: it seems possible that correspondent *A* was Hardman and correspondent *B* Oliphant or Blowitz. It certainly seems likely, if we look at the situation in its context—the prestige of *The Times* and the urgent need of the new Third Republic for friends abroad—that Blowitz had links with the French government. His various reporting feats are more simply explained as political leaks than as feats of detective agility.

After 1870 the conditions of work of foreign and war correspondents changed. They were changed on the political plane: with the Franco-Prussian War wars in general in western Europe came to an end for a generation. Diplomatic relations and tensions between the powers continued to be the staple of the foreign pages of the London papers: in western Europe there was plenty of scope for the foreign correspondent, but none for the war correspondent. The war correspondents of the 1870s and 1880s found themselves working much further afield—in South Africa, the Balkans, or the North-West Frontier.

Their work was also transformed by the development of technology. Telegraphic links were established, to the Black Sea in 1856, and to India in 1869. The habit of using the telegraphs routinely had been established, by the *Daily News* in

Britain in the first place, in the Franco-Prussian war. The use of the telegraphs led to changes in techniques and in expectations. Beatty-Kingston, who had been employed by the *Daily Telegraph*, in 1890 described the change in the life of 'Our Own Correspondent' thus:

In his case the demand for literary style had been all but done away with by the telegraph, which has robbed him of his most agreeable and sympathetic function and converted him into a laconic compounder of epitomes. Little more than a decade ago the newspaper proprietors and their clients the general public valued good descriptive matter, sketches of character, and studies of national or local manners, customs and peculiarities, at least as highly as dry digests ... telegrams are costly commodities and the use of electricity has superinduced a tendency to summarize in the reader as well as in the purveyor of news.[41]

The change was from the long and personal letter to the short and dispassionate, and frequent summary of the current state of affairs. By the time of Tel-el-Kebir the new style was established: Macdonald of *The Times* rebuked their own correspondent, who had described his own adventures: the 'reports of the Standard correspondent were distinguished by their solid business like details'.[42] A letter to Escott from E. D. J. Wilson of the *Standard* gives the background '... we have spent infinitely more money in providing war news and have dished them up in a far better style than was in vogue during the Russo-Turkish war.'[43]

A third development, which had its effects on the supply of news, was the great increase in circulations since the 1860s, and therefore presumably of resources. Telegraphy was very expensive, but the resources to pay for it had also grown. Nevertheless, in spite of all these considerations, the handling of the Penjdeh incident, as it blew up in the spring of 1885, did not represent any really marked change from earlier examples.

4. The Penjdeh question, 1885

The essential features of the situation were familiar enough to the political public from the previous crisis of 1879. Afghanis-

---

[41] W. Beatty-Kingston, *A Journalist's Jottings*, 2 v., 1890, ii, 356.
[42] *The Times* archives, letter dated 9 Sept. 1882 to E. Cant-Wall.
[43] Escott MSS, BL Add. MS 58795, letter dated 26 Sept. 1882.

tan formed a buffer state between Russian Turkestan and British India, and in January and February 1885 it was widely believed that Russia was preparing to move forward into Afghanistan, taking advantage of the British involvement in the Sudan. To report directly on the truth of the report would present great problems: Russian Turkestan was closed to foreign journalists (though Edmund O'Donovan of the *Daily News* had travelled as far as Merv in disguise in 1879, from whence he had had to be rescued by the Foreign Office).[44] On the Indian side there was no similar problem. Calcutta had a large British population from among whom most London newspapers found correspondents. At the time the crisis developed, a British frontier-delimiting expedition was at work, under the command of Sir Peter Lumsden, on the Russo-Afghan border. *The Times*, with its flair for doing things in style, also had a correspondent with this expedition. There were no other reports, not even from Reuters, from the possible scene of action.[45] The papers also had their regular resident correspondents in the European capitals, and, as a threat of war began to be taken seriously at the end of March, papers printed relevant comments and news items from widely scattered places.

The sending of despatches from the Afghan frontier in 1885 is itself a spectacular illustration of the technical advances which had been made. From Lumsden's base at Gulran, messages could be brought in three days on a 'fast camel' to Meshed in north-east Persia, from whence there was a telegraphic link to London.[46] On 10 April *The Times* published a despatch from Gulran which had been dated 3 April. Had events turned out differently they would have been able to display an equal technical virtuosity in the Sudan. They had their own correspondent in Khartoum, Frank le Poer Power, who sent home despatches until all communications were cut off: 'I telegraph every week to London', he wrote to his

---

[44] Edmund Downey, *Twenty Years Ago*, 1905, has a chapter on O'Donovan, 118–40. He also appears, in a different light, in the Le Poer Power MSS, BL Add. M 58069.

[45] Though the *Illustrated London News* had an artist with the Lumsden expedition, and the *Daily Telegraph* published on 6 Mar. what it claimed to be a view of Penjdeh, copied from his work.

[46] *Daily Telegraph*, 4 Mar. 1885.

brother.[47] Outside, the field telegraph wires were advancing with Wolseley's army, and there were daily reports in the London papers. The contrast between these situations and the anecdotes of the mid-century, where boats put out from Cork to meet the American steamers, and journalists hire special trains, is profound. Speedy access to the news from the heart of the area of crisis was now normal and to be expected.

If we turn from the mechanics of news transmission to the contents of the foreign correspondence being printed, the change is less noticeable. Those reports on the Afghan question that came from St Petersburg were consistently reassuring. On 20 March *The Times* correspondent reported that 'The general opinion here is that Russia cannot retire with dignity without some move from Mr. Gladstone.' On 29 March he reported that troop movements were relatively slight, and contrasted the Russian calm with English war fever. On 30th he wrote that there were great hopes of a peaceful solution, and that the Russian emphasis on the problem was that it was merely one of law and order in that area. Other papers reported similarly: the *Standard* on 17 March had been told 'on the highest authority' that everyone in St Petersburg wanted peace. (This was directly opposed to the belligerence and alarmism of the paper's editorial policy.) On 2 April *The Times* correspondent was able to explain why he had written as he had done: it was the result of Russian censorship. A sentence in a despatch of 15 March, printed in the *Standard*, gives off an unmistakable scent of censorship: 'If I continue to quote the angry phrases of the unofficial [Russian] press [who were prophesying war] it is rather with a view to point out their foolishness.'

Reports from India were far fuller in *The Times* than elsewhere. The correspondent in Calcutta took a diametrically opposed view of the situation, and his reports, taken in conjunction with those from St Petersburg, must have made confusing reading. On 28 March he wrote that

[47] Le Poer Power MSS, letter dated 13 Nov. 1883. This small collection gives a remarkable firsthand picture of foreign correspondents at work. Power had been engaged as assistant by Edmund O'Donovan to accompany him, on behalf of the *Daily News*, first to Khartoum, and then to Central Asia. They fell out in Khartoum, O'Donovan proving to drink 'only ... absinthe, 3 or 4 bottles at a time without water' (letter dated 9 October 1883). Power then began to write for *The Times*, with whom he had already been in contact. O'Donovan died at El Obeid (November 1883), and Power was murdered, before the fall of Khartoum, in October 1884.

The general opinion in India is that it is not of the least use to make a
fuss about the Russians withdrawing ... and that the really important point is that they all this while are reinforcing their troops ... but
the vacillating spirit which appears to pervade the Cabinet has not
affected the Indian government ... If any doubt has ever been felt
regarding the feeling of the natives that doubt no longer exists. It is
abundantly clear that their feeling is one of the most enthusiastic
loyalty. Hindoos and Mahomedans are quite shrewd enough to see
that they would gain nothing by Russia's success.

On 25 and 28 March more reports from Calcutta were printed
on the excited preparations going ahead in India. On 29th
there was a report on the folly of a decision to stop the building
of the railway to Quetta. It seems clear that the correspondents
in Russia and India were acting, willingly or unwillingly,
merely as spokesmen for locally held policies.[48]

Reports from other places were divided in the same way: on
17 March the *Standard* printed reports from Vienna stressing
the peacefulness of the Russians, and stressing that local
opinion hoped that Britain would back down, and from Berlin
saying that 'All the independent organs of public opinion, and
even the majority of diplomatists, are now convinced that the
Afghan frontier question cannot be solved otherwise than by
arms.' In Vienna and Berlin, however, the correspondents were
able to maintain a personal detachment from the local views: it
was clear to the reader what they were being offered. An
isolated report from Odessa, in *The Times* of 9 April, throws the
propagandist quality of the rest into relief: it believed in
Russia's warlike intentions, but the writer also backed his
opinion with information on the way in which the Russians
could move troops and supplies to the Afghan border. Presumably it was easier to escape the censor away from St
Petersburg.

The reporting of the Penjdeh incident shows, once again,
that good political contacts brought great advantages. The
presence of a correspondent with the Lumsden expedition

---

[48] An anecdote told by Rudyard Kipling (*Something of Myself*, 1937, 51) gives a
picture of the background of British journalism in India: he worked on a paper in
Lahore and, on being hissed in the Club on account of the paper's editorial line, was
defended by someone who said '"The boy's only doing what he's paid to do" ...
Someone said kindly "You damned young ass! Don't you know that your paper has the
Government printing-contract?"'

could have given *The Times* great and exclusive advantages, though in the event he had little of interest to report. How was *The Times* able to get into such positions? It was partly, no doubt, because they were known to be the most willing to spend money on such speculative enterprises. But it stemmed also from the combination of good contacts and the, as it were, Erastian attitude of its management towards powers that be. In India the firm resistance to Russian advance, supported editorially by *The Times*, was also held by Roberts, who became Commander-in-Chief in 1885. A more likely contact, however, was Lord Dufferin, who had arrived in India as Governor-General the year before, with Donald Mackenzie Wallace as his secretary. (The latter had left his post with *The Times*, but was to return to it as head of its Foreign Department in 1891.) The defence of the frontier, and in particular the completion of the Quetta railway, were two of Dufferin's major concerns.[49]

The incident throws two interesting general questions into relief. The first concerns the practical operation of censorship, shown so clearly in Russia, and perhaps to be suspected in Berlin and Vienna. Despatches might be tampered with, and the correspondent be slow to find out what happened. For example, there was a complaint from London in May 1884 that the Spanish government had delayed telegrams and sent substitutes instead.[50] It is also true that telegraphy, which appeared to offer the press so much in the way of immediacy and supervision, from London, of the correspondent, could also be a weapon in the hands of the authorities. So long as the news went by post there were many ways of evading censorship, such as the sending of letters to alternative addresses. It went at the speed of normal travel, and in exceptional circumstances could be taken by messenger.[51] The existence of the telegraph killed the news value of postal despatches and the telegraph was easily controlled. Wolseley's skill in handling war correspondents combined affability in keeping them in touch with events and a tight hold over the telegraph. The news-

[49] *DNB*.

[50] *The Times* archives.

[51] See for example the account of how Blowitz smuggled the text of the Treaty of Berlin away, in Giles, *Prince of Journalists*, 109–12.

papers in January 1885 maintained an optimistic tone right up
to the news of the fall of Khartoum, at a time when sober
critical reflection might have told them that all was not going
well.[52] Had the correspondent with Lumsden been minded to
write critically he might have had difficulty in getting his news
out; it is a fair guess that the fast camels were organized by the
army.

The reports of the Paris Commune and of the Afghan
question illustrate another important general characteristic of
the foreign news, namely the way in which it was presented
once it reached London. A modern reader is struck, not so
much by the biased character of the reports, some of which
might be encountered today, as by the fact that they were
offered in a bald, unreconciled, form with no attempt to
analyse or explain things to the general reader. To present
contradictory reports, as they were received, has the merit of
honesty, but some political education would have been necessary to deduce from them what was happening.

The explanation probably lies in the way in which newspapers spent the money they devoted to news-gathering. The
only newspaper for which adequate information exists is *The
Times*, but since the other London papers presented their news
in a similar way (and since sub-editors moved from one paper
to another with ease) we can take *The Times* as representative
in this respect. In the 1870s and 1880s it spent an enormous
proportion of its outlay on foreign news, regularly exceeding
the amount spent on home news. Typical figures might be
about £20,000 for foreign news against £17,000 for 'office
expenses, reporting, and linage', for a half year.[53] At times of
crisis the foreign news would cost a great deal more: in the
second half of 1882, at the time of Wolseley's expedition
against Arabi Pasha, it rose to £33,000. The foreign expenses
were predominantly incurred on telegraphy: to give a specific
example the telegrams describing the Prince of Wales's visit to
India in 1875 cost *The Times* £3,231, while Russell, the
correspondent, was paid a fee of £800.[54] Any reporting from

[52] For instance, the *Standard* on 12 Jan. 'All is well in Khartoum. Gordon's steamers
ply without any serious interruption down to Metemmeh and bring in supplies.' In fact
Omdurman capitulated for lack of food on 15th.

[53] *The Times* archives.

[54] *The Times* archives.

South Africa, India, or the Far East was extremely expensive.

On the other hand the office staff was very small. *The Times* employed one man, Edward Cant-Wall, to sub-edit, single-handed, the news which came by telegraph, both from the paper's own correspondents and from Reuters. The news from India would presumably have come in early in the day's proceedings, but a single person could hardly have had the time to do more than arrange the various items on the page— even if more had been expected. The *History of the Times* makes it clear that, before the creation of the Foreign Department in 1891, the foreign news was printed in the form in which it arrived.[55] It appears that it would have been felt improper to tamper with the work of the correspondents. This can be compared with the habit, general at this time, in the provincial and London press, of printing successive Reuters telegrams, on the same or kindred subjects, one below the other in the same column. The use of the telegrams as the raw material from which to make a connected account, or the re-writing of a story as later news came in, were developments of the future. The Victorian system was extravagant in its use of resources and offered no barrier to propaganda.

Newspapers continued to depend on the good offices of governments in their quest for news. From a government's point of view it was important to have favourable reports: the curious story of Bismarck's interview with Austin suggest how greatly politicians could stand in need of such a mouthpiece. The question then arises, how were the celebrated feats of investigative journalism, when governments' misdeeds were exposed by the press, managed? A close look at two of them suggests that they were no exceptions to the rule.

Delane invited W. H. Russell to travel to the East with the British forces in February 1854, and he landed at Gallipoli with them in April.[56] At that time *The Times* was a firm supporter of the Aberdeen administration. In June he landed with the troops at Varna. There he was observed from an unusual angle by E. L. Godkin, at that time the special correspondent of the *Daily News*, who, while complaining that journalists were being treated as 'a sort of parias [sic], friendless individuals who

---

[55] *The History of the Times*, III, *The Twentieth Century Test*, 1947, 125 ff.
[56] Dasent, *Delane*, I, 170, 178.

might be pitched into with perfect impunity' contrasted their treatment with 'the English camp at Devna, where the *Times* correspondent receives rations for himself and three horses from the commissariat, by order of the home government.'[57] Like Arrivabene, he was, initially at least, the privileged correspondent of a friendly paper.

There is a hint of management from London in Russell's letters from the Crimea. Delane himself went out there in August and September and saw the landing in the Crimea in September. On his return to London he saw Newcastle, the Secretary for War, and warned him of the approaching winter hardships. When no notice was taken of him he joined the outcry against the Government and the campaign behind Palmerston. Russell's attacks on mismanagement of the war began in December. By May 1855, when the new government was in power, Dr Prendergast, serving with the forces, noticed that Russell's writings 'have not the same intense interest that they formerly had. Some restrictions upon his imparting of information is manifested therein.'[58]

Another celebrated investigation was carried out by the American, J. A. MacGahan, in 1876. 'As "Special Commissioner" for the *Daily News* MacGahan made for the scene of the massacres where he arrived on 25 July.'[59] From his reports the *Daily News* derived great honour. It is, on the face of it, unlikely that it would have been practicable for an American journalist to travel in a region which was in rebellion against the Turkish government, to investigate atrocities which they were anxious to conceal. The exact circumstances were slightly different. An American missionary college, Robert College in Constantinople, specialized in teaching Bulgarian children. News of the atrocities filtered through to the college, which was anxious to find out the facts. They persuaded the American consul, Schuyler, to investigate. According to Edwin Pears, the *Daily News* regular correspondent,

... beyond any doubt difficulties would have been placed in my way by the Turkish Government: probably they would even have refused to give me the necessary local passport. The selection of Mr.

[57] Ogden, *E. L. Godkin*, 60–1.
[58] BL Add. MS 59849 f. 91 (11 May 1855).
[59] R. T. Shannon, *Gladstone and the Bulgarian Agitation 1876*, 1963, 42.

McGahan was a happy one. He was a friend of Mr. Schuyler's. Both of them had been in Central Asia and knew something of Russia, and neither of them could be charged with having any prejudices against the Turks. Mr. Schuyler went on behalf of his Government and Mr. McGahan accompanied him.[60]

To quote these two examples in no way depreciates the importance of their reporting, but illustrates their dependence on government support.

In times of peace, the practical advantages to be gained from friendly relations with foreign powers were less marked, and it is harder to trace the extent of such secret influences. In May 1874 the *Printer's Register*, retailing printer's gossip in an article entitled 'Nobbling the Press', believed that 'a newer London daily is said to be in German pay,' that the French government had approached a London paper and failed, that an Indian nawab had a London evening paper in his pay, and the Turks were established 'in a quarter where it is least to be expected'. The last of these, the link between the *Morning Post* and the Turks, which can be traced back as far as the Crimea, certainly continued. Reginald Brett noted in his diary in 1876 that the Turkish Ambassador in London, Musurus Pasha 'had rented Combe Wood from Borthwick so Beust said to him "La Turquie a loué le Morning Post, et le Morning Post a loué la Turquie"'.[61] As late as 1895, when all the London newspapers were reporting the Armenian massacres extensively, the old association still held good. The *Morning Post* did not print news of the massacres, except a despatch from Turkey on 11 February saying that all was quiet. To gloss over news of this magnitude suggests that the Turks had some substantial hold over the paper: it can have done little good to the reputation of the *Morning Post*.

The connection between W. T. Stead and the Russians has already been mentioned. It was shown in the way in which the *Pall Mall Gazette* constantly acted as their apologist. Madame Novikov was a frequent contributor: her provocative style of argument is illustrated in an article of January 1885 which argued that British government in Ireland was like Russian

[60] Edwin Pears, *Forty Years in Constantinople . . . 1873–1915*, 1916, 18.
[61] *Journals and Letters*, I, 39.

rule in Poland. Two extracts from a summary (of which the author is not known) of the evolution of the Afghan dispute read like a caricature: 'February 1884. The Merv Turkomans ask the Russians to protect and govern Merv', and 'March 23–4, 1884 ... the Saryk Turkomans offer themselves to the Great White Czar. M. Lessar tells them the Russians do not want them.'[62]

The Times was regarded as friendly to the French government, though whether this support was restricted to a party or to particular individuals is not known. There is thus, partly by a process of exclusion, a probability that the 'newer London daily' believed to be in touch with the Germans was the *Daily Telegraph*. It has been described, for the period *c*. 1890 to 1914 as 'the least consistently Germanophobe' of the Conservative morning dailies.[63] A letter from Granville of 18 April 1872, to Hill of the *Daily News*, runs 'The "Telegraph" is not inspired by us but I should think is so by Bernstorff' (the German Ambassador in London).[64] A more substantial hint comes in a report from the British Ambassador in Berlin that the correspondent of the *Daily Telegraph* there was frequently receiving leaked information from the German Foreign Office, and that this never appeared as coming from Berlin, but as coming from an outside correspondent or from some other European capital.[65] This suggests that the management of the *Daily Telegraph* were cognisant of the situation. There is also evidence that Bismarck tried to make a mouthpiece of other papers: the story of his interview with Austin is one example. Another is an entry in Brett's diary in 1878, noting how his brother had

met a few evenings before, Greenwood, editor of the *Pall Mall Gazette*, [when it was a Conservative paper] who told him one curious thing. Bismarck, hearing that he was in Berlin, sent for him and praised the *Pall Mall*, saying that it was the only independent newspaper within his acquaintance. He offered him the run of the public offices, all the information he could give him, on the condition

---

[62] *Pall Mall Gazette*. For examples of Madame Novikov's writing see 13 and 29 May, and 5 June 1884; 15 Jan., 12 and 24 Feb. 1885. The extract about the Turkomans is from the issue of 9 Apr. 1885. For Lessar see p. 164 above.

[63] Oron J. Hale, *Publicity and Diplomacy*, 1940, 26.

[64] Granville MSS, PRO 30/29/426.

[65] C. L. Smith, *The Embassy of Sir William White at Constantinople, 1886–1891*, Oxford, 1957, 71.

that once a month a German professor should be allowed to write an article in the *Pall Mall* to state the 'facts' of German policy; no argument, only facts. Greenwood refused.[66]

Governmental influence, British or foreign, was to some extent inevitable: diplomatic news on which the newspapers concentrated could hardly avoid being coloured by the way in which the chief participants expressed themselves. The man in the street might absorb the interpretation he was being offered, but to the politicians, if they were aware of what was going on, there was a good range of views to choose from. The news from the agencies presented different problems. The Reuters network had grown up in the middle of the century, step by step with the cable system, and its style of reporting was fully adapted to it.[67] (By comparison *The Times* network in the mid-century was ancillary to the Foreign Office's diplomatic network.) Reuters was, as it still is today, as much concerned with business as with political and general news. It had the largest number of agents in the largest number of places, and provided the framework of information on which foreign news pages were constructed. It was the system most likely to pick up news from any unexpected quarter—the natural catastrophe, or the political uprising in a place not yet in the news. Its news was short and factual, sent by wire in telegraphic form. The numbers of words transmitted—77 daily from India in 1869 and 40 from Australia in 1872—illustrate how highly condensed it was in the earliest days.[68]

The general evolution of the press in the last thirty or forty years of the century was likely to enlarge Reuters share of the total news-gathering process. On one hand, telegraphic rates continued to be very high, as a proportion of a newspaper's total expenses. On the other hand, the general course of historical change was involving Europeans more and more with the remoter parts of the world, particularly with tropical Africa and the Far East: to both these regions the rates were very high indeed.[69] *The Times* was peculiarly short of money after it had to find costs of £200,000 for the Parnell Special

---

[66] *Journals and Letters*, I, 55.

[67] See Graham Storey, *Reuters Century*, 1951; and Michael Palmer, 'The British press and international news, 1851–99' in Boyce *et al. Newspaper History*, 1978, 205–19.

[68] Storey, 63, 69.

[69] See chapter I.

Commission in 1889, but the manager, Macdonald, had been worrying about excessive telegraph costs well before that time, and trying to cut down on new foreign appointments. (For example, referring to Bombay, the paper could not afford a '"Special" all to ourselves', the reasons being 'chief among them the cost of the wire with the comparatively small amount of matter which it yields.')[70] Correspondents were limited in the amount they might send by telegraph. Where the provincial press was concerned, they had been provided with Reuters telegrams since 1868 through an agreement made between the agency and the Press Association. The London papers made individual arrangements with Reuters but took their service. They established their own correspondents in new areas as it became necessary, but the general picture of the world's affairs was being increasingly shaped by Reuters.[71]

Their news was as sensitive to political influence as anyone else's. The agency's own business, as its centenary history makes clear, was not particularly profitable.[72] It was unlike a newspaper which could benefit automatically from increased sales or advertising revenue. Reuters income came from a series of bargains struck with large organizations—newspaper managements or other agencies. It was also dependent, in a way which a newspaper, with its all-round range of contents was not, for its reputation and income on its ability to deliver the news reliably, quickly, and comprehensively. It needed to maintain good relations with government-run news agencies and telegraph systems. Thus they were easily drawn into contact with governments. The history of Reuters states that they received subsidies from the Khedive of Egypt and the Viceroy of India down to 1900 to help pay for the provision of news to those places, though the arrangement could also have involved some official influence over whatever they sent back to England. Another potential source of influence was the news-sharing agreement made in 1870 between Reuters, covering the English-speaking world, the British Empire and the Far East, the French Havas agency, covering southern Europe and Latin America, and the Wolff agency in Germany, dealing

[70] *The Times* archives, Macdonald's letter-book, 17 May 1884.
[71] See Palmer, *Newspaper History*, 208 ff.
[72] Storey, 87 ff.

with Scandinavia and Russia.[73] Havas and Wolff were both official agencies. This added another layer of selection and interpretation to the news as it finally reached the reader.

In what ways could such influences actually operate? Reuters, unlike the newspapers, could not print and distribute their news to the public. Also, they sent short and factual messages (including factual statements of diplomatic situations), rather than the essays in which kites might be flown and tension increased or eased. To that extent a politician profited more from a direct link with a journalist or proprietor. Nevertheless, agency news could affect the shape of events. If a friendly government gave an agency priority on the wire, a statement favourable to it might set the tone of subsequent discussion. One example, taken from Macdonald's correspondence to Colquhoun, *The Times* correspondent in Hanoi, states that the latter's despatch, dated 29 January and published 13 March 1884, had been opened by the French but forwarded

without any Russian process of mutilation. The French public at home will be able to learn a good deal otherwise left in the dark as to the operation of their troops in the East. You will also see from the leader that your telegrams have been delayed and they have been careful to give Reuter precedence over you in announcing the fall of Bac-Nish.[74]

The foreign news of the London papers was therefore compounded of a mixture of ingredients: from Reuters, from their 'own correspondents', and from the comments of British political figures, as and when they were available. The amount of sifting and digestion which the editorial staff could carry out was, generally speaking, small. At *The Times*, the creation of the Foreign Department in 1891 imposed control over the correspondents and supervised what was printed, but this came near the end of the period under discussion in this book.

News in the provincial press was more derivative. They did not employ their own correspondents abroad. Occasionally they sent special correspondents on limited assignments; the *Manchester Guardian* had a correspondent besieged in Metz in 1870, and sent a correspondent to cover the Italian campaign

[73] Storey, 91, 53.
[74] *The Times* archives.

in Abyssinia in 1896,[75] but these were exceptional. Occasionally they printed contributions from people who were correspondents in the literal sense—from local people who found themselves caught up in crises abroad and wrote home about their experiences. There are also particular foreign features in some papers, such as the impressive range of business information printed in the *Manchester Guardian* in the middle of the century, from the cotton exporting ports of the southern United States. But with such exceptions as these, it remains true that the provincial press derived its foreign news from Reuters, through the Press Association, and from the reprinting and digestion of paragraphs from the London papers.[76] The readers of a provincial daily therefore received, sometimes a day later, a digest of a variety of London papers. In a large well-run paper they would see half or two-thirds of a page of foreign news in normal times. The smallest evening papers, and even the weekly papers, would have a short column, three or four inches long, of foreign telegrams supplied probably by the Central News. Foreign news therefore was widely distributed.

It was subject, however, to a far wider margin of error than home news. It is not possible to make general comparisons of the qualities of home and foreign news, but home news was subject to safeguards which were generally known and understood. Parliament was a place where political rumours could be publicly questioned and statements demanded—something for which there was no international equivalent. At home, politicians briefing their friends or leaking information (as the case might be) were operating within known rules and with limited powers: there was nothing to correspond with the holding up of telegrams or censorship to which the present chapter has referred.

To ask what effects these varied forms of international influence and interference had on the general course of events is to pose an impossibly wide question. One can suggest some generally mitigating factors. There was a variety of influences, some of them conflicting, at work: the pro-Turkishness of the *Morning Post* was counterbalanced by the Russianism of the *Pall Mall Gazette*. Secondly, and importantly, the associations,

[75] Ayerst, *Guardian. Biography of a Newspaper*, 1971, 160; and *Guardian* archives.
[76] Oron J. Hale, 30 ff.' and chapter VI above.

or at any rate some of them, were well known, as is clear from a number of the episodes recorded in this chapter. The politically educated might pick their way through to a balanced impression of the situation.

A general effect, which can be demonstrated, is the way in which the coverage of foreign events reflected the diplomatic map of Europe. Foreign news was primarily of diplomatic moves and reactions, and particularly concentrated on Continental Europe. An exceptional non-diplomatic event, such as the assassination of the Tsar in 1881, might attract great attention, but in general the reader learnt a great deal about foreign policy and little about foreign places and people (though the Tsar's death was followed, particularly in the *Daily Telegraph*, by quantities of sensational reporting of anarchist groups and student revolutionary hideouts). The lack of interest in the Americas, or in Australia, discussed in a previous chapter, may be related to this tendency. European diplomatic news, apart from other considerations, was more convenient: it was cheaper to transmit and arrived earlier in the day, and American news suffered. According to the *Printer's Register*, 'This indifference to American affairs is but poorly compensated for by all the telegraphic rubbish concerning the Three Emperors, the Bonapartists, Bulgars, Montenegrins, and other semi-barbarians.'[77] Two papers at least had private wires to Paris, *The Times* by 1874 and the *Standard* by 1879.[78] The comparative neglect of American affairs was described in the following terms by Joseph Hatton, London correspondent of the *New York Times*:

Hitherto *The Times* was the only journal which had a regular cable correspondent (at Philadelphia) in the United States, and *The Times*'s dispatches were often singularly meagre. It was one of the complaints of Americans in England that while the London newspapers published daily reports from all the great capitals of the Old World, they almost ignored the doings of the New. Washington keeps clear of European politics, and is, happily for America, not a factor in the burning questions that agitate England in the East. For these reasons

[77] *Printer's Register*, Sept. 1879.
[78] Ibid., June 1874, and Jan. 1879.

American news had not been hitherto regarded as especially interesting to English readers.[79]

The *Standard* responded to this situation by establishing a daily cable service from New York in June 1881, and was able to reap a reward a month later when it printed five columns, sent by cable, on the assassination of President Garfield.[80] Nevertheless, in spite of this initiative, it remained generally true that the foreign news presented to British readers was closely tied to diplomatic questions.

[79] Joseph Hatton, *Journalistic London*, 1882, 143. He also quoted *Harper's Weekly* of 25 June 1881, 'American travellers in Europe know what it is to take up a London daily paper and find the news of the United States compressed into a few lines, and packed away in an obscure corner.' (Ibid., 144.)

[80] Ibid.

XI

Handling the News

THE process of collecting news—both home and foreign—was thus strongly affected by external pressures: the newspaper which was in good standing with an authority which had something to tell received a good deal more than the occasional oddment of exclusive information; and conversely the investigative journalist had massive difficulties to surmount. This is a situation, however, which must not be presented out of proportion. As a previous chapter showed, over very large areas of public life access by the press was fully accepted and conventional. Publicity was actively sought by important groups and interests. It was not difficult to collect news to fill columns: the problems lay with its interpretation and control.

It is therefore necessary to look at the situation from another side and consider in more detail the way in which the news was presented, and the extent to which techniques developed over the period covered by this study. The first question must concern the amount of space devoted to the various categories of news. Some papers increased in size. In the 1870s the penny papers had normally been of eight pages, with possibly two extra on Saturdays. By the 1890s the most prosperous, like the *Manchester Guardian* or the *Daily Telegraph*, varied between ten and twelve pages, further narrowing the gap between them and the threepenny *Times*. In general those parts not concerned with party politics were tending to grow.

The general scale of sports reporting grew substantially in the last thirty years of the nineteenth century, partly as the result of the expanding numbers of organized sports. In the middle of the century the sporting news of the London papers was limited: to take a specific example, in the second and third weeks of October 1864 *The Times* printed daily between three-quarters and one-and-a-half columns of racing news, confined to the meetings at Lincoln and Newmarket, and, (showing the paper's cosmopolitan style) Longchamps. There was also news from Tattersall's. The *Daily Telegraph* and the *Standard* carried

reports from rather more meetings. Both had some cricket reports and the *Standard* had news of 'aquatics' (rowing) and a forthcoming prize-fight in Dublin. By the 1890s, while the amount of space had not greatly altered, the range of activities covered was much wider. The *Daily Chronicle* by 1895 gave, in addition to the racing news, reports on yachting, rowing, lacrosse, football, hockey, angling, billiards, athletics, and cycling. *The Times* covered a similar list: the *Daily News* covered chess as well.

In the provinces in the 1860s racing news was reported in much the same way as in London. In subsequent years, however, sports reporting grew to occupy a more central place in the provincial paper than it did in London; the evening papers established in the 1870s gained immediately from the fact that they could offer a results service the same day. By the 1880s some were advertising the range and quality of their sporting news in the directories: some examples are the *Nottingham Journal*, the *Nottingham Daily Guardian*, and the *Yorkshire Post*, the 'chief organ for this class of news in the north of England'.[1] An example of the increasing resources being put into sports reporting is in the *Newcastle Daily Chronicle*, which on the relevant days of the week devoted two out of an eight-page paper to sport, while the *Evening Chronicle*, under the same management, had a special 'Football Edition' on Saturdays. By 1895 the London *Daily Chronicle* gave, in addition to news of racing, reports on yachting, rowing, lacrosse, football, hockey, angling, billiards, athletics, and cycling. The *Daily News* dealt with a similar list—and chess as well.

The evolution of the City pages was in some ways similar: in the mid-century the London papers had business sections, which give good clues to their readerships: in October 1864 the *Daily Telegraph* had two columns daily on the Stock Exchange, and on Saturday a section called the 'Money Market' which was directed not to the business man, but to the average reader with savings to invest. The *Standard* had a rather fuller list of share prices. *The Times* had, as early as the 1860s, an impressive business section. As well as London prices it printed share prices from the provincial stock exchanges. It had reports of the commodity markets: cereal prices from Mark Lane, prices

[1] *Mitchell's Newspaper Directory.*

from the provincial cattle markets, and short reports, (perhaps each a dozen lines long) of the state of commerce, collected from sixteen provincial centres. The pages included an occasional analytical piece—on Friday 14 October 1864, for example, an analysis of the United States' public debt. The contrast between the two papers is one between *The Times*, the paper for the City merchant, and the *Daily Telegraph*, the paper for the clerk and the shopkeeper. By the 1890s the City pages had grown in range and sophistication in the penny papers, while *The Times*'s pages were not substantially different.

These two subjects, therefore tended to consume certainly more journalistic effort, and effectively more space at the end of the century. What subjects were making way for them? The most conspicuous decline was in parliamentary reporting.

Table 11.1. *Length of Parliamentary reports (to the nearest 250 words)**

	Hansard	The Times	Daily Telegraph	Leeds Mercury
1865				
24 April	16,750	18,500	6,750	750
4 May	30,250	26,500	11,500	3,250
1875				
7 May (The Budget)	66,000	26,500	18,750	5,750
14 June	43,500	26,250	11,000	2,000
1885				
15 April	30,750	6,250	500	2,000
28 April	46,500	20,750	4,750	Nil.
1895				
4 April	58,750	41,250	2,000	3,000
26 April	23,500	11,750	2,500	Nil.

* These figures represent a rough count of the total Parliamentary proceedings of the day, Lords and Commons, and any ancillary matter about private bills, petitions, etc.

Table 11.1 tells a clear story. In 1865 *The Times* was on one occasion longer than *Hansard*, showing that *Hansard* was not yet a verbatim record. *The Times* was always longer than the *Daily Telegraph*. The provincial paper quoted here, the *Leeds Mercury*, was a serious Liberal paper, edited in the 1880s by Wemyss Reid and owned by the Baines family. Except on a special occasion, such as the Budget, its parliamentary report was slight. The more popular papers, particularly the halfpenny evenings, had

little or no parliamentary reporting. In 1878–80, the reporting of proceedings was considered by Select Committees of both Houses, and as a result *Hansard*'s reports acquired an official status.[2] After this time the amount printed in the *Daily Telegraph* and the *Leeds Mercury* declined noticeably, except on special occasions. These reports of proceedings were to a certain extent replaced by political commentary and parliamentary sketches— though the latter were nothing new, an early example being E. M. Whitty's sketches in the *Leader* in 1852–3.[3]

The impression that parliamentary reporting was giving way to news about politicians is probably correct. A number of letters in the Cowen collection suggest this; they come from Cowen, whose interest in politics was serious, to his London office. In January 1887, on Lord Randolph Churchill's resignation as Chancellor of the Exchequer, he wrote:

The main interest will centre in what Lord Randolph says—give a brief summary of his speech, and a description of the proceedings generally, with respect to his explanation. This will be the most interesting part of the night's doings. Give something also about Smith's demeanour as Leader, as it will be interesting, and anything about Goschen that can be said will also be useful . . . Don't make the summaries too long.

Similarly, in September 1888 with the Parnell Commission, 'I dare say the business will pale in interest as it goes on', and next day, 'I wish at your convenience during the next few days you would write a description of the court where the Parnell Commission will sit, of the general appearance of the place and so forth; also as much about the judges as you know—their appearance, manner of address, demeanour, and anything personal about them.' and in November, 'The Parnell Commission is more interesting than Parliament.'[4]

In these quotations we can see that the hard substance of debates is losing out to a general notion of what will interest the readers—not what they say, but the way that they say it. It

---

[2] Parliamentary papers 1878 (327) xvii, 1878–9 (203) xii, 1880 (HL 66)·vii, sess. 2. The practical result was that *Hansard*'s shorthand writer was moved down from the Press Gallery to a place where the speeches could be clearly heard, inaudibility in the Gallery being a constant subject of complaint.

[3] Reprinted as *St. Stephen's in the Fifties*, 1906.

[4] Cowen MSS, letters of 24 Jan. 1887 (D 365), 9 Oct. 1888 (D 400), and 23 Nov. 1888 (D 404).

might be expected that the long verbatim reports of political speeches and meetings would be going the same way. It is difficult to demonstrate a trend over the period as a whole; for one thing the occasions which would attract a full report occur at irregular intervals. On some specimen days in October 1864 long reports—of over a thousand words—on items of home news were printed in *The Times*, the *Standard*, and the *Daily Telegraph*[5] on the subjects listed in Table 11.2.

Table 11.2. *Number of words printed (to the nearest 25)*

	The Times	Standard	Daily Telegraph
Tuesday, 4 October 1864			
Royal Visit	3,750	2,900	2,675
Erith explosion	1,100	2,625	1,850
Mr Doulton at Lambeth	1,650	—	—
Ireland	1,450	—	—
Agricultural show St Ives	—	1,675	—
Saturday, 8 October			
Royal visit	—	2,900	2,000
Erith explosion	1,450	—	1,800
Agricultural show, St Ives	1,600	—	—
Ireland	1,275	—	—
Colliers' strike	—	—	1,200
Meeting of metropolitan Board of Works	2,000	2,500	—
Thursday, 13 October			
Cutting first turf Devon and Somerset Railway	—	2,000	—
Mr Gladstone at Bolton	6,350	7,500	6,550
Church Congress, Bristol	4,350	3,325	—
Irish murder	—	2,400	—
Ireland	3,900	—	550
G. von Bunsen at North Walsham	3,200	—	—

[5] These days were chosen on different days of the week, to avoid Christmas or the holiday season, and to avoid any exceptional conditions such as a General Election.

The events in Table 11.2 need explanation. The Prince and Princess of Wales were making a social visit to Sweden and the Princess's home in Denmark, and it was being fully reported in the press.[6] The explosion, at a munitions dump at Erith, Kent, had occurred on the previous Saturday, and the longest reports of the accident had appeared on the previous day, 3 October: they had described the damage done and the rush of sightseers to the place by train on Sunday. Doulton, the china manufacturer, was MP for Lambeth, and had been explaining his support for Gladstone to his constituents. The agricultural show at St Ives, Huntingdonshire, had been the occasion of a speech by Lord Robert Montagu, a Conservative politician, describing his work on a Royal Commission on the disposal of sewage. Both these speeches had a certain, though not outstanding, significance at the time and were reported verbatim. The Church Congress was an annual event, held in a different town each year. Reporters from *The Times* and the *Standard* had gone to Bristol, and, as with the political meetings, sent in verbatim reports. G. von. Bunsen, Prussian Minister in London had been speaking on the Schleswig–Holstein question. There remains the visit of Gladstone to Bolton, where he opened a public park. The visit, the opening of his tour of South Lancashire, was a well-known episode in his career, was accompanied by reporters, and was fully reported in the London and provincial papers. If we look at the table as a whole we see that there are only five occasions on which reporters were sent out of London, on the royal visit, to St Ives, to Bolton, to North Walsham, and to the Church Congress. Their reports were verbatim in the strictest sense; not only was the text of the main speech given, but also the various introductory remarks or impromptu exchanges. The descriptions of the Erith explosion included penny-a-lining of the most prolix kind: the *Daily Telegraph* reporter needed 73 lines to describe the rush of sightseers at the London railway station. Two sentences may give the flavour of the whole:

Of the wearied and hard-worked servants of the railway company it is only due to say that they did their arduous duty well. At the Belvedere station tickets, so far as they could be, were collected by some of the company's servants assisted by two or three policemen,

[6] See chapter VIII.

the station-master at this place moving the down trains on as soon as possible to keep the line clear, and then having them shunted on to the up line.[7]

In none of these reports can one see evidence of sub-editorial pruning: the impression we receive is that there was not a great deal of pressure on space, and that, once a reporter had been sent to cover an event, everything that he sent in might as well be printed.

These reports on home affairs may be compared with those from another trio of days thirty years later, in 1894 as shown in Table 11.3.

Table 11.3 *Number of words printed*

	The Times	Standard	Daily Telegraph
Monday, 15 October 1894			
Sir H. James at Heywood	2,275	—	375
Church Congress	2,500	—	—
W. O'Brien in Ireland	—	1,825	—
Thursday, 18 October			
Diocesan Conferences (several reports grouped together)	1,425	—	—
Shaw Lefevre at Bradford	325	1,875	—
Tuesday, 30 October			
Shaw Lefevre at Liverpool	1,150	2,675	—
Morley on Irish dynamiters	2,125	2,900	2,350

It cannot be claimed that the figures in Table 11.3 demonstrate any startling change over thirty years, though there is a proportionate reduction, particularly in *The Times*. Newspapers were still capable of printing extremely long reports; on 30 October *The Times* published nearly four columns on the Austro-Hungarian military manœuvres, and on the next day the *Daily Telegraph* devoted over three columns to a speech by Lord Salisbury at Edinburgh.

Thus, by the 1890s and the eve of publication of the *Daily Mail*, newspapers still appear, in general, as compilations of discrete items with little attempt to organize, let alone manipu-

[7] A comment in the *Bucks Herald* of 8 Oct. is worth quoting; 'the penny-a-liners, who have filled the papers with the most preposterous tales about broken windows, smashed shutters, children shot out of bed and other marvels in districts which I know to have been quite unaffected by the catastrophe'.

late, the news in pursuit of an editorial objective—which to a modern reader may sound wholly to the good. We can get some sense of how things were about to change from some of Northcliffe's early correspondence with the editorial staff of the *Daily Mail*: for example, in 1909, 'I looked in vain for "World's Press" on the subject ... It is the old habit of failure to follow up ...' or, a complaint about '... your man in London, who seems to limit his sphere to very few journals. I no longer see quotations from Japanese and Russian papers and very few from American and Canadian papers. A system I built up myself of arranging these papers, as far back as the year 1897, seems to have disappeared.' Two years later, 'The point of the Seamen's strike, which has never been simply explained in the "Daily Mail" at all—and which ought to be explained every day in a few lines—is the stoppage of the food supplies.'[8]

Consistently through these quotations runs the idea that the material of the news is there to be shaped into a coherent body of reading. Such influences as that of Brett over Stead, or Musurus Pasha over the *Morning Post*, were kept at bay, at the price of substituting the close control of the editor or proprietor—according to the individual personalities involved. The main thrust of Northcliffe's letters is directed against the subeditors: they are the people who fail to make points effectively: 'The possibility of our being able to issue eight page papers with success is entirely one of editing and sub-editing.'

Northcliffe also had the capacity to create an event through the adroit use of his own newspaper resources. Some of these schemes—the search for the *Daily Mail* hat and the *Daily Mail* rose—have precedents in the competitions run in the 1880s by *Tit-Bits* and *Answers*. Another, with a political point, and perhaps more innovative, was projected as follows:

There is already in type, a story of the Daily Mail Empire Cup ...

Circular letters were sent to the Lord Mayors and Mayors of all the principal towns some time ago, asking how Empire Day was to be celebrated.

Letters were also forwarded to the Clerks of the County Councils throughout the Kingdom asking what was proposed to be done in the schools on Empire day.

[8] Northcliffe MSS, BL Add. MS 62198, letters to Marlowe dated 7 Mar. 1909, and 30 June 1911.

Correspondents of the big centres have been asked for stories on how Empire Day is to be celebrated.

Already sufficient information has been collected for a first class news article. This is being held back until the Daily Mail Empire Cup article has appeared.[9]

This kind of thing, the creation of an event by the careful deployment of the paper's own resources, could probably have been done equally well in the nineteenth century by the management of the larger newspapers. In fact, both here, and in the reiteration of the need to follow up a story, the close similarity of Northcliffe's methods to those of Stead is clear. Stead's 'church', which was to investigate the lack of reading-matter in workhouses,[10] and his relentless pursuit of the naval expenditure question, were similar in spirit. The difference is that Northcliffe was a successful entrepreneur, doing what he liked with his own, and Stead was not. Stead and Northcliffe are both often referred to as founders of 'sensationalism', unjustly, for concentration on the amazing and the shocking had existed long before: they were important figures in newspaper history because they both fully understood how to use the instruments they conducted.

This failure to appreciate the full opportunities which were open can be illustrated in a number of ways. By the last quarter of the nineteenth century there was a large, trained labour force employed in the collection and presentation of news:[11] London papers had their provincial correspondents, and the agencies had their organizations. They thus had the kind of network which could have produced answers to questions of current social and political interest that no other agency could have handled: the kind of inquiry carried out into Empire Day plans could have been mounted into agricultural distress, the prospects of political parties, attitudes to different kinds of schooling—or similar subjects.

It is also shown in their handling of information once it had been collected. Press-cutting newspaper libraries go back to the beginning of this century: it may be significant that the one which has been acquired by the British Library as the most

[9] Ibid., 29 Apr. 1909.
[10] See p. 49 above.
[11] For figures in the industry see chapter II.

generally useful and accessible was built up by the popular *Daily Express*.[12] Libraries may have existed in the newspaper offices of the nineteenth century, and perhaps in the reorganized Foreign Department of *The Times* after 1891. They do not, however, appear in the many accounts of journalists' work: indifference to their value is neatly shown in J. A. Spender's description of Sir Edward Cook, who

... had a mind in which everything seemed to be indexed and was instantly available, whenever it was wanted. For the office he invented a system of what he called 'clag-books' (the origin of the name I never could discover), in which clippings from all sorts of newspapers and periodicals about persons and things were daily posted. In addition, he had his own private 'clag'—clippings made with his own hand and stored in envelopes which he kept at home.[13]

J. W. Robertson Scott, another established journalist, from another notable journalistic family, added a further detail, 'The clag-books were invented by Stead, and were kept, with reference books, by the devoted Miss Hetherington.'[14] The noticeable feature of these comments is, not that they describe another of Stead's innovations, but their tone of amusement at the oddity of Cook's collection; the oddity consisting in the keeping of cuttings as much as in the name. The idea that effective commentary on events needs sometimes to be done with reference to previous events seems to be missing.

The general impression left by reading in the nineteenth-century press—even to the end of the century— is of its weakness in generalizing and sifting capacities, which was shown sometimes in its inability to digest reports from different places or to build up information over a period of time. This weakness, together perhaps with some of the underlying attitudes of the time, is shown in a simple example in reports of exceptional weather conditions. Storms and heatwaves today may make the headlines for a short time. On such occasions items from a variety of places are woven together into a general account; possibly different types of account are juxtaposed— one scientific, explaining long-term climatic changes, another

[12] For a general account of these collections see Gordon Phillips, 'A national press archive' in Boyce *et al.* eds., *Newspaper history*, 339–42.

[13] *Life, Journalism, and Politics*, 1927, I, 33.

[14] *Life and Death of a Newspaper*, 1952, 269.

describing local experiences. In the late nineteenth century we are likely to find, at best, reports from different places printed one below the other in the same column: it is equally likely that they appear scattered, filling up corners on different pages. It needed the imagination of a Northcliffe or a Stead to see the possibilities of such information. An example of one such event which failed to emerge may be quoted. At the New Year of 1894–5 there was a prolonged gale, which did damage in many places. The *Daily Telegraph* collected reports from perhaps a dozen places from Scotland to Bilbao, and printed them in one column on 1 January and then dropped the subject. As the gales died down, reports of ships overdue began to come in, and appeared in the *Newcastle Daily Chronicle*, and *Eastern Morning News* of Hull, and possibly papers in other ports, on 2 and 3 January. (These continued until about 12 January.) On 4 January the *Yorkshire Post*, which had, exceptionally, printed an interesting general article on the storms in the north on New Year's Day, again produced a general report. Collating the various reports of ships presumed lost, from the Tyne to East Anglia, it worked out that over 400 lives might have been lost. This appalling total was reported in the Newcastle *Evening Chronicle* on the same day and in the *Eastern Morning News* next morning. It did not appear in the *Yorkshire Evening Post* of the 4th, or the *Newcastle Daily Chronicle* the following day. It did not make any impact on the London papers nor on provincial papers outside the immediate area—such as the *Manchester Guardian* or the *Birmingham Daily Post*. This suggests, as well as an indifference to human loss of life, the haphazard and casual way in which news, outside certain standard topics, tended to be put together.

In general, then, it seems that the incoming news continued to be handled, down to the end of the century, in the traditional fashion, with little in the way of collation and condensation. Sports news and business news had emerged as integral parts of the well-informed daily newspaper, and had developed their own conventions of presentation and content. Particularly in the halfpenny press, a style of journalism which did not pretend to be the poor man's substitute for *The Times* was developing. There had been reductions—proportionately greater in popular papers, but also to an extent in *The Times*, in

the scale of reporting of Parliamentary debates, and of meetings and speeches. What was lacking—as could also be seen to be lacking in the handling of briefings from politicians at home and abroad[15]—was independence of mind. The Victorian picture of a free press exploring malpractice proves to be a poor guide to reality. The emphases and interests which the London dailies represented were those of the political society in which editorial staff moved. (This emerges very clearly from the paragraphs of social gossip or sections on 'London day by day': the writer's standpoint is that of the well-connected man of affairs, showing whimsical amusement at the behaviour of the crowd.)

The unspoken assumptions and limitations of the London papers may be studied from another angle: from the kind of bias shown in their selection of topics for report. One such bias in foreign news, towards those countries and questions with which Britain was diplomatically involved, at the expense of other matters, has been discussed in the last chapter.

Another, which becomes clear to anyone trying to use the London papers as a record of general events, is the bias towards the capital and away from the provinces. If we return to the specimen days of October 1864 mentioned earlier in this chapter we can count the items of provincial news appearing on those days, and the results are not impressive. It is difficult at times to decide where 'provincial' begins and ends: in these lists there have been excluded: by-elections (usually seen as an aspect of party politics), market trends (often seen as a facet of City news), and news from within the Home Counties, which could hardly be called provincial.

In *The Times* of 4 October 1864 there were:

Nottingham Goose Fair	125 words
Nottingham railway accident	225
Trade at Bacup	75
Rivalry of the Tyne and Wear navigation authorities	375
Three short sections where a number of short items were printed together	1275

[15] See chapters IX and X.

On 8 October:

Archaeological find at Salisbury	175
Trade at Nottingham	75
A rare hawk seen at Wick	100
Lord Russell as Lord Rector at Aberdeen	50
Duke of Cambridge visits Dover	400
Trials of steamships on the Clyde	100
Similar trials on the Tyne	300
Pickpocket arrested in Manchester	125
Letter from the Poor Law Board about the cotton famine	575

It would be tedious to continue this listing, which illustrates so well the unchanging interests of *The Times* and its readers. On 13 October it printed, among items in another similar miscellany, 400 words on the Wolverhampton ironmasters' quarterly meeting, held to fix wages under the sliding-scale arrangements employed at that time.

The *Standard* offered a similar service, though the individual items were different: on 4 October:

Harvest in Yorkshire	300
Late riots in Belfast	150
A whale stranded in Rothesay	150
Inquest at Liverpool	150
Pit accident at Madeley	325

On 8 October:

Bankruptcy at Liverpool	25
Incendiarism in Lincolnshire and Yorkshire	650
Fortifications at Milford Haven	50
Two youths accused of bathing indecently in Scotland	325
Fire at Boscobel	200
Two sections of miscellaneous small items; together	750

On 13 October the *Standard* also mentioned the meeting of the Staffordshire iron-masters (300 words) and printed a short report on Weyhill Fair (350 words).

The *Daily Telegraph*'s coverage of provincial news was still slighter.

On 4 October:

Inquest at Liverpool	125
Brother Ignatius at Manchester	525
Pit accident at Madeley	225
Convict leaps from train at Crewe	175

On 8 October:

Railway accident at Crewe	125
Duke of Cambridge visits Dover	300
Warwick colliers' strike	1,175

On 13 October:

Murder in Ireland	550
Brutal attack in Wednesbury	200
Unveiling of memorial window in Devonshire	375

Certain conclusions emerge, even from this tiny sample. The first is the miscellaneous character of the items: there are only two or three topics that appear in more then one list. In fact these items are often taken with acknowledgement, sometimes perhaps without, from the provincial press. They appear normally at the bottom of a page, and are apparently used to fill up a column. Miscellaneous as they are, they nevertheless include at least two items which might have deserved more space: even without their modern connotations of social tension, the late riot in Belfast and the incendiarism in Lincolnshire and Yorkshire might seem more newsworthy. Neither of these events was mentioned by more than one paper. Then again, apart from the reference to the Tyne and Wear navigation authorities, none of the papers refers to the great disputes about public works and municipal politics, or to the local agitations that filled the columns of the provincial press. Altogether the amount of the space (other than advertisements) occupied by provincial news amounted to between 2 per cent and 4 per cent—the figure of 4 per cent being unusually high since it was inflated by the report in the *Daily Telegraph* of the colliers' strike, a genuine piece of provincial news, treated fully. The long reports, mentioned earlier, on Gladstone at Bolton, the Church Congress, and the agricultural congress, have been excluded as they seem to be more appropriately seen as national events.

This small sample gives a fair impression of the way in which news was regularly handled: a few topics were treated exhaustively, and news which was not related to the interests of Londoners (including their City interests) was treated perfunctorily. It perhaps under-estimates the range of topics treated over a period. *The Times*, and even more the other two papers, were slow to extend their interests outside their established field of national and international politics, but they nevertheless made occasional excursions. *The Times* by 1864 ran, as has been shown, a regular column of Irish news, in the process giving, perhaps, more attention to Irish than to English provincial affairs; and on 24 October published a column of over 2,000 words on distress in Lancashire, collating evidence from five separate cotton towns. Nevertheless, such surveys were not frequent.

By 1894 the relative positions of London and provincial news might be expected to have altered substantially. Two reform acts had increased the weight of provincial industrial areas in the House of Commons; the provincial press had grown greatly in numbers of titles and circulation, and the development of news agencies should have made the routine scanning of provincial events simpler. Had the demand been there, the machinery to supply it would or could have been available. A summary of provincial news items similar to that carried out in 1864 yields these results:

On 15 October, 1894, *The Times*:

Accident at Leith	400
Shipbuilding at Belfast	300
Section including items on Oxford, a drought at Leicester, and speech at Oldham	450
Opening of Thirlmere reservoir	325
Centenary of Ushaw college	475
Explosion at Darlington	100

On 18 October

Leicester drought	300
Mining news, Pontypridd	175
Miscellaneous provincial news section	1,475
Disasters at sea	575

| University news | 400 |
| Liverpool School Board | 100 |

On 30 October:

| Miscellaneous provincial news | 275 |
| Liverpool court case | 175 |

The *Standard*, on the other hand, showed a significant development:

On 15 October:

Column 'The Provinces'	2,150
Accident at Leicester	100
Salmon hatchery, Chester	100
Cost of opening ceremony, Manchester Ship Canal	100
Miscellaneous	325
Opening of Thirlmere reservoir	811

On 18 October:

| 'The Provinces' | 1,900 |

On 30 October:

| 'The Provinces' | 2,125 |
| Court case, Liverpool | 225 |

The provincial news in the *Daily Telegraph* continued to be negligible.

On 15 October:

Accident at Leith	225
Opening of Thirlmere reservoir	225
Explosion at Birkenhead	50

On 18 October:

| Land conference, Belfast | 275 |

On 30 October there was, effectively, no provincial news.

Of the three papers under discussion, the *Standard* had developed a regular news column entitled 'The Provinces', which it had been running at least since 1885: the individual items in it might be similar to those that appeared in the other papers, but the existence of the column meant at least that the editor recognized provincial news as an integral part of his paper.

Palmer's *Index* to *The Times* makes possible other angles of approach. The total number of entries in the two periods, for a number of provincial towns, and relating to their political and economic affairs, are as shown in Table 11.4.

Table 11.4

	1864	1894
	(October–December quarter)	
Belfast	13	3
Birmingham	12	5
Bristol	0	0
Glasgow	2	0
Manchester	6	5
Norwich	1	2
Nottingham	2	0
Oxford*	0	0
Plymouth	0	0
Sheffield	6	0

* Other than the University, for which there were about fifty entries in the last quarter of 1864.

The impression of indifference is reinforced by the lists of topics handled in leading articles. In the last quarter of 1864 there were published eighteen articles on topics which might be considered provincial. There were five on the cotton famine, three on provincial reform meetings, five on industrial disputes, three on the drainage of towns, and two on Sabbatarianism in Scotland. In the October–December quarter of 1894 the list was much smaller: there were five altogether, on a cotton-workers' ballot, the meeting of the Incorporated Law Society at Bristol, the Manchester Ship Canal, the Scottish coal strike, and an article on 'Newcastle and Dublin' on politics. In each period rather more than 200 leading articles were published in all.

These ways of trying to assess the space given by newspapers to different kinds of event are open to the criticism that the samples are too small and may be unrepresentative. But they are straws which are all pointing the same way: and they support contemporary provincial criticisms of the metropolitan press—for example those of Joseph Chamberlain quoted in chapter IX.

To talk of distortion in the discussion of topics is to enter into more controversial territory: there are not many subjects about which an objective standard of truth could easily be agreed. A statement which might appear factual might well have some political intention, as for example the comments about Gladstone's health at a time when the succession to the Liberal leadership was becoming a matter of public speculation. We can talk with more confidence about distortion if we measure the actions of the press against something other than our own assessment of what would be a fair account of events. Two tests are suggested: first, can we show occasions on which the press misled in such a way that the public was taken by surprise by the course of events, and secondly, did they fail to take up pointers, from the proceedings of parliament for example? If they did fail, how far was it deliberate and how far inadvertent? These questions will be considered in relation to three periods, 1879–80, 1885–6, and 1893–5 and in relation to the reporting of domestic affairs.

The years 1879–80 are familiar to any student as years of crisis and a turning point: there was depression in industry, a very cold spring in 1879, a collapse of wheat prices in the summer, and the formation of the Land League in October, 1879. These troubles were followed by the Liberal victory in the General Election of April 1880 and Gladstone's eventual return to power, with a range of Radical supporters, and by the emergence of a powerful Parnellite party in the House of Commons. How well did the press cover these events? This question, as it stands, could only be answered by an exhaustive investigation, but it will be narrowed down to a study of the main articles (leading articles and others) and longer reports in the main London papers. Events reported in uncoordinated small paragraphs in odd corners of the paper could be as readily missed by contemporaries as by modern readers.

In December 1878, when the number of the unemployed were rising to the usual mid-winter peak, the stagnation of trade was raised in a parliamentary question by four MPs, and they received the reply that it was not as serious as it had been in 1868. This was not reported in *The Times*, and did not elicit any discussion on the leader page. During the opening months of 1879, which were very cold and snowy, *The Times* published

two leading articles on the commercial situation. Thereafter they published no leading articles until the autumn, though the depression deepened, and the unemployment rate was the highest for any year in the half-century down to 1914.[16] In the Commons the state of the economy was raised in debate on 22 May, and the *Daily News* published a leading article on the same question on the 26th; apart from that none of the papers under discussion reported anything, other than spasmodic small references to individual firms during the summer. In October the first signs that the recession was ending began to appear: there was renewed activity on the Stock Exchange and share prices began to rise. This recovery was fully reported in all the papers under discussion; in *The Times* there was, for the first time, a series of leading articles in October to December 1879, systematically discussing the reasons for the paper's belief in recovery. The presence of these articles underlines the lack of guidance and information to the paper's readers earlier in the year.

This chronology suggests the process of news-gathering that was at work. In the autumn of 1878, and through most of 1879, evidence of the recession could be obtained, possibly from accounts of unusual distress in London's East End, but chiefly from the provinces in the form of news of short-time working, closure of firms, or of strikes (notably a long strike of the Durham miners in April and May 1879), strikes which were in most cases stimulated by proposals by the employers for reductions in wages. On 14 April *The Times* published a leading article on trade disputes, in which the paper argued that wage reductions were a necessary part of the process of overcoming the recession. Apart from that, there was no general discussion of the economic trend. The news of closures and short-time working might be printed in isolated short reports in various corners of the paper, no attempt being made to present a co-ordinated account of the recession as a general phenomenon. The *Daily Telegraph* and the *Standard* handled the economic situation in much the same way; the *Daily News* occasionally presented a collected list of economic developments in an organized manner, though it did not do this at all frequently. Politicians taking their information from the daily press

[16] W. Ashworth, *An Economic History of England, 1870–1939*, 1960, 193.

could well be excused their failure to appreciate the situation.

When the first signs of recovery appeared in the autumn, all
the papers gave greater weight and emphasis to them. Partly,
perhaps, this was because they wished to give good news, but
partly it was because the signs of recovery appeared in the City,
in a quarter where they were in contact with the experts. City
news got into the papers: related happenings in the provinces
or in the East End did not. The onset of the recession had been
noticed in the City pages in 1878. This kind of reporting may
have been satisfactory to the London business man, but
politically it was misleading. It illustrates the effects of the news
values of the time, that Gladstone should have fought the 1880
General Election on the issues of Disraeli's foreign adventures.

The same narrow field of vision, or unwillingness to look at
what was politically unwelcome, can be seen in Irish affairs.
Conditions had been deteriorating in Ireland, as earnings from
migrant Irish labour in England went down with the onset of
the depression, as wheat prices fell and the potato crop also
failed in 1878–9. (The number of evictions rose from 980 in
1878 to 1,238 in 1879.)[17] The revival of the land agitation,
which became conspicuous in the 1880s, can be traced from the
spring of 1879: Parnell and Davitt were addressing meetings in
April 1879, which were reported briefly in the London papers.
On 4 July there was a full debate in the House of Commons on
the English agricultural collapse, which was fully discussed in
leading articles in *The Times*, the *Daily Telegraph*, the *Daily
News*, and the *Standard*. On this occasion there was an attempt
by Irish representatives to draw parliament's attention to the
Irish situation. The attempt drew from James Lowther, the
Irish Chief Secretary, a reply that Irish agricultural problems
were less serious than English ones, and that there was no
question of legislation to reduce Irish rents. This was briefly
reported by some of the papers. On 12 July a skirmish between
Irish and English MPs in the House received a much fuller
report. On 7 August the Irish members again raised the
question of Irish agriculture, on the adjournment, stressing
that near-famine conditions were prevailing in some parts of
the country. This earned a two-inch report from the *Daily News*
and the *Standard*; the *Daily Telegraph* ignored it altogether.

[17] F. S. L. Lyons, *Ireland since the Famine*, 1971, 160.

This indifference can be contrasted with the interest in the press in those topics which were canvassed by publicists and lobbyists. Parnell stood aside from such circles, and it is hard to see how a nationalist leader could have done otherwise. The Irish cause was propelled by public support in Ireland and the Irish vote in Britain, and supporters could be approached through the local press. The only Irish politician to move in circles where politicians and journalists met socially seems to have been Justin McCarthy, a leader-writer on the *Daily News*, the only major London paper to support Home Rule in 1886. This is not to suggest that anti-Irish feeling could be determined or even substantially changed by newspapers; but merely to say that this route to favourable publicity was not used by the Irish.

At the beginning of October the 'no rent' agitation in Ireland began in earnest. On 6 October a 'monster meeting' at Maryborough, Queen's County, was reported at length (one and a quarter columns) in the *Daily Telegraph, Standard, Daily News*, and *The Times*. By the end of November special correspondents of the *Standard, Daily Telegraph, Manchester Guardian, New York Herald*, and no doubt other papers, were in Ireland investigating and reporting for themselves; in the case of the *New York Herald* this led to the establishment of a relief fund in the United States.[18] The tone of the British reporting was still sceptical: for example *The Times* said on 23 October that the agitation was 'brief and frothy'; the *Daily Telegraph* wrote on 1 December, 'The tenantry are undoubtedly—as I have seen for myself—in extreme distress in many parts and like to be told that it is foreign tyranny and oppressive land legislation that have brought them to starvation and not their own hereditary want of thrift and the bad seasons.'

Throughout the year the coverage of the Irish question had lagged behind events. There had been clear signals in parliament in the middle of the year that there was trouble ahead: the only effective reporting began when there was a display of violence in the House of Commons in August, and even more when organized political agitation began in October. A significant comment came in the *Daily Telegraph* on 27 October, when

---

[18] According to T. M. Healy it raised £40,000 (*Letters and Leaders of my Day*, 2 vols., 1928, I, 92).

it reported that the Parisian *République française* had a leading article on Ireland saying that 'In the present instance the Irish question is far more discussed in the foreign press than it is in England itself.'

In the second period under discussion, 1885–6, the Irish question was at the centre of national politics and was fully treated in the press as a whole. Comparisons can, however, be made of the way in which industrial affairs were reported in 1885 and 1879–80. 1885–6 was again the trough of the depression. It was again a time of pressure on wages, and strikes, particularly in the Lancashire cotton industry, in resistance to these reductions. In July demand in parliament led to the appointment of the Royal Commission on the Depression of Industry. A widespread but unorganized interest in protective tariffs had been expressed from the late 1870s. Newspapers, particularly the *Standard*, had already been printing a great deal on German tariff questions in 1879; and the Conservatives had made a survey of opinion in the West Riding after their electoral defeat in 1880.[19] Manufacturing and commercial questions were therefore the object of increasing political interest. Social questions had also become more generally canvassed and, simply, more fashionable, with the publication of Henry George's *Progress and Poverty* in 1882, and Andrew Mearns's *Bitter Cry of Outcast London* in 1883, and with the setting up of the Royal Commission on the Housing of the Working Classes, chaired by Lord Salisbury, in 1884. It would not be surprising therefore if newspapers gave more attention to the recession in 1885–6 than they had done in 1879. Analysis of *The Times*'s leading articles shows that they published four on the depression in January and early February 1885, and two on the unemployed in London and on work for the unemployed (using that word) in February and March. Then they published one leading article on the trade depression in each of the months May and June; two on working-class housing in July, in connection with a bill before the Commons, and four on the trade depression in connection with the appointment of the Royal Commission on the Depression of Industry. These show a greater interest in such subjects than had been shown in 1879, in line with the greater parliamentary interest. It was

[19] Copy in Hambleden MSS, PS 7/80, Aug. 1881.

nevertheless slight when compared with the thirty-one leading articles published on the Afghan frontier question in the first half of the year.

The London papers' lack of interest in news of this kind, and unwillingness to spend energy or resources in finding it, might not have changed very much, as a detailed study of provincial strikes shows. In the late summer of 1885 the attempt to reduce wages in the cotton industry led to a prolonged strike by cotton workers in Oldham and the surrounding area. In Bolton the threat of a strike was averted at the last moment. At the same time there were strikes in the Staffordshire potteries, in Durham, and in the shipbuilding industry in Newcastle. 'Still more strikes, still more destitution ... from Oldham and Dundee, from Newcastle and Staffordshire, from all quarters comes the same sad tale.' This was how Hyndman's journal *Justice* described it on 12 September. This unrest coincided with Joseph Chamberlain's election tour, making speeches on behalf of his 'Unauthorised Programme', which was a major topic in the news. The only London newspaper to notice the unrest was *The Times*. It published three relevant articles in September; one on the Oldham strike on the 1st, one on the Royal Commission on the 8th, and one on the 14th on the strike in Newcastle. As well as this it published three in September on the annual meeting of the TUC. The only other paper to comment at all on the industrial situation was the *Daily News*, which published a leading article on steel production on 3 September. In general the newspapers either wrote on foreign affairs, or published articles appropriate to the 'silly season'; for example in the *Daily Telegraph* someone, probably Sala, was writing about an oyster which had been caught with two mice inside its shell. Another holiday topic was whether ladies would be capable of commanding the ships of the Royal Navy. In the news columns there were sporadic short references to industrial events, especially in the *Standard*'s regular column of provincial news.

This failure to make effective generalizations can be compared with similar failures in newspapers in the regions primarily affected: if we look at the *Oldham Chronicle* we find a full account of the day-to-day situation of the strikers in Oldham and the surrounding area—descriptions of soup kitchens, or of

the numbers of people on strike, and lengthy discussions of the precise points at issue. In the *Manchester Evening News* (published some eight miles away and circulating in some of the outlying Oldham districts), we find reports ranging from two inches to ten inches in length on the development of events in the neighbouring town. The *Bolton Evening News*, which, before the local cotton spinners settled for a 5 per cent reduction in wages, was describing the same situation as in Oldham, published notices perhaps two or three sentences long about the Oldham strike. The *Leeds Daily News* in the West Riding woollen region, but only about thirty miles from Oldham, published information about strikes in Dundee and Ilkeston, but nothing about Oldham. London papers were bad at putting together information from the provinces, but the provinces were equally bad at reporting news of each other. Each place was preoccupied with its own affairs. Only a committed socialist, it seems, could see these various events in a coherent form.

In the beginning of 1886 there was a series of disorders connected with the depression; in January troops were brought in to keep order between strikers and blacklegs in the slate quarries of North Wales—this was quite fully reported by *The Times* and the *Daily News*. On 8–10 February (Monday to Wednesday) there followed the famous series of riots when, after a meeting of the unemployed in Trafalgar Square, part of the crowd broke away and went on the rampage in Pall Mall and St James's Street and on into Mayfair.[20] The riots were helped by two days of fog on 9 and 10 February, after which they subsided. These events in the centre of the capital transformed the attitudes of the newspapers: all the papers under discussion could talk of little else in that week and for days after, and they began to give prominence to the subject in general: on 17 February *The Times* began a series of articles on 'Out-of-Work London', and the *Daily News* published an account summarizing and evaluating reports of riots in nine different provincial places. There could hardly be a clearer example of the extent to which London papers focused their interests on London: it needed the shock of the Pall Mall riots

[20] See chapter V.

for them to see that the unemployed were a significant problem.

By the 1890s the handling of these questions had developed a little further. It is worth looking by now also at the *Daily Chronicle*, which, since its acquisition by Edward Lloyd in 1876, had been growing in circulation and prestige as the Liberal–Radical morning paper. Two particular episodes may be considered: first the Bradford conference in January 1893, when the Independent Labour Party was established. There were already two ILP members in the House of Commons, since the election of 1892, so there was something in the already existing situation at Westminster to draw the newspapers' attention to it, but, nevertheless, the conference was a meeting, in a fairly remote provincial town, of what might have seemed a fairly obscure pressure group. Nevertheless, all the papers studied gave about a column to reports of the proceedings, by their own reporters. Two gave it a leading article, the *Daily News*, which was sympathetic, and the *Daily Telegraph*, which was disparaging.

A further test of the character of reporting can be made in connection with a strike of boot and shoe operatives in March and April 1895. This was an event which has a place in the history of trade unionism, but its reporting is significant for two other reasons: first, it did not involve workers in one of the traditional and picturesque heavy industries of the Industrial Revolution; factory-made shoes were an innovation of the previous twenty years, and journalists would have needed to be alert and informed to notice the significance of the strike. Secondly, the strike itself was significant in beginning simultaneously in a number of centres—Leicester, Northampton, Wellingborough, and minor boot and shoe centres in Northamptonshire. In contrast to the handling of strikes in 1878–9 and 1885–6, *The Times* at once treated the strike as a single event, publishing an account from 'an occasional correspondent' (that is a free-lance expert commissioned for the task), which assessed the questions in dispute, and described what had happened in the different centres. This was the kind of report which we expect today, but which had not been seen in the 1870s and 1880s. As for the *Daily Chronicle*, its industrial reporting was at the other extreme from the haphazard and

uninterested reporting shown in the 1870s and 1880s. In the 1890s the *Daily Chronicle* introduced a regular daily feature, 'The Labour Movement', in which varied items were collected together. For example (when there might have been a shortage of other news) the column included a report of a sermon delivered by Canon Scott Holland to the unemployed in St Paul's Cathedral. The variety of disputes, disturbances, and accounts of events in charitable Settlements, illustrate the kind of thing which had failed to get into the newspapers before. The *Daily Chronicle* had its sights firmly fixed on events in the boot and shoe industry.

With the passage of time, the London papers had improved their ability to diagnose and report such labour questions. To a certain extent they were reflecting a shift in public interest. In the 1870s the treatment of industrial troubles in general, and more especially of strikes, in the press was hampered by lack of an appropriate set of ideas in the minds of the writers. In one of the few leading articles in *The Times*, on 23 November 1878, the writer wondered if it were true that there was such a thing as a trade cycle in Britain, whether it was inevitably of ten years' duration, and whether cycles of some kind occurred in other countries as well. This suggests that he had no accepted idea of how the recession had arisen. People were agreed however on the way out of it: the economy was 'a self-supporting, self-acting social system': resistance to reductions in wages would delay the natural process of reduction in prices which would in due course set the wheels of recovery again in motion. Thus, there was no remedy to put forward: the recession was part of a natural and inevitable process whose nature was not understood. It is easier to report news associated with some proposed form of action—had the strikes of 1879–80 given support to the programme of an established pressure group they would have probably been given more space. (It would be worth comparing the reporting of provincial affairs in 1879 with that of the 1840s, when the programme of free trade was being put forward, or with that in the cotton famine. when distress was certainly there, in the same places, but when it could be attributed to a stand being taken on a great moral issue.) By the end of the 1880s the criticism of Ricardian economics, which was being expressed on a number of fronts,

and the livelier sympathy being shown for the poor, made it more likely that newspapers would exert themselves to find out facts. Since most of Britain's major large-scale industry lay outside London, these investigations automatically did something to redress the London-centred bias of the London papers.

The reporting of economic difficulties may also have suffered—though this is not so clear—from the lack of convenient indicators. Today there is the regular publication of unemployment figures: in the nineteenth century there was no equivalent of this; the unemployment percentages derived from trade union records which are used today by historians are calculations carried out a generation later. Nor does it seem that they could get any very clear-cut day-to-day guidance on provincial affairs from City pages. Very few British industrial shares were quoted on the London Stock Exchange: some were quoted locally on provincial exchanges, some family firms were not quoted at all. The list of share prices in the London papers concentrated on government stocks, railway companies, and overseas stocks of various kinds.

In general, then, the choice of what to emphasize rested more on what was current politically than on attempts to try and find out the state of the nation: and sometimes, as in 1879, press investigation lagged well behind the raising of questions in parliament. The importance of party politics in determining what newspapers would investigate is shown in the later history of the Irish land question: by 1888 'Bloody Balfour's' handling of Irish disorders was the subject of party dispute at Westminster, and we find reference in *Hansard* to complaints that newspapermen had been prevented from witnessing eviction scenes, or equally significantly, that *The Times* reporter had been given a privileged position in seeing them.[21] These scenes, which had been ignored in the 1870s, were now the object of press competition. The press paid more attention to Ireland and the English provinces because politicians were doing so too. Nevertheless, when all these points have been weighed, a development in the techniques of reporting can be seen. The *Daily Chronicle* was able, without the aid of unemployment figures, to present a picture of labour which was its own creation, and which, by collecting individual scraps of infor-

[21] *Hansard*, vol. 329, col. 198 (20 July 1888).

mation, offered a new topic for public debate: the columns on the Labour Movement deserve a place in the history of investigative journalism. According to H. W. Massingham, who may well have worked on that column, 'The Labour News is the most extensive and most carefully edited that any paper presents to its readers. It has the confidence of the trade unions and London working men more than any since the *Northern Star*.'[22] *The Times* was also by the 1890s much more likely to publish articles in which the paper offered surveys, which were apparently independently prepared, of the general progress of events.

Over thirty years, therefore, there had been changes in the handling of the news, but it was hardly spectacular. The volume of material collected might be increasing, and editorial staffs (from the few facts we know) increasing also.[23] But the general formulas on which newspapers were constructed had hardly changed. It remained true that newspaper pages were filled with reports, which might be effectively verbatim, of meetings and speeches; that London papers showed little interest in the provinces; and that provincial papers themselves were local in their interests. If there was a greater awareness of social questions in the 1890s it was because the subject was growing in importance in Westminster politics. It could be argued that the style developed by *The Times*, under Delane's editorship, of parliamentary and diplomatic news and commentary directed to the interests of the well-to-do Londoner, was generally followed to the end of the century.

Where there was discernible change was at the other end of the market. Provincial papers grew faster than London ones, and halfpenny evenings more than morning ones.[24] These evening papers changed profoundly over the last thirty years of the century. In the 1870s they had come into being to recirculate, cheaply, the previous day's news, sometimes using the morning paper's plates for the purpose. In the following years they continued on the whole to reprint news secondhand, where they were linked to a morning paper. By the end of the century they had developed their modern style, with separate

[22] Massingham, 121–2.
[23] See chapter IV.
[24] See chapter II.

editorial staffs, separate reports, and concentrated on the same day's news, especially in sport. They were developing a different range of news interests, more local, more sporting, less concerned with London life, adapted to the general run of the provincial public.

XII

Conclusion

IN the second half of the nineteenth century the newspaper became established as part of the normal furniture of life for all classes; and by 'newspaper' would have been understood a paper owned by the reader and most probably appearing daily. It was considered reasonable by those in authority that prisoners, workhouse inmates, and members of the Forces should be provided with newspapers.[1] (There survives among Wolseley's papers a satirical Forces' newspaper, the *Wady Halfa Gazette*, with laboured jokes about electoral reform among the pyramids, produced for the entertainment of the troops.) Figures of circulation are patchy and uncertain: we can form reasonable estimates for the main successful London and provincial papers, but the total volume of local papers, weekly papers, short-lived papers, and publications such as the *Wady Halfa Gazette*, would be impossible to guess.

There cannot be any doubt about the widespread and lively absorption in news of many sorts in late Victorian Britain. It was shown in many ways: in the anecdote of the Shaftesbury News Club,[2] in papers started up to report particular events, such as those which concentrated on the Tichborne Case, and in special editions—the *Daily News* thought it worth while in 1880 to print a special edition with the result of the Boat Race (and a defeat of the Afghans). The most convincing evidence of a solid public interest in the news is that so many well-known episodes of late Victorian history only make sense against a background in which news was circulating widely: the Bulgarian agitation, the Midlothian speeches, and the Khaki election are obvious examples. So is the story of the Queen's unpopularity in the 1870s: how often had anti-royal feeling been provoked by individuals' frustrated attempts to see her pass? And how often had newspapers told them of her absence?

In this advance of the newspapers to a central position in

[1] See chapter II.
[2] See p. 96 above.

public life political considerations played their part, though the full ramifications of the process are not yet clear. The technical printing and telegraphic developments of the 1860s and 1870s came at a providential time for party politicians. Cheap, up-to-the-minute, and interesting newspapers were becoming easier to provide at precisely the time when the parties were faced with new problems in handling urban electorates. Conversely, the party magnates and managers provided a source of newspaper finance. It is not known how frequently this happened, nor can the effects of the political connection be assessed with much precision: it certainly will have helped to promote competition and political variety among newspapers; how far it actually restricted the range of what was reported is another question.

In these ways newspapers developed in the later nineteenth century in a favourable environment: in the general writing on the subject there was no longer the suggestion that they were engines of potential sedition. A second general reflection must concern the energy and drive with which they were developed. The proprietors were willing to invest in the new technologies—the web rotary presses, the private wires, and later the telephone. The specialized skills involved in collecting the news, putting it together in print, and distributing it, were developed apparently without strain. We do not read complaints in correspondence about the difficulty of finding competent people to run the rapidly increasing number of new publications—though it is a difficulty which might have been expected. Newspapers are also distinguished by the courage and enterprise with which they embarked on assignments whose difficulty we tend to overlook: for example, in the spring of 1885 many papers had their correspondents with Wolseley on the Upper Nile. They left at the end of February after the fall of Khartoum.[3] By the end of March someone was sending despatches to the *Standard* from Meshed in north-east Persia.[4] Whether one person went from one place to the other, or whether the *Standard* employed two correspondents, difficult and expensive journeys to remote areas were involved. War

---

[3] Preston, *In Relief of Gordon*. 163.

[4] See issue of 31 Mar. They were also printing dispatches from Suakin on the Red Sea at the same time.

correspondents have a reputation for self-advertisement,[5] and their exploits tend to be played down, but in fact they needed great courage, and their employment was very expensive.[6]

Newspaper history is also distinguished by its record of co-operative action by the proprietors. It was not uncommon in Victorian Britain for businessmen to band together, often in order to put pressure on the government: one may cite the General Shipowners' Society acting in defence of the Navigation Acts, or the many occasions on which the Manchester Chamber of Commerce memorialized the government. Joint working arrangements existed in the banking and railway world. But the history of the Provincial Newspaper Society shows common action to an exceptional extent—in agitating in the 1850s for the abolition of the remaining taxes on newspapers, and in the 1860s for the acquisition of the telegraphs by the Post Office. The creation of the Press Association in a form which enabled it quickly to occupy a central position in the dissemination of news is an outstanding example of co-operative action—not, as with the clearing-house operations of the banks and railways, a rationalization of arrangements at the frontiers of different organizations, but an agreement to accept a common supply of the main ingredients of the members' productions.

This picture of vigour and enterprise stands in striking contrast to the ways in which news was commonly handled in the later nineteenth century. The Victorian newspaper with, by modern standards, a small circulation, could be expected to deploy its resources frugally: the characteristic news item—a report of a meeting of which there had been advance notice—was, from this point of view, a sound investment of resources. At the other extreme, investigative journalism might involve time wasted in following false trails. It is also necessary to be cautious in generalization: no one can sample more than a small fraction of the acres of printed material which have survived. Nevertheless, with these qualifications in mind, it remains true that managements rarely showed vigour and

---

[5] This is well illustrated by the titles of some of their reminiscences: Archibald Forbes, *Souvenirs of some Continents*, 1885; or J. E. H. Skinner, (also of the *Daily News*) *After the Storm*, 1866, and *Roughing it in Crete*, 1868.

[6] See chapter X.

initiative. At all the various points at which the present study
has tried to unravel the route by which the newspapers got hold
of news, and the way in which they presented it to the public, it
can be shown that influence exerted by politicians, or lobbyists,
met with little effective criticism or resistance. The reasons for
this may vary: sometimes the voice of a lobby may not have
been recognized for what it was, sometimes it may have exactly
expressed what an editor wished to print, sometimes it may
have been printed along the line of least resistance. In their
range of interests newspapers followed current fashions: it is
very hard to find topics which they were the first to introduce
into public debate.

It is a paradox, though an understandable one, that, in
proportion as the newspapers grew in social acceptance, being
no longer taxed or suspected, so they declined in critical vigour.
At the beginning of the century there was a popular press,
stamped and unstamped, which enjoyed good sales, and which
filled its columns with streams of criticism of tax-eaters,
shopocrats, millocrats, and base lying Whigs. Such papers
carried very little general news, and concentrated their attack
on what had been said in Parliament. By the end of the century
there were popular halfpenny papers, mostly in the evening,
with summaries of the day's international and national news,
and devoting much space to football news and romantic serials.
A similar process of settling-down perhaps affected the London
papers: the *Daily Telegraph* had begun as a Radical–Liberal
paper, and *The Times* had been the 'Thunderer' in the days of
Barnes's editorship. Much of this change must be connected
with changes in the attitudes of the reading public. Some
of it, however, in the London dailies at least, would be
connected with the public appetite for inside news, and the
assumption that a true view of the situation could only be
obtained through confidential hints from those in the know. If
inside information was essential, journalists were unlikely to
antagonize their contacts unduly, though they might favour
one political group against another, or one foreign power, or
attack a fallen idol who had no future usefulness anyway.
Contacts like Carnarvon and Granville operated within the old
conventions of political patronage, Carnarvon sending his

favoured journalists parcels of pheasants and venison, but not inviting them for the shooting.[7] Had the politicians been pestered or driven into corners they might have broken the contacts off. Similarly, in foreign affairs newspapers received information from *émigré* sources, or from foreign governments; it might be suspect, but if they rejected it they might be left with nothing.

Such a position of dependence may be the normal condition of political journalism: it would have been the same in the early nineteenth century, and today 'sources close to' public figures are reported prominently in the newspapers. The paradox was that this situation of real dependence—shown, for example most painfully in Morley's pleas for help quoted in an earlier chapter[8]—should coexist with the exalted nineteenth-century belief in the press as the impartial investigator of truth and righter of wrong.

[7] Carnarvon MSS, BL Add. MS 60776, letter dated 8 Aug. 1878 (to Meredith Townsend), 60777 2 Feb. and 22 July 1889 (W. T. Stead), 60779, 24 Dec. 1880 (T. H. S. Escott).

[8] See p. 187 above.

Bibliography

THESE lists are of the manuscript and printed sources cited in the text. They are not a general bibliography of the subject: for that there is a very full list in the *New Cambridge Bibliography of English Literature*, vol. III, Cambridge, 1969, cols. 1755–1866. For information on particular newspapers the most useful sources are the press directories: *Mitchell's Newspaper Press Directory* (from 1846), *May's London Press Dictionary* (from 1871, and from 1890 taken over by *Willing's Press Guide*), and *Deacon's Newspaper Handbook* (from 1877). Probably more widely accessible is the British Library's published *Catalogue of the Newspaper Library*, 1975, 8 vols., and, in conjunction with it, the catalogue *Microfilms of Newspapers and Journals for Sale, 1983–4*, listing the rapidly increasing number of titles which may be read on microfilm.

MANUSCRIPTS

Alfred Austin MSS, Bristol University Library.
A. H. Burgess's Letter-Book, Manchester Central Library.
Carnarvon MSS, British Library.
Joseph Chamberlain MSS, Birmingham University Library.
Cowen MSS, Tyne and Wear Record Office.
Dilke MSS, British Library.
Disraeli MSS, Bodleian Library.
Escott MSS, British Library.
Gladstone MSS, British Library.
Herbert Gladstone MSS, British Library.
Granville MSS, Public Record Office.
Guardian archives, Manchester University Library.
Montague Guest MSS, British Library.
Hambleden MSS, W. H. Smith and Son, Ltd.
Hamilton MSS, British Library.
Iddesleigh MSS, British Library.
Leader MSS, Sheffield Central Library.
Manchester Town Hall Opening Celebrations Documents, Manchester Central Library.
National Liberal Club archives, Bristol University Library.
Northcliff MSS, British Library.

Peel MSS, British Library.
Le Poer Power MSS, British Library.
Prendergast MSS, British Library.
E. R. Russell MSS, British Library.
Saunders MSS, Churchill College, Cambridge.
W. H. Smith archives, W. H. Smith and Son, Ltd.
The Times archives.
H. J. Wilson MSS, Sheffield Central Library.
Wolseley MSS, Hove Public Library.
Yates's Diary, British Library.

PUBLIC RECORD OFFICE

BT 13/11 practice over advertising in newspapers.
BT 13/16 Communications to newspapers, and the foundation of the
  Board of Trade Journal.
BT 13/27 Communications to newspapers.
FO 83/814 Communications to newspapers, 1870–1884, continued in
FO 83/1328, 1885–94, and
FO 83/2028, 1895–1905.
HO 45/9864/B13734 Communications to the press and government
  advertising list.
T1/7385/B Papers relating to prohibition of civil servants' communi-
  cations to the press (Treasury Minute 8466/73), and official
  communications to newspapers.
T1/13802 Provisions of newspapers for use by government depart-
  ments.
WO31/38 Regulations, 1878, including conduct of war correspon-
  dents, continued in
WO33/32.

OFFICIAL PUBLICATIONS

Hansard's Parliamentary Debates.
Statistique générale de la Télégraphie, pub. annually, Berne, 1874– .
Select Committee on the Post Office (Telegraph Department), 1876 (357)
  XIII.
Select Committee on Parliamentary Reporting, 1878 (327) XVII, 1878–9
  (203) XII, 1880 (H. L. 66) VII Sess. 2.
Royal Commission on the Press, Parliamentary papers, 1947–8 XIV–XV;
  1948–9, XX.
Royal Commission on the Press, Parliamentary papers, 1961–2 XXI–
  XXII.

CONTEMPORARY WORKS

Where no place of publication is given London should be understood.

Adams, William E. A., *Memoirs of a Social Atom*, 2 vols., 1902.

Arrivabene, Charles (Carlo), *Italy under Victor Emmanuel*, 2 vols., 1862.

Aspden, Hartley, *Fifty Years a Journalist*, n.d.

Atkinson, John C., *Forty Years in a Moorland Parish*, 1891.

Austin, Alfred, *Autobiography*, 2 vols., 1911.

Bahlman, Dudley W. R., *The Diary of Sir Edward Hamilton*, 2 vols. Oxford, 1972.

Barker, Alfred, *The Newspaper World*, 1890.

Beatty-Kingston, William, *A Journalist's Jottings*, 2 vols. 1890.

—— *Men, Cities, and Events* [1895].

Blunt, Wilfrid Scawen, *Secret History of the English Occupation of Egypt*, 2nd edn. 1907.

Boon, John, *Victorian, Edwardians, and Georgians*, 2 vols., 1927.

Brett, Maurice V. and Oliver S. B., *Journals and Letters of Reginald, Viscount Esher*, 4 vols., 1934–8.

Brett, Reginald, see Brett, above.

Brodrick, George C., *Memories and Impressions, 1831–1900*, 1900.

Bussey, Harry F., *Sixty Years of Journalism*, Bristol, 1906.

Campbell, Duncan, *Reminiscences of an Octogenarian Highlander*, Inverness, 1910.

Clarke, Tom, *My Northcliffe Diary*, 1931.

Cline, Clarence L. (ed.), *Letters of George Meredith*, 3 vols., Oxford, 1970.

Cobbe, Frances Power, *Life of Frances Power Cobbe, by Herself*, 2 vols., 1894.

Cobbett, William, *Rural Rides*, 1830, Everyman edn., 2 vols., n.d.

—— *History of the Regency and Reign of King George the Fourth*, 2 vols., 1830–4.

Cooper, Charles A., *An Editor's Retrospect*, 1896.

Dasent, Arthur I., *John Thadeus Delane*, 2 vols., 1908.

Downey, Edmund, *Twenty Years Ago*, 1905.

Escott, Thomas H. S., *Platform, Press, Politics and Play*, Bristol, n.d.

—— *Club Makers and Club Members*, 1914.

—— (A Foreign Resident, pseud.), *Society in London*, 1885.

Forbes, Archibald, *Souvenirs of some Continents*, 1885.

—— *Memories and Studies of War and Peace*, 1895.

Frost, Thomas, *Reminiscences of a Country Journalist*, 1886.

Gallenga, Antonio, *Episodes of my Second Life*, 2 vols., 1884.

Gardiner, Alfred G., *The Life of Sir William Harcourt*, 2 vols., 1923.

Gaskell, Elizabeth, *Life of Charlotte Brontë*, 1857, Everyman edn., 1908.

Gissing, George, *New Grub Street*, 1891, Penguin edn., 1968.

Gladstone, W. E., *Diaries*, see under Matthew; correspondence under Ramm.

Gordon, Peter (ed.), *The Red Earl: the Papers of the Fifth Earl Spencer, 1835–1910*, I, 1981.

Granville, Earl, see under Ramm.

Griffiths, Arthur, *Clubs and Clubmen*, 1907.

Greville C. C. F., see under Strachey and Fulford.

Hamilton, Sir Edward, see under Bahlman.

Hatton, Joseph, *Journalistic London*, 1882.

Healy, Timothy M., *Letters and Leaders of my Day*, 2 vols., 1928.

Hirst, Francis W., *Early Life and Letters of John Morley*, 2 vols., 1927.

Hoole, William S. (ed.), *Lawley Covers the Confederacy*, Tuscaloosa, 1964.

Hyndman, Henry M., *The Record of an Adventurous Life*, 1911.

Jackson, Mason, *The Pictorial Press, its Origin and Progress*, 1885.

Jefferies, Richard, *Hodge and his Masters*, 1880.

Jones, Kennedy, *Fleet Street and Downing Street*, n.d.

Kipling, Rudyard, *Something of Myself*, 1937.

Lloyd, Edward, *A Glimpse into Paper-Making and Journalism* [1895].

Low, Sidney, and Ker, William P., *Samuel Henry Jeyes, his Personality and Work, 1915*.

Lucas, Reginald, *Lord Glenesk and the Morning Post*, 1910.

Lucy, Sir Henry W., *Peeps at Parliament*, 1904.

—— *Sixty Years in the Wilderness*, 1909.

M'Callum, J. Leslie, *James Annand M.P., a Tribute*, 1908.

McCarthy, Justin, *Our Book of Memories: Letters of Justin McCarthy to Mrs Campbell Praed*, 1912.

—— and Robinson, Sir John, *The Daily News Jubilee*, 1896.

Massingham, Henry W., *The London Daily Press*, 1892.

Matthew, Henry Colin G. (ed.), *The Gladstone Diaries*, vols V–VIII, 1864–4, Oxford, 1978–82.

Meredith, George, see under Cline.

Meynell, Wilfred, ('John Oldcastle' pseud.) *Journals and Journalism, with a Guide for Literary Beginners*, 1880.

Morley, John, 'Anonymous journalism', in *Fortnightly Review*, VIII, 1867.

Nicoll, Sir William R., *James Macdonell, Journalist*, 1890.

Noble, Mark, *Short Sketches of the Eminent Men of the North of England*, Newcastle, 1885.

Ogden, Rollo (ed.), *The Life and Letters of E. L. Godkin*, 2 vols., 1907.

Pears, Sir Edwin, *Forty Years in Constantinople . . . 1873–1915*, 1916.

Pike, Godfrey Holden, *John Cassell*, 1894.

Ponsonby, Sir Frederick, *Letters of the Empress Frederick*, 1928.

Preston, Adrian (ed.), *In Relief of Gordon. Lord Wolseley's Campaign Journal . . . 1884–1885*, 1967.

Ramm, Agatha (ed.), *The Political Correspondence of Mr. Gladstone and Lord Granville*, 1868–76, Camden 3 ser. lxxxi–ii, 2 vols. 1952; and *1876–1886*, 2 vols., Oxford, 1962.

Reid, Stuart J. (ed.), *The Memoirs of Sir Wemyss Reid*, 1905.

Reid, Sir T. Wemyss, *The Life of the Right Honourable William Edward Forster*, 2 vols., 1888.

Robinson, Sir John R., *Fifty Years in Fleet Street*, 1904.

Rowntree, Benjamin Seebohm, *Poverty, a Study of Town Life*, 4th edn., 1902.

Russell, William Howard, *My Diary During the Last Great War*, 1874.

Sala, George A., *The Life and Adventures of George Augustus Sala, written by Himself*, 2 vols., 1895.

Simonis, H., *Street of Ink*, 1917.

Sinclair, Alexander, *Fifty Years of Newspaper Life: being chiefly Reminiscences of that Time*, Glasgow, privately printed [1895?].

Skinner, John E. H.,*After the Storm*, 2 vols., 1866.

—— *Roughing it in Crete*, 1868.

Smith, Wareham, *Spilt Ink*, 1932.

Spencer, Earl, see under Gordon.

Spender, J. A., *Life, Journalism, and Politics*, 2 vols., 1927.

Stanley, Lord, see under Vincent.

Strachey, Lytton and Fulford, Roger (eds.), *The Greville Memoirs, 1814–1860*, 8 vols., 1938.

Thorold, Algar, *The Life of Henry Labouchere*, 1913.

Vincent, John, *Disraeli, Derby and the Conservative Party, Journals and Memoirs of Edward Henry, Lord Stanley, 1849–69*. Hassocks, 1978.

Watson, Aaron, *A Newspaper Man's Memories*, n.d.

Watts, Alfred Alaric, *Alaric Watts, a Narrative of his Life*, 2 vols., 1884.

Whitty, Edward M., *St. Stephen's in the Fifties*, 1906.

Wolseley, see under Preston.

MODERN WORKS

Ashworth, William, *An Economic History of England, 1870–1939*, 1960.

Aspinall, Arthur, 'The social status of journalists at the beginning of the nineteenth century', *Review of English Studies*, XXI, 1945.

—— *Politics and the Press, c. 1780–1850*, 1949.

Asquith, Ivon, 'Advertising and the press in the late eighteenth and early nineteenth centuries: James Perry and the *Morning Chronicle* 1790–1821', *Historical Journal*, XVIII, 4, 1975.

—— 'The Whig party and the press in the early nineteenth century', *Bulletin of the Institute of Historical Research*, November, 1976.

Ayerst, David, *Guardian, Biography of a Newspaper*, 1971.

Baylen, Joseph O., 'W. T. Stead as publisher and editor of the *Review of Reviews*', *Victorian Periodicals Newsletter*, Bloomington, Ind., 1978–80.

Bennett, Geoffrey, *Charlie B.*, 1968, (Beresford).

Berlin, Sir Isaiah, *Karl Marx*, Oxford, 1939.

Berridge, Virginia, 'Popular Sunday papers and mid-Victorian society' in Boyce *et al.*, *Newspaper History*, 247–64.

Boyce, George, Curran, James and Wingate, Pauline, *Newspaper History*, 1978.

Brewer, John, *Party Ideology and Popular Politics at the Accession of George III*, Cambridge, 1976.

Brown, Lucy, 'The treatment of the news in mid-Victorian newspapers', *Transactions of the Royal Historical Society*, 5th ser., XXVII, 1977.

Burnham, Lord, *Peterborough Court*, 1955.

Chilston, Lord, *W. H. Smith*, 1965.

Codding, George A. *The International Telecommunications Union*, Leiden, 1952.

Cooke, Alistair B. and Vincent, John, *The Governing Passion*, Brighton and New York, 1974.

Crapster, Basil L. 'Thomas Hamber, 1828–1902, Tory journalist', in *Victorian Periodicals Newsletter*, Bloomington, Ind. 1978–80.

Elton, Lord, *General Gordon*, 1954.

Fisher, Lord, see under Marder.

Flint, John, *Cecil Rhodes*, 1976.

Foster, John, *Class Struggle and the Industrial Revolution*, [1974].

Fraser, Peter, *Lord Esher, a Political Biography*, 1973.

Gash, Norman, *Sir Robert Peel*, 1972.

Gibb, Mildren A. and Beckwith, Frank, *The Yorkshire Post: Two Centuries*, 1954.

Giles, Frank, *A Prince of Journalists: the Life and Times of de Blowitz*, 1962.

Gittings, Robert, *Young Thomas Hardy*, 1975, Penguin edn. 1978.

—— *The Older Hardy*, 1978, Penguin edn., 1980.

Hadley, W. E., 'Northamptonshire memories', in *Northamptonshire Past and Present*, II (1956), 123–30.

Hale, Oron J., *Publicity and Diplomacy*, 1940.

Hanham, Harold J., *Elections and Party Managements: Politics in the Time of Disraeli and Gladstone*, 1959.

Henderson, Philip, *The Life of Laurence Oliphant*, 1956.

Hollingworth, Brian, *Songs of the People: Lancashire Dialect Poetry of the Industrial Revolution*, Manchester, 1977.

Howe, Ellic, *Newspaper Printing in the Nineteenth Century*, 1943.

Keir, David L. and Lawson, Frederick H., *Cases in Constitutional law*, 1948 edn.

Koss, Stephen, *The Rise and Fall of the Political Press in Britain*: I, *The Nineteenth Century, 1981*, II *The Twentieth Century, 1984*.

Leavis, Queenie D., *Fiction and the Reading Public*, 1932.

Lee, Alan J., *The Origins of the Popular Press, 1855–1914*, 1976.

Longford, Elizabeth, *Victoria R. I.*, 1964.

Lucas, P. J. 'Furness newspapers in mid-Victorian England' in Peter Bell (ed.), *Victorian Lancashire*, Newton Abbot, 1974.

Lyons, Francis S. L., 'Parnellism and Crime' in *Transactions of the Royal Historical Society*, 5th ser., XXIV, 1974.

—— *Ireland since the Famine*, 1971.

Mackay, Ruddock, *Fisher of Kilverstone*, Oxford, 1973.

McKibbin, Ross, 'Working class gambling in Britain, 1880–1939' in *Past and Present*, no. 82, 1979.

Magnus, Sir Philip, *King Edward the Seventh*, 1964, Penguin edn. 1967.

Marder, Arthur, *Fear God and Dread Nought: . . . the Correspondence of Admiral of the Fleet Lord Fisher of Kilverstone*, 3 vols., 1952–9.

Mills, John Saxon, *Sir Edward Cook K. B. E.; a Biography*, 1921.

Naylor, Leonard E., *The Irrepressible Victorian: the Story of Thomas Gibson Bowles*, 1965.

Nevett, Terry R., *Advertising in Britain*, 1982.

Ogilvy-Webb, Marjorie, *The Government Explains*, 1965.

Palmer, Michael, 'The British press and international news 1851–99; of agencies and newspapers' in Boyce *et al.*, *Newspaper History*.

Pares, Richard, *King George III and the Politicians*, Oxford, 1953, 30.

Paul, Humphrey, 'Random Northamptonshire reminiscences' in *Northamptonshire Past and Present*, II, 1955.

Phillips, Gordon, 'A national press archive' in Boyce *et al.*, *Newspaper History*.

Porter, A. N., 'Sir Alfred Milner and the Press, 1897–1899', in *Historical Journal*, XVI, 1973.

Preston, Adrian, 'Wolseley: the Khartoum relief expedition and the defence of India, 1885–1900', in *Journal of Imperial and Commonwealth History*, May 1978.

Robinson, R., and Gallagher, J., *Africa and the Victorians*, 1961.

Saul, S. B., *The Myth of the Great Depression*, 1969.

Scott, George, *Reporter Anonymous: the Story of the Press Association*, 1968.

Scott, J. W. Robertson, *The Life and Death of a Newspaper*, 1952.

Seguin, J-P., *Nouvelles à sensation: canards du* XIXe *siècle*, Paris, 1959.

Seymour-Ure, Colin, *The Press, Politics and the Public*, 1968.

Shannon, Richard T., *Gladstone and the Bulgarian Agitation*, 1963.

Smith, Colin L., *The Embassy of Sir William White at Constantinople, 1886–1891*, Oxford, 1957.

Stansky, Peter D. L., *Ambitions and Strategies: the Struggle for the Leadership of the Liberal Party in the 1890s*, Oxford, 1964.

Steiner, Zara, *The Foreign Office and Foreign Policy*, Cambridge, 1969.

Storey, Graham, *Reuters Century*, 1951.

Thompson, Paul, *Socialists, Liberals and Labour, the Struggle for London*, 1967.

Times, The History of the, 5 vols., 1935–52.

Tunstall, Jeremy, *The Westminster Lobby Correspondents*, 1970.

Ward, Humphrey, *History of the Athenaeum, 1824–1925*, 1926.

Wadsworth, Alfred P., 'Newspaper circulations, 1800–1954', *Manchester Statistical Society Transactions*, 1954–5.

Wellesley Index to Victorian Periodicals, Toronto, 1966– .

Index of Newspapers and Periodicals mentioned in the Text

All the Year Round 108
Altrincham and Bowdon Guardian 117
Answers 251
Ashton Evening Reporter 19, 100

Band of Hope Review and Sunday Scholar's Friend 48
Barnsley Chronicle, circulation 53
Barnsley Independent 101
Barrow Times 82
Berwick Advertiser 81
Birmingham Daily Post 44, 69, 89; reporting on Sunday 99, 123, 150; political
     contacts 194–5, 254
Birmingham Journal 88
Blackburn Patriot, and party politics 73
Blackwood's Magazine 28
Blue Budget 66
Board of Trade Journal 156
Bolton Evening Guardian (*Bolton Guardian* after 1880) 60; and Henry Lucy 125
Bolton Evening News 60, 109; industrial news 267
Bolton Journal (amalgamated with *Guardian* 1893) 109
Border Advertiser (Galashiels) 81
Borough of Oldham Vindicator and Lancashire Ten Hours' Advocate 58
Bradford Advertiser 76
Bradford Daily Telegraph 26 n.3; circulation 43, 41, 53; and party politics 60
Bradford Observer (*Yorkshire Daily Observer* after 1901) 41; and 1868 election 60,
     151, 155 n.39
Bradford Review, and party politics 73
Bradford Times 41
[Brighton] *Argus* 60
Brighton Examiner 81
Brighton Guardian 81
Bristol Evening News 98
British Lion 66
Bucks Advertiser (Aylesbury) 73, 81
Bucks Herald 15, 28, 250 n.7
Bury and Suffolk Standard, circulation 53
Buxton Advertiser and High Peak Chronicle, and Duke of Devonshire 71

Cape Times (Cape Town) 212
[Cardiff] *Western Mail*, circulation 53; and Lord Bute 70

Carlisle Journal 81
Cassell's Magazine 83
Catholic Progress, in HM prisons 48
Central Press 118, 125
Chambers's Journal 133
Civil Service Review 153
Clerkenwell News 61; see also *Daily Chronicle*
Cologne Gazette 242
Congleton and Macclesfield Mercury 73
Conservative Journal and Church of England Gazette 66
Contemporary Review 107–8; and W. T. Stead 187, 193
Cornhill Magazine 107–8, 133
Cumberland Pacquet and Ware's Whitehaven Advertiser (in 1896 *West Cumberland Post*) 81

Daily Chronicle (formerly *Clerkenwell News*), advertising rates 19–20, 36, 39, 50; features 106; inside knowledge 198–203; sporting news 245; industrial reporting 268–9, 271
Daily Express, library 253
Daily Gazette for Middlesbrough, Stockton and District 109 n.21
Daily Mail 12, 17; branded goods advertisements 21; circulation 27, 33, 86; popular style 102; news editing 250–2
Daily News, machinery 9; advertisements 19; display advertisements 22; circulation 31, 39–43, 51, 52; and party politics 61–5; staff 75–7; editor's position 90–1, 102; features 106; shares news with *New York Tribune* 115, and with *Morning Post* 116, 131, 133; and Maurice 141 143, 157; and Gladstone 177–82, 185; inside knowledge 196–203; in Sudan 207; and Sardinia 217–21; American Civil War 222; Franco-Prussian War 224, 227; Merv 229, 344; Bulgarian atrocities 235; sports news 245–6; industrial news 261–8; Irish distress 263–5; special editions 273
Daily Telegraph, machinery 9–10; advertisements 17, 20; circulation 31, 36, 39–43, 50, 52; government advertisements 56–7, 61; price 62; graduates 78; editorial control 90; features 106, 116; and G. A. Sala 130, 133; and Wolseley 140–1, 145, 157; interviews 160–1, 164; and Gladstone 171–6; 182, 185; inside knowledge 196–203; in Sudan 207; foreign correspondence 210–11; and Italian War 221, 224; and Bismarck 237; sensationalism 242; number of pages 244; sports and City news 244–6; long reports 248–50; weather 254; provincial news 256–9; industrial news 261–71; Irish distress 263–5; radical beginnings 276
The Day 61
Derby Gazette 73
Derby Telegraph 60
Derbyshire Chronicle 73
Devon Evening Express 19
Doncaster Reporter 73
Dorset County Chronicle 76

East Anglian Echo (Bury St Edmund's) 73

East Lancashire Echo (Bury) 19
Eastern Morning News (Hull) 33; and J. L. Garvin 77; associated *Western
   Morning News* 116–17; weather reports 254
Eastern Weekly Express (after 1871 *Eastern Weekly Press*) (Norwich) 73
Echo, circulation 30, 35, 42–3, 52; politics 66; editor's position 92
Economist 173
Edinburgh Evening Courant 130
Edinburgh Review 107–9
Essex Examiner, Kentish Courier and Home Counties Advertiser (Grays, Essex) 73
Evening News (London) 35, 67
Evening Standard 42, 52, 110
Evening Star of Gwent and South Wales Times (Newport) 81, 109 n.21
Evening Times (Glasgow) 34

Family Herald 80
Featherstone Observer 81
Financial Times 41
Fortnightly Review 89, 108, 114, 128–9, 143, 153; and Chamberlain 194
Freeman's Journal (Dublin) 44, 115

Galignani's Messenger, and George Saunders 114
Gateshead Observer 73
Glasgow Herald, production costs 9–12; paper prices 13; advertisements 19;
   circulation 32, 34; at National Liberal Club 44, 46, 53, 66, 69; staff 83, 86;
   news sharing with *Standard* 115; on Foreign Office and Admiralty lists 155;
   war preparations 157
Glasgow Mail, see *North British Daily Mail*
Glasgow News 66–67; and Duke of Buccleuch 70
Globe 42; and party politics 66, 110, 131
[Gloucester] *Citizen* 109 n.21
Gloucestershire Echo (Cheltenham) 60
Good Words 108, 113 n.2
Graphic 137, 144

Halifax Courier 73
Hertfordshire County Chronicle (a localized edition of the *County Chronicle*) 81
Home Words on the Waters (not listed in BL catalogue) 48
Huddersfield Chronicle (after 1871 *Huddersfield Daily Chronicle*) 73, 123
Hull Advertiser 15

Illustrated London News 30, 97, 144; danger to war correspondents 224
Illustrated Police News 30
Imperial Review 66
Investor's Guardian and Limited Liability Review 57
Ipswich Journal, and George Meredith 76
Irish Monthly (not listed in BL catalogue) 48

John Bull, and Brontës 27; and government advertising 56; advance news 209

Justice criticizes Queen Victoria 146; industrial news 266

Kentish Express (Ashford) circulation, 53

Lancashire Daily Express and Standard (before 1885 *Blackburn Evening Express*), circulation 26 n.3
Leeds Daily News circulation 26 n.2; industrial news 267
Leeds Express (*Leeds Evening Express* 1867–76 and 1884–1901), circulation 26 n.2, 60
Leeds Intelligencer (see also *Yorkshire Post*) 27, 32, 60
Leeds Mercury 4; circulation 27, 33, 41, 44, 69, 89; editor's position 91, 146, 149; Hawarden Kite 167; political contacts 194
Leeds Times 73
Leicester Daily Mercury 60; reporting on Sunday 99
Leisure Hour, in ships and prisons 48
Literary Gazette 76
[Liverpool] *Albion* 41, 75, 81; politics 88; and Canning 162
[Liverpool] *Daily Post*, circulation 32, 44, 53, 69; political contacts 194
Liverpool Echo, circulation 53, 60
Liverpool Mail 74
Liverpool Mercury 44
Lloyd's Weekly Newspaper 42, 46–8, 52; and politics 66; news content 96, 114; and Queen Victoria 137
[London] *Gazette* 54
London Journal 80

Macmillan's Magazine 107
Manchester Courier, machinery 10, 41, 46
[Manchester] *Evening Mail* 60
Manchester Evening News, circulation 34–5, 60; industrial news 267
Manchester Examiner 41, 46; and politics 72, 74, 76, 81; reporting on Sunday 99
Manchester Guardian, new machinery 9; telegraphy costs 14, 16, 19; circulation 32, 34, 35, 37; in Bradford 41; at National Liberal Club 44, 53, 69; its politics 72; and graduates 78; staff 83–4, 86, 89, 102; reporters' diaries 103, 115, 123; on Foreign Office list 154; and war preparations 157; special correspondent 240, 254; enlarged 244; and Ireland 264
[Manchester] *Telegraphic News* 81
Midland Counties Evening Express (Wolverhampton) 19, 60
Moniteur Officiel 221
Morning Advertiser 115
Morning Chronicle 15; and Peelites 61, 77, 33, 152; and Napoleon III 217
Morning Herald 116; and American Civil War 222
Morning Leader 36
Morning Star 64; supports North in American Civil War 222

National Press Journal (not listed in BL catalogue) 44, 118
National Reformer 80

National Review 108, 183

Newcastle Daily Chronicle 20; circulation 32; at National Liberal Club 44, 45–6, 53; politics 71–2, of its staff 88; editorial control 93; Trafalgar Square meeting 104; features 107, 115; different agencies employed 120, 122, 150; sports 245; weather 254

[Newcastle] *Evening Chronicle* 75, 245, 254

Newcastle Courant 81

Newcastle Daily Leader 46, 70–2; staff 86, 113

Newsbasket; the monthly journal of W. H. Smith and Son 50

News of the World 27, 42; news content 96

New York Evening Post 170

New York Herald, and Beresford 142; interviews 165

New York Times 242

New York Tribune, and *Daily News* 115; interviews 165, 179, 211

Nineteenth Century 107–8

Norfolk Herald (after 1867 *Norwich Dispatch*) 74

Northampton Mercury Daily Reporter (after 1885 *Northampton Daily Reporter*) 61, 92

Northampton Daily Chronicle and Evening Herald 61

North British Daily Mail (Glasgow) 44

North Cheshire Herald (Glossop) 74

North-East Daily Gazette (Middlesbrough) 34, 53

Northern Daily Express (Newcastle), staff 83; and Saunders 116

Northern Echo (Darlington) 33, 46, 53, 57, 81; praised by Bright 125; and Gladstone 176, 188

Northern Star 50, 271

Norwich Mercury 81

Nottingham Daily Express 93

Nottingham Daily Guardian, sports reporting 245

Nottingham Journal, sports reporting 245

Oldham Chronicle 20, 34; party politics 58–60, 76; industrial news 266

Oldham Evening Express 58

Oldham Standard, party politics 58–9, 74, 117

Pall Mall Gazette, new machines 10; loss of advertising revenue 23, 35, 42, 45, 68, 77; and J. A. Spender 79; politics of staff 87; influence 110–11, 131, 135; and George Saunders 114–15; interviews 162–4, 185; sources of news 187–93, 201, 210, 221; and Bismarck 237; and the Russians 237

[Penzance] *Evening Tidings* (*Tidings*, 1873–86) 47

The People, and Conservatives, 67, 72

Peterborough Times 74

Petit Journal (Paris) 130

Plymouth Mail 81

The Press 61

Preston Guardian 53, 81

Preston Herald 74

Printer's Register 9, 11, 12, 16–17, 30, 46, 66, 70, 78, 82, 97; on the *Sun* 203; on
   Dreikaiserbund 242
Public Advertiser 54
Punch 128, 135

Quarterly Review 107, 109, 161
Queen 113 n.2
Quiver 113 n.2

République française 265
Review of Reviews, and workhouse reading 48, 108, 188
Reynolds's Newspaper, advertisements 17, 27; circulation 42, 44, 46; politics 66;
   news content 96
Rochdale Observer 74
Runcorn and Widnes Examiner 74
Runcorn and Widnes Guardian 117

St. James's Gazette 35, 68, 110, 185
Saturday Review 125
Scarborough Daily Post 46
Scarborough Evening News and Daily Mercury 46
Scotsman 44, 46, 49, 53, 69, 89; features 107, 155; political information
   194–202
Scottish Leader 44
Sheffield Daily Telegraph,circulation 27, 30, 33, 53, 123
Sheffield Evening Post 89
Sheffield Evening Star 60, 101–2
Sheffield Independent 27, 51; and parties 59; editorial control 93, 101; and Henry
   Lucy 125, 150; and official news 154
Shields Advocate (South Shields) 81
Shields Daily News (North Shields) 74
South Wales Daily News (Cardiff), and Henry Lucy 125
Speaker 109
Spectator 109, 113, n.2, 128, 185
Sporting Times 125
Staffordshire Daily Sentinel (Hanley), circulation 26 n.3, 60, 69
Stalybridge and Dukinfield Standard 117
Standard, and advertisements 16, 19–20; circulation 31, 39–43, 45; price
   reduced 61–5, 69, 80, 82, 87, 93; reporting 102, 114; shares news with
   Glasgow Herald 115, 116, 131–3; and Wolseley 140; war preparations 157;
   war correspondence 159, 274, 172, 181; and Conservatives 183–7; inside
   knowledge 196–203; in Sudan 207; foreign correspondence 213; Italian
   War 221; American Civil War 222; Franco-Prussian War 224–5, 228;
   India 230; New York service 243; sports 245; long reports 248–50;
   provincial news 256–9; industrial news 261–6; Irish distress 263–5
Star 35, 110
Star of Gwent see *Evening Star of Gwent*

Statesman 130
Strand Magazine, contributions from Queen Victoria 137, 140; 'illustrated interviews' 162
Sun 66, 118; inside information 203
Sunderland Times 81
Sussex Daily News (Brighton) 44

Taunton Courier 81
Temple Bar 77
The Times, Walter press 8–10; paper prices 13; cost of foreign cables 15, 233; income from advertisements 16–18, 23; circulation 27, 31, 39–43, 50, 52; government advertising 55, 61; and Oxford 78; staff 84; their politics 88, 90, 276; editorial control 88; news content 96, 100–2; Trafalgar Square meeting 103; foreign reporting 105; features 106, 114, 116, 124, 128, 130, 133–4, 136, 138; and Frederick Maurice 141; peak sales 147; *Wason v. Walter* 148; Lobby correspondent 152; Admiralty news 155; war preparations 157; offered official help with war correspondence 159, 163–4, 166; Gladstone corrects 173, 175; and Conservatives 182, 184; and Carnarvon 185; inside knowledge 196–203, 207; foreign correspondence 210–17; and Italian War, 1859, 219–20; American Civil War 222–3; Franco-Prussian War 224–7; India 228–32; resources put into foreign correspondence 233–4; Crimean War 234–5; Foreign Department 240; sports and City news 244–6; long reports 248–50, 255; provincial news 255–60; industrial news 261–71; Irish reports 263–5
Tit-Bits, advertisements 17, 102, 251
Truth 77, 110, 113 n.2
Tyneside Daily Echo (Newcastle after 1880) 60

United Ireland (before 1881 *Flag of Ireland*) 44

Victorian Periodicals Newsletter 63 n.23, 188 n.51
Vanity Fair 110, 128

Wady Halfa Gazette 273
Wakefield Express 81
Wakefield Free Press 74
Warrington Guardian 12, 117
Weekly Dispatch 42
Weekly Mail (London) 66
Weekly Times 42
Western Daily Mercury (Plymouth) 44
Western Daily Press (Bristol), Sunday reporting 99
Western Gazette (Yeovil), circulation 53
Western Morning News (Plymouth) 33, 44; and *Eastern Morning News* 116–17, 155, n.39
Westminster Gazette 35, 110–13
West Sussex Gazette and Advertiser, circulation 53
Worcester Daily Times 60

[Worcester] *Evening Post* 98
The World 45, 110, 113 n.2; and Escott 114; criticizes Prince of Wales 135, 162, 174

Yorkshire Gazette (York) 28
Yorkshire Evening Post (Leeds) 254
Yorkshire Post (Leeds, see also *Leeds Intelligencer*) 32–4, 41, 45; circulation 53; government advertisements 57; party politics 60, 66; staff 83; features 107; sport 245; weather 254

Index

Abbot, Charles, Speaker, and printing of Parlimentary papers 148

Adam, W. P., Liberal Whip 194

Adams, W. E. (*Newcastle Evening Chronicle*), career 75; memories of Fleet Street 80

Admiralty 56; and official information 155, 157–8; and naval estimates, 1894, 200–2; *see also* 'Truth about the Navy'

Adullamites, and *The Day* 61

advertising 15–24; space devoted to 16–17; categories of 17–21; rates 19; display advertisements 21; government advertising 55–7

Afghanistan, 1885, 156–7; interviews on 164, 178–9, 197, 228–32

Alabama arbitration, briefing on 177, 179

Albert, Prince Consort, on foreign powers and the press 217

Alexander III, Tsar, seats at coronation 136; interviewed by Stead 162

Alexandria, bombardment of, 1882, 136; advance warning 177

Allott, H. 59

American and English News Agency 119

American Civil War, and *Standard* 63; and Lancashire readers 97; British reporting of 222

American news 99; *Standard* daily cable service, 1881, 242–3

Anderson, G. 159

Annand, James (*Newcastle Daily Leader*) 70, 72

anonymous journalism 3, 108

Armstrong, Sir George, and the *Globe* and *The People* 67

Arnold, Arthur (*Echo*) 35

Arnold, Edwin (*Daily Telegraph*), pro-Turkish sympathies 175; and Carnarvon, ibid., 185

Arnold-Forster, H. O. and W. T. Stead 188

Arrivabene, Carlo (*Daily News*) 219

Arundel Club 129

Ashanti War, 1874 97

Ashley, C. H. and Wright, William, agency for sporting results 124

Aspden, Hartley, journalist, career 76; reports royal visit 146

Aspinall, Arthur 54–5; on social status of journalists 133

Asquith, H. H., and government advertising 56

Astor, W. W. 87, 110

Athenaeum Club, journalist members 128

Atkinson, Revd J. C., on newspapers in N. Yorks 28

Austin, Alfred (*Standard*), political views 87, 108; and Wolseley 140; Bismarck 160, 224–5, 237; and Salisbury 183, 204; in British embassies 213

Australian and New Zealand news 98

Austro-Italian War 218 ff.

Baines family (*Leeds Mercury*) 119, 134, 246; Edward Baines MP 149

Baker, Major-General Sir Samuel 190

Baker, Valentine 190

Balfour, A. J. 131; and the *Standard* 183–4, 204

Ballantyne, Thomas (*Statesman*) 130

Barnes, Thomas (*The Times*) 133–4

Bean, William (*Liverpool Albion*) 162

Beatty-Kingston, William (*Daily Telegraph*), interviews Pius IX and Victor Emmanuel 160–1; in Franco-Prussian War 224; on telegraphy 228

Beaverbrook, Lord (*Daily Express*), and graduates 79; vendettas and blacklists 94

Bell, C. F. Moberly (*The Times*), at bombardment of Alexandria 138, 207; background 210

Bell, J. H. (*Northern Echo*) 57

Bennett, James Gordon (*New York Herald*) 165

Beresford, Lord Charles 131, 138–9; active in Commons Lobby 152

Bernstorff, Albrecht von, German am-

bassador in London, and *Daily Telegraph* 237

Birmingham Improvement Bill, 1876, 193

Bismarck, Herbert von 131; Otto von, and Austin 160, 224–5, 215; and Greenwood 237

Black, William (*Daily News*) 133

Blowitz, H. S. Opper de (*The Times*) 210, 213; Paris appointment 226–7

Blue Books, distribution to press 138, 154–5

Blumenfeld, R. D. (*Daily Express*) 132

Blunt, Wilfrid Scawen, criticizes foreign correspondents 214

Board of Customs 56

Board of Trade 56; establishment of *Board of Trade Journal* 156

Boon, John (Central News), experiences as lobby correspondent 151, 156; Gladstone's press conference, 1886, 218

Borthwick, Algernon (Lord Glenesk, *Morning Post*) 10, 90, 93; and the Turks 236

Bourke, Algernon, and *The Times* 182

Bowles, Thomas Gibson (*Vanity Fair*) 128

Brackenbury, Major-General Henry, and journalists 141

Bradford, newspaper reading in, 1867, 40–1; party politics and newspapers in 60

Bradlaugh, Henry 60

branded goods 20–1

Brett, Reginald (Viscount Esher), and *Daily Telegraph* 176; and W. T. Stead 189–92; on *Morning Post* and the Turks 236, 237

Bright, John praises *Northern Echo* 125

Brodrick, G. C. (*The Times*) in 1860s, 76; entry to journalism 79; on leader-writing and personal views 88

Brontë, Charlotte 27–8

Brougham, Lord 161

Browne, G. L. (*Bucks Herald*) 28

Bryce, James, contribution to *Fortnightly Review* 171

Buccleuch, 5th Duke of, and *Glasgow News* 70

Buckle, G. E. (*The Times*), Pigott forgeries 90, 128

Bulgarian atrocities, effects on circulations 40, 59; on new publications 60, 156; war news after 159; and the *Daily Telegraph* 174–5; *Daily News*'s reports on 235

Bullock-Hall, foreign correspondent 221

Bullock press 8–9

Bunce, Sir James Thackray, (*Birmingham Daily Post*) 89; and Chamberlain 194–5

Bundock, C. S. (National Union of Journalists), evidence on staffing levels 82

Bunsen, Georg von, Prussian minister in London, and Austin 225; speech reported 248–9

Burdett-Coutts, Baroness, interviewed 162

Burgess, A. H., costs of running a small paper 83

Burleigh, Bennet (*Daily Telegraph*) 217

Burnand, F. C. (*Punch*) 128, 135

Burnham, Lord, *see* Levy-Lawson

Bussey, H. F., journalist, career 81

Bute, 3rd Earl of 54

Bute, 3rd Marquis of, and *Western Mail*, Cardiff 70

Cables, cost of 14–15, 233

Cambridge, Duke of, Commander-in-Chief 139–40

Campbell, Duncan (*Bradford Advertiser*), career 76

Cant-Wall, Edward (*The Times*) 234

Carlton Club, and newspapers in 1830s 65; excludes Press Association 123, 127

Carlyle, Thomas, on sub-editors 85

Carnarvon, 4th Earl of, pursued by W. T. Stead 163–4; and *Daily Telegraph* 175; friendships with journalists 185, 276

Cassell, John 29

Cavour, Count 218, 220

censorship, in war 158–60, 232–3; by foreign governments 230, 240

Central News, and telegraphs 14; report Trafalgar Square riots, 1886, 104; and Central Press 117–18; subscribers and tariff 120–2; and official information 155, 207

Central Press 117–18; and the *Sun* 203

Chamberlain, Joseph, and government advertising 56; and Sheffield newspapers 59–60, 107, 111; leaks infor-

Chamberlain (*cont.*):
mation to Escott 131; its extent 185–6; and *Birmingham Daily Post* 150, 194–5; at Colonial Office 156; refuses interview 165; criticizes F. H. Hill 181, 185; provincial contacts 193–4, 203
Chenery, Thomas (*The Times*) 90; complains of Eber 211
Childers, H. C. E. 194
Chirol, Valentine (*The Times*) 211
Churchill, Lord Randolph 127; reports of his resignation, 1887, 247
Church Missionary Society 198
circulation, early 19th century 7–8, 26ff; weekly papers 27–8; and reading habits 29–31; and newspaper prices 31–4; relative growth, London and the provinces 35; provincial circulation areas 45–8; prisons, ships, and workhouses 48–9; statistics 52–3
City news, development 245–6, 262, 269
civil servants, debarred from writing for press, 1873, 153–4
Clifford, Frederick (*Sheffield Daily Telegraph*), chairman, Press Association 123
clubs, London and provincial, and journalist members 127–9
Cobbe, Frances Power (*Daily News*) 77
Cobbett, William, and parliamentary reporting 2, 217; refers to reporters and editors 85; given a dinner in 1802, 133; on reports of royal occasions 147
Cockburn, Chief Justice 148
Colonial Office, information to the press 155
Connolly, Pierce, anti-Catholic propagandist, and *Daily Telegraph* 210
Conservative party and newspapers 62–4; Central Office and the *National Review* 108
Cook, Sir Edward (*Pall Mall Gazette* and *Daily News*), career 77–9; politics 87; editorial independence 93; 'clagbooks' 253
Cooke, A. B., 196
Cooper, Charles (*Scotsman*) 89, 194; on authority of provincial press 196; on Gladstone's retirement 202
'copy-taster', first use of the term 85

Corry, Montague, and Edward Levy 175
Cosmopolitan Club 131
Costello, Dudley (*Daily News*) 130
Court Circular 146
Courtney, Leonard 79
Cowen, Joseph (*Newcastle Daily Chronicle*) 20, 44; and politics of paper 71–2; and leader-writing 88, 93; on reporting Sunday events 99; Trafalgar Square 104; and penny-a-liners 113; and special correspondents 115; use of agencies 119, 122; on journalists and House of Commons 150, 152
Crawford (*Daily News*), Mrs Emily, 77; G. M., in Paris in 1870, 90
Crimean War news 158, 234–5
Croker, J. Wilson 133, 161
Crompton, T. B., paper manufacturer 10, 89
Cubitt, George, MP 67

Dale, Revd R. W. 99
Dasent, G. W. (*The Times*) 128
Delane, John Thadeus (*The Times*) 78, 88; as editor 89–90, 128; and Carnarvon 185; Gallenga 226; sends Russell to the Crimea 234
Derby, 14th Earl of, *Daily News* and fall of 1859 administration 220
Derry, J. (*Nottingham Daily Express*) 93
Devonshire, Dukes of, and *Buxton Advertiser* 71
Dicey, A. V., and *Northampton Daily Reporter* 92
Dicey, Edward (*Daily Telegraph*), pro-Turkish sympathies 175
Dilke, Charles Wentworth 218
Dilke, Sir Charles Wentworth, 2nd bart. 185; on briefing of journalists 187; and Gordon 190–1
Disraeli, Benjamin 15, 28; and *The Press* 61, 62; refuses to be interviewed 164; gives advance copies of speech to *The Times* 182, 209
Dixie, Sir Beaumont 77; Lady Florence and *Morning Post* 77
Dufferin and Ava, 1st Marquis of, to Cairo with Wallace 212; policies in India 232
Du Maurier, George 129

Durham, 1st Earl of 134

East Africa Company 198–9
Eastern Question, *see* Bulgarian atrocities
Eber, Ferdinand (*The Times*), influenced by Hungarian sentiment 211; at Magenta 219
Edinburgh, Alfred Duke of, and journalists 135; wedding reports 145
'editor', first use of word 85; constrained by proprietors 89–93
Education Act, 1870 10
Egan, Pierce, journalist 134
Egyptian debt, views on 197
Ellis, H. C. (*Northern Echo*), advice on running a provincial paper 27, 33, 51, n. 55; curriculum vitae 81
Employer's Liability Bill, 1894, 199, 201
employment in printing and journalism 37–8
Ensor, Sir Robert 35; on *Manchester Guardian* 92; and editorial independence 94
Erith explosion, 1864, reports 249–50
Escott, T. H. S. (*Fortnightly Review, Standard* and others), independence as editor of *Fortnightly Review* 90, 107, 109; works for several publications at the same time, 114–15, 127, 129; and Edward Hamilton 131; conversation with Hartington 132; and royal family 135; and Brackenbury 141–2; extent of information to Chamberlain 185–6, 228
Evans, Sebastian (*The People*) 67
evening papers, growth of 33–6

'features', first use of the term 158; proportion relative to news 106–7
Fife, Duke of 135
'Fire' Fowler 113
Fisher, Admiral 'Jacky' 138; contact with Stead 189, 193
Fitzroy, E. A. (*John Bull*) 56
Football League, league tables and newspapers 125
Forbes, Archibald (*Daily News*) 95, 217; in Franco-Prussian War 224, 275 n. 5
foreign correspondents, and diplomatic service 211–13, 242–3
Foreign Office and official information 155–7, 208

Forster, W. E. 42; association with Wemyss Reid 184
Franco-Prussian War, and demand for war news 63–5, 97; reporting of 223–5
Frederick, Crown Prince of Prussia, interviewed by W. H. Russell 161
freedom of information 2, 147–9, 168–9, 214–16
free-lance literary earnings 113
Fremantle, Sir Charles 153
Friederichs, Hulda (*Pall Mall Gazette*), chief interviewer 162
Frith, W. P., RA, 'Private view of the Royal Academy' 130
Frost, Thomas, radical journalist, career 75; principles in leader-writing 88–9; example of writing 101; on Canning 162

Gallenga, Antonio (*Daily News, The Times*) on interviews 163; work for *Daily News* 218; for *The Times* 219; in American Civil War 223; in Franco-Prussian War 226
Garfield, President of the United States, *Standard*'s reports of death 243
Garibaldi 221
Garnett family (*Manchester Guardian*) 10, 134
Garrett, Edmund (*Cape Times*) and Milner 212
Garrick Club 128, 131
Garvin, J. L., entry into journalism 77
General Shipowners' Society 275
George, Henry 92–4, 117
Giffen, Robert (*The Times*) 153
Gladstone, Herbert, and government advertising 56, 131; Hawarden Kite 167, 207–8
Gladstone, W. E. 35, 61, 69, 131; reporters on his special train 146; and interviews 165–6; and press intrusions 167; and E. L. Godkin 170–1; dealings with Thornton Hunt 171–3, 204; and W. T. Stead from 1876, 176; complains of leaks to *Standard* 186; and Egyptian debt 197; Uganda 198; his retirement 199–203; favours Press Association 207
Glyn, George Carr (Liberal whip), on

Glyn (*cont.*):
  interviews 161; suspects *Daily Tele-graph* 173–4
Godkin, E. L. (*Daily News, New York Evening Post*), on Gladstone and the press 170; reports American Civil War 222; on W. H. Russell 234
Godley, J. A., secretary to Gladstone 165
Gordon, General, introduced to W. T. Stead 189–91; message from Khartoum 206
government advertising, *see* advertising
Granville, 2nd Earl, contact with F. H. Hill 177–8; regrets his dismissal 181; and leaks to *Standard* 186; on need for consultation 186, 205; and Gordon 190; on *Daily Telegraph* 237, 276
Greenwood, Frederick (*Pall Mall Gazette*), and Carnarvon 185; and Bismarck 237
Greville, C. C. 134
Griffin, Sir Lepel, Indian civil servant, offers to write for *Fortnightly Review* 110
Grosvenor, Lord Richard (Liberal Whip), and government advertising 56; briefs Lucy 179; arranges press reporting for Gladstone's speeches 207
Guest, Montague 128

Hall, Sidney (*Graphic*) 137
Hamber, 'Capt.' (*Standard*) 63
Hamilton, Edward, secretary to Gladstone, links with Escott 131, 134; briefing of *Daily News* 178–80, 204–5
Hamilton, George, and *Standard* 62
Hammond, J. L. 79
Hanham, H. J. 45
Hannay, James (*Edinburgh Evening Courant*) 130
Hansard's parliamentary debates 4, 148; 246–7
Harcourt, Sir William, writes for press 76; and F. H. Hill 184 n. 38; and Uganda 198, 203
Hardman, Frederick (*The Times*) 130; and Paris Commune 226
Hardy, Thomas, advised to write for press 76, 129
Harmsworth, Alfred, Lord Northcliffe (*Daily Mail*), and advertising revenue 17; display type 21; circulation

figures 27; on *The Times* 213; conduct of the *Daily Mail* 251–2
Harper, George (*Huddersfield Chronicle*), chairman of Press Association 123
Hartington, Marquis of, relations with Escott 131–2; and *Daily Telegraph* 176, 189, and Egyptian debt 197
Hatfield, Herts, newspaper reading in, 1876, 42
Havas news agency 120–4, 239
Healy, T. M., writes Parnell's interview 165; and American journalists 167
Henry, Mitchell, on Lobby 150
Henty, G. A. (*Standard*), political views 87, 217; in Italy, 1886, 221; in Franco-Prussian War 224
Heywood, Abel 24; costs of running a small paper 83
Hill, Frank Harrison (*Daily News*) 131; and Liberal administrations 177–82; criticisms and dismissal 181, 204–5
Hirst, Francis W. 79
Hirst, Jonathan (*Oldham Chronicle*) 58
Hobhouse, L. T. 79
Hobson, J. A. 79
Hoe press 8–9
Home Office 56
Hotze, Henry, Confederate agent 63, 223
House of Commons, newspapers in Library 44; Press Gallery 149–50; Lobby 150–2
Hozier, Capt. H., and war reporting 158; in Franco-Prussian War 224
Hunt, Henry ('Orator') 147
Hunt, Leigh 171
Hunt, Thornton Leigh (*Daily Telegraph*), and Gladstone 171–3, 204
Hutton, R. H. (*Spectator*) 128
Hyndman, H. M. (*Pall Mall Gazette, Justice*) on royal press release 146; in Italy, 1866, 221

India, news from 230–2; Reuters and 238–9
Inland Revenue 56
interviews, character and development of 160–6

Jackson, Mason (*Illustrated London News*),

difficulties of war correspondents 223–4

Jaffray, John (*Birmingham Daily Post*), chairman of Press Association 123

Jefferies, Richard 82

Jerome, Jennie 130

Jeyes, Samuel (*Standard*) 80

Johnstone, James, and the *Standard* 62–3, 93

Jones, Kennedy (*Evening News* and *Daily Mail*) 86, 146, 156

journalists, education and background 76–80; career patterns 81–2; size of newspaper staffs 82–7; first use of term 85; specialization 85; political loyalties 87–9; power of the proprietors 89–94; English style 100–102; social status 127 ff.; in clubs 128; and royalty 135; and services 137; *see also* foreign correspondents

Junior Carlton Club 127

Keudell, Baron von 225

Khedive of Egypt, and Reuters 239

Koss, Stephen 55, 61–3

Labouchere, Henry (*Daily News, Truth*) 22, 44, 60; and *Daily News* 64–5, 90–1; and Havas 124; in the Lobby 151, 165; on need for editors to consult politicians 186

Lavino, William (*Daily Telegraph, The Times*), foreign correspondent 210

Lawley, Francis (*Daily Telegraph*) 140; reports American Civil War for *The Times* 222–3

Leach, Francis (*Barrow Times*) 82

Leader, J. D. (*Sheffield Independent*), newspapers in Sheffield 59; family 134

'leader-writer', early use of term 85

Leavis, Mrs Q. D. 102

Lee, Alan 55, 61

Leighton, Sir Frederick, PRA, interviewed 162

Le Marchant, Sir Denis, Bt. 134

Leopold, King of the Belgians 134

Lessar, Russian diplomatist, interviewed by Press Association 164, 237

Levy, Edward, Lord Burnham (*Daily Telegraph*), as editor 90; and Eastern Question 174–5; supports W. H. Smith 175, 204

Levy-Lawson family 10, 61, 93

Lewes, G. H. 171

Liberal party and newspapers 69

Liberal Press Agency (later National Press Agency) 118

Lingen, R. R. 153

linotype 11

Linton, Mrs Lynn (*Morning Chronicle*) 77, 210

literacy, and growth of press 7, 29–30, 48–9

Lloyd, Edward (*Lloyd's Weekly Newspaper*), and paper mill 12; interviewed 162

London Press Club 129

Lowe, Robert 153

Lucy, Sir Henry (*Daily News*), career 75; as editor 91–2; works simultaneously for variety of publications 114–15; contacts with Liberal leaders 125, 132; on Press Gallery 149; and interviews 165; gets advice from Liberal Whip 179, 186

Lumsden, Sir Peter, in Afghanistan 157, 229–32; assistant interviewed 164

McCarthy, Justin (*Daily News*) 75; social contacts 143; interviewed in United States 167, 264

Macdonald, John (*The Times*), and advertising 23; and Pigott forgeries 90, 136; on public opinion in 1878, 175; complains of agencies 207, 212, 215, 240

Macdonell, James (*Northern Daily Express, Daily Telegraph*) principles and leader-writing 88, 90, 116–17

McGahan, J. A. (*Daily News*), and Bulgarian atrocities 235

Mackay, Charles, (*The Times*), correspondent in New York 223

Mackie, Alexander (*Cheshire Guardian et al.*), syndicated publishing 117

Maginn, William (*Standard*) 69

Maiden Tribute case 188

Manchester Chamber of Commerce 275

Manchester Town Hall, seating plan at opening 144

Manning, Cardinal, writes in *Nineteenth Century* 108

Marlborough, 7th Duke, proposes to establish newspaper 130

Martineau, Harriet (*Daily News*) 77

Marx, Karl 211
Massingham, H. W. (*Daily Chronicle*) 20, 35, 87
Maurice, Major Frederick, as correspondent of *Daily News* 141; survey of war reporting problems, 1878, 158
May, Thomas Erskine 153
Meredith, George, writes for *Ipswich Journal* 76; war correspondent in Italy, 1866, 221
Miall, Edward 42
Mill, John Stuart 176
Milner, Alfred 132; and Edmund Garrett 212
Morley, Arnold (*Daily News*) 90
Morley, John, entry into journalism 76; career 107, 128; social contacts 131, 186; need for guidance 187, 203, 277
Morley, Samuel (*Daily News*) 64, 91
Morris, Mowbray (*The Times*) 319
Mudford, William (*Standard*) 63–5, 93; social contacts 131, 133, 268; and Chamberlain 186
Mundella, A. J. 59
Musurus Pasha, Turkish ambassador, and *Morning Post* 236

Napoleon III, and interviews 161; and *Standard* 217, 221; bans foreign correspondents 219, 223
National Liberal Club, newspapers taken 44; popularity of the *Pall Mall Gazette* in 110
National Press Agency, *see* Liberal Press Agency
National Union of Journalists, evidence to Royal Commission on Press, on education of journalists 79; on staffing levels 82
naval rearmament and the press 138–9, 188–9, 199–201
Nevinson, Henry 79
Newcastle, 5th Duke of, visited by Delane 235
Newnes, George (*Strand Magazine* etc.) 137; publishes interviews 162; and *Review of Reviews* 188
news 1–3, Victorian appetite for stimulated 95–8; range of interests, and limitations 98–100; objectivity 102–4; foreign news, 105 *and* Chapter X passim; proportions of

news and features 105–7; news of economic affairs 261–71
newspaper chains 116–17
newspaper libraries 253
Northbrook, Lord 189, 192
Northcliffe, Lord (*Daily Mail*), *see* Harmsworth, Alfred
Novikov, Madame Olga, and Stead 188, 193; contributions to *Pall Mall Gazette* 236

O'Donovan, Edmund (*Daily News*), journey to Merv 229; in Khartoum 230
official government information, 19th century arrangements 152–8; and Press Association 208–9
Oldham, Lancs., newspapers and party politics in 58–9, 117
Oliphant, Laurence (*The Times*), in Paris 226

Paget, Sir Augustus 213
Palmerston, Viscount, and *Morning Post* 61, 161, 172, 186
paper, raw materials 11–12, prices 13, paper duties 11
Paris Commune, 1871, 225–7, 233
Parkinson, J. C. 133
Parliament, decline in space given to reporting of debates 246–7, 255; increased numbers of parliamentary questions 206 n. 83; *see also* House of Commons
Parnell, Charles Stuart, avoids interview 165, 264
Parnell Commission 247
party politics 54–7; and provincial papers 57–61; and metropolitan 61–7; concern over working-class support 68; effects on character of papers 70–3; and editorial independence 87–94; and official news 227 n. 39, 181–2, 259
Patterson, Robert H. (*Globe* and *Glasgow News*) 130
Paul, Herbert (*Daily News*), background 76, 79
Payn, James (*Chambers's Journal, Cornhill*) 133
Pears, Sir Edwin (*Daily News*) 210; and atrocities 235
Pease family, and *Northern Echo* 57
Peel, Sir Robert 161

Peelites, and *Morning Chronicle* 61
Penjdeh question 4, 228–32
'penny-a-liners', and sub-editors 85; share of news-gathering 112–14; example 249–50
Permissive Bill, in 1892, 198
Perry, James (*Morning Chronicle*) 15, 133
Pius IX, interview with *Daily Telegraph* 160
Post Office telegraph revenue 14
Power, Frank le Poer (*The Times*), in the Sudan 229–30
Praed, Mrs Campbell, on American journalists 167–8
Prendergast, Dr, opinion of *The Times* 96; on W. H. Russell 235
Press Association 4; and telegraphs 14; and government advertising 56; reports Trafalgar Square meeting, 1886, 103–4, 112; history 121–3; complaint of bias 123; and official information 157–8, 206–8; routine interviews 164; favoured by Gladstone 207; agreement with Reuters 122, 239, 275
press conferences 206–8
Press Gallery, *see* House of Commons
press intrusions 166–8
provincial news published in London 255–60
Provincial Newspaper Society, and mechanical type-setting 11; and supplies of newsprint 12
provincial press and foreign news 241
Prussian government and war correspondents 224

reading habits, *see* literacy
Reeve, Henry (*The Times*), and Carnarvon 185
Reform Act, 1867, and newspapers for working class 60, 63, 68
Reform Club, admits Press Association to meeting 1894, 123; journalist members 127–8; 'press-gang' lunches 133
Reid, Hugh Gilzean, newspaper proprietor 11; career 81
Reid, Sir Thomas Wemyss (*Leeds Mercury*) 33; career 76, 89; memories of *Northern Daily Express* 83; politics 87; restrictions on, at *Leeds Mercury* 91; and 'press-gang' 133, 146; on Press

Gallery 149; Hawarden Kite 167; and W. E. Forster 184, 246
religious news 99
Rennie, Wallace (*Oldham Chronicle*) 58; career 76
reporters, early references to 85
reporting, general conventions 102–5; of state occasions 144–5; of trials 147; parliamentary 147–52, 246–7; verbatim speeches 246; of provinces in London 255–60; depression of 1879, 261–3, 1885–6, 265–8; social questions, 1890s 269–71; Irish questions 263–4, 270
Reuters News Agency 4, 102, 120; agreement with PA 122; expansion to 1900, 238–9; subsidies, Egypt and India 239
Rhodes, Cecil, and W. T. Stead 188, 193
Rideout, W. J. (*Morning Post*) 10, 89
'Ring' in Army 139–42
Robert College, Constantinople 235
Roberts, General Lord 140; handling of war correspondents 159; and Indian news 232
Robinson, Sir John (*Daily News*), career 76; and editorial policy 91, 133
Rolle, Mark 70
Rose, George, speaks of 'editor', 1803, 85
Rose, Philip, Conservative Whip, and *Standard*, 1859, 62, 64, 66
Rosebery, 5th Earl, friend of E. T. Cook at Oxford 78; and Uganda 198–9, 203
Ross, Lt. James, proposals on war reporting 158
rotary presses, development and costs 8–11
Royal Commission on Press, 1947–8, 35, 70; education of journalists 79; on staffing levels 82; editorial independence 94; newspaper chains 117
Royal Family 134–7; reports of state occasions 145; weddings 145–7
Ruffini [Giovanni?] (*Daily News*) 218
Russell, E. R. (*Liverpool Daily Post*), and Chamberlain 194
Russell, Sir William Howard (*The Times*, *Daily Telegraph*), and Crimea 2, 234–5, 128; accompanies Prince of Wales to Egypt and India 136, 233; and Wolseley 141; interviews Prussian Crown Prince 161, 217; difficul-

Russell (*cont.*)
ties in American Civil War 223; and in Franco-Prussian War 224
Russia, reports from 230; and *Pall Mall Gazette* 236

St James's Club 128, 131
Sala, George Augustus (*Daily Telegraph*) 130, 133, 135–6; and Wolseley 140, 145; interviews Napoleon III and Garibaldi 161, 162; tours United States 217; correspondent in Italy 221
Salisbury, 3rd Marquis, writes for press 77, 155; and the *Standard* 183, 204; report of speech 250
Salvation Army, and W. T. Stead 188
Sardinia and *Daily News* 217–21
Saunders, George, foreign correspondent, works for variety of papers simultaneously 114–15, 210; and embassies 214; working day 215
Saunders, William, newspaper and news agency proprietor 33; opinion of Henry George 92; syndicated newspapers 116–17; chairman of Press Association 123
Savage Club 129
Schuyler, US consul in Constantinople 235
Scott, C. P. (*Manchester Guardian*) 33; politics of 72; early career 78–9; becomes editor 89; quoted 92, 103; Scott family 119
Scott, J. W. Robertson, on E. T. Cook's 'clag-books' 253
Seymour, Horace, secretary to Gladstone 207
Shaftesbury News Club 96, 273
Sheffield, party politics and newspapers in 59
Shields, Thomas (*Bradford Daily Telegraph*) 60
Simonis, H. 51, 87; and 'penny-a-liners' 113, 209
Sinclair, Alexander (*Glasgow Herald*) 19, 32
Smith, W. H. (Lord Hambleden) 29; and Sir George Armstrong 67, 68; and Pigott forgeries 90, 183
Smith, Messrs W. H. and Son, distribution of London papers 35; Daily Number Book 39–40; sales in Brad-

ford and Hatfield 41–3; recirculation of old papers 50, 175
Spencer, 5th Earl, on royal visit to Sweden 145; and naval rearmament 200–1, 207
Spender, J. A. (*Eastern Morning News*), entry into journalism 77, 79; politics 87; and *Eastern Morning News* 92, 112, 132; on Sir E. Cook 93, 253; as free-lance journalist 112; and 'Jacky' Fisher 138
Spicer, correspondent in Italy 221
sporting news, increase 124–5, 244–5
stamp duty, repeal 3, 26, 31
Stanley, Edward 217
Stansky, P. 198
Stead, W. T. (*Northern Echo, Pall Mall Gazette, Review of Reviews*) 23, 33; workhouse reading 48–9; career 76; politics 87, 108, 110; and G. Saunders 114, 133; 'Truth about the Navy' 138, 192; interviews 160–4; and Carnarvon 163, 185; and Gladstone 165, 176; and advisers to *Pall Mall Gazette* 187–93; Russian influence 236; investigative enterprises 252
Stephen, [Harry?] interviewed by Press Association 164
Stephen, Sir James Fitzjames 79
Stephen, Sir Leslie 79
Stockdale v. Hansard (1839) 148
'sub-editor', early use of term 85
Sudan, briefing on 178; and W. T. Stead 189–91; withdrawal from 197, 229–30; control of news from 233 n. 52, 274
syndicated news and newspapers 115–17

Taylor family (*Manchester Guardian*) 10, 134; J. E. Taylor's influence on editorials 92, 119; chairman of Press Association 123
telegraphy 11; costs 13–15; and Press Association 121; effects on foreign correspondence 227, 233
Tess of the D'Urbervilles 109
Thackeray, W. M., on sub-editors 85
Thiers, L.-A., recommends Blowitz 226
Thistlewood, Arthur 147
Thompson, Henry Yates (*Pall Mall Gazette*), printing machinery 10;

advertising revenue 23, 87; ignored 193

Thomson, William, Archbishop of York, invites the press 146

Thursfield, Sir James (*The Times* naval correspondent) 138

Tillotsons (*Bolton Journal*) publish fiction 109

Townsend, George (*Standard*) 62

Townsend, Meredith (*Spectator*), and Carnarvon 185

Trafalgar Square meeting, 1886, 103

Treasury minute of 1873, *see* civil servants

Trevelyan, Sir Charles, writes to the papers 152

Trollope, Thomas Adolphus (*Standard*), correspondent in Rome 213

'Truth about the Navy' 138, 192

Tucker, Marwood, Conservative newspaper proprietor 67

Turks, and *Morning Post* 217, 236

Uganda question 198–9, 203

United States Constitution 2

Victor Emmanuel, King of Savoy, interview with *Daily Telegraph* 160, 163

Victoria, Crown Princess of Prussia, press contacts 135

Victoria, Queen, contacts with press 137; press releases 146; intrusions on 166, 202, 206; on foreign powers and press 217

Vincent, J. R. 196

Wales, Edward Prince of, dines with journalists 135, 136; and Beresford 139; reports of his wedding 145, 146; press intrusions 166; visits to India and Egypt 136; and Scandinavia 145, 249

Walford, F. G. 153

Wallace, Sir Donald Mackenzie (*The Times*) 175, 210, 212; and India 232

Walter family (*The Times*), Arthur 212; John, III 88; and Pigott forgeries 90

Walter press 8–9

War Office, and government advertising 56, 157

war reporting 158–60, 216

Wason v. Walter (1868), 148

Watson, Aaron (*Newcastle Daily Chronicle* and others), politics and leader-writing 88; on Press Gallery 149; on Lobby correspondents 151

Watts, Alaric, newspaper proprietor 65, 69

weather reports 253–4

Wescomb, Charles (*Plymouth Journal*, *Globe*) 67

West, Sir Algernon, secretary to Gladstone 201

Wheeler's Press Agency 119

White, Arnold (*Daily Express*) naval correspondent 138

Whitefriars Club 129

Whitty family (*Liverpool Journal*, *Liverpool Daily Post*) 134; E. M. Whitty's parliamentary sketches 247

Wilkes, John 148

Williams, Charles (*Graphic*), and Wolseley 141

Wilson, E. D. J. (*The Times*) 133; on war news 228

Wilson, H. J. 14, 16, 26, 51, 59, 81, 83; and editorial control 92; offers help as MP 150

Wolff news agency 120, 239

Wolseley, General Sir Garnet, cultivates press 139–42, 154, 159; and Stead and Gordon 189, 206; controls telegraph 232

women in journalism 77

Wood, General Sir Evelyn 191

Wright, William, *see* Ashley, C. H.

Yates, Edmund (*The World*), reports Escott's discussions with Hartington 132; attacks Prince of Wales 135; 'celebrities at home' 162; refused interview by Disraeli 164

Yorkshire Conservative Newspaper Company (*Yorkshire Post*) 60

D1607752